Rudolf Steiner's Philosophy

Andrew Welburn

Rudolf Steiner's Philosophy

and the Crisis of Contemporary Thought

Floris Books

First published in 2004 by Floris Books
© 2004 Andrew Welburn

Andrew Welburn has asserted his right under the
Copyright, Designs and Patents Act 1988
to be identified as the Author of this Work.

British Library CIP Data available

ISBN 0-86315-436-0

Printed in Great Britain
by Cromwell Press, Trowbridge

For Owen Barfield, friend and inspirer

Contents

God Appears & God is Light
To those Poor Souls who dwell in Night
But does a Human Form Display
To those who Dwell in Realms of Day

William Blake

Preface

In calling my opening chapter to Rudolf Steiner's thought 'An Ecology of Knowing,' I should perhaps make it clear straightaway that the reader will find in it nothing in the way of facts and figures concerning the decline of rain-forests or the pollution of our seas. The title draws attention rather to the deeper problem of our way of thinking about our own relation to the world. For so long as we continue to think in the ways that have brought us to the brink of ecological disaster — thinking in terms of manipulation, detachment, looking-on from outside — we can do little more than tinker with issues that really demand a radical approach. Yet few thinkers have gone very far toward a reappraisal of the kind which Rudolf Steiner made. The scientists fear that there can be no real knowledge if we turn our backs on 'objectivity,' and are dubious of the complexities that go with knowledge from within; the moralists share the evaluation of knowledge as cold and alien to compassion, and seek some overriding imperative or restraining order on the progress of science. To some, at least, Rudolf Steiner has come to seem all the more relevant as the opposing parties grow further apart. What we need is a standpoint which gives us knowledge, but in a way that keeps us in touch with a humane perspective, putting that knowledge into the context of the balance of forces which give us our place in the cosmos. Knowledge, after all, is human knowledge for human purposes. Steiner helps explain its human meaning and so, as he puts, gives us back to ourselves — and explains also the inherent dynamic within knowing which can tempt us to forget its origination from a special angle, making us think that only our perspective is real or that it alone matters.

The ecological movement already owes much to ideas which

Rudolf Steiner introduced. Although the practical applications of Steiner's thought are too far-reaching to be pursued in this book, the profoundly ecological nature of his approach to agriculture, medicine, nutrition and other aspects of our lifestyle is clear. It may be noted in particular that modern ecological thinking owes much to the impact of two followers of Steiner's ideas. It was Steiner's pupil D.N. Dunlop who founded the organization which has since turned into the World Energy Council, stemming from the World Power Conference of 1924.[1] And it was another of Steiner's pupils, Walter Johannes Stein, who, working with Dunlop in England in the 1930's, first clearly saw the 'energy problem' as one requiring a comprehensive understanding of planetary resources and the factors affecting global development.[2]

The issues affecting how we think about the environment, however, are as wide as philosophy itself. What I have attempted therefore is an outline account of how we can understand the objective aspects of knowledge and its human origins, the free development of the human individuality, without any fixed goal but with an unlimited potential that is related to the very nature of the evolving universe, and an ability to perceive specific value in actions and experiences that affect the world and ourselves, as Steiner characterized them in his philosophical books and lectures. I have attempted to do so without going into much technical philosophical detail (even had I felt qualified to do so!), but rather in a series of overlapping considerations to show the implication of Steiner's approach and its way of relating the fundamental questions of knowledge and moral freedom in his special, illuminating way. There was at one stage a thought of including mention of those philosophers who have advanced Steiner's ideas — Owen Barfield, Oskar Hansen, Jonathan Westphal, Georg Kühlewind, Bernardo Gut, to name but a few — and so point the reader to the detailed arguments which have since been advanced in the areas on which he touched. But time and space, to which philosophers have traditionally been hostile, turned against this idea in their turn. What has emerged is at least an effort to see Steiner's thought in its potential wholeness of vision for our time.

In calling for a 'rethinking' of Steiner's thought in my open-

ing chapter I might seem to be denying my own case for his continued relevance, let alone increasing it. But this contradiction is
only a shallow one. It is precisely because his ideas are still so
relevant that they need to be formulated anew in terms of the
struggles and insights of the modern world. In his own time, he
turned those ideas against the fashionable Kantianism which
tried to limit all knowledge to the kind of external truth which
scientists then affirmed. Nowadays the pretensions of science
are expressed in quite other ways. Steiner was never against science, but he would have protested against the abuses of science
no doubt in necessarily different terms. Or in morals: the slogan
of 'ethical individualism' which he then pitted against the 'formalist' ethics of rules and imperatives, to my mind no longer
immediately brings to mind the really important features of
Steiner's ethical thought. What we need to have brought out for
us nowadays is not so much further emphasis on individualism
in the manner of Max Stirner, as an explanation that Steiner
advocates a deeper sense of being oneself: one that does not just
break loose from rules and regulations, but that is able to find
out of direct moral perception the insights we need to make
individualism once more a creative part of shared reality, a
social whole.

In the exposition of his thought I have therefore largely
avoided trying to summarize what his philosophy meant at the
time, in favour of showing how precisely such ideas are needed
in the crucial arguments that have gone on since. I have adopted
the device of imagining Steiner eavesdropping, as it were, on
certain significant developments, whether in physics, psychology, or socio-ethical anthropology. The general idea of 'the self
in development' presented itself as way of showing the inter-
connectedness, in Steiner's thought, of these several aspects —
avoiding the one-sided suggestion of 'individualism' in ethics,
and bringing out the link to developmental and structural-mor-
phological approaches which help integrate the human standpoint into the wider world. It would certainly be possible to
write a book on Rudolf Steiner in his contemporary setting. But
when Eduard von Hartmann, for instance, responded by trying
to pigeon-hole Steiner and opted for the cumbersome label
'epistemological monist,' does it really prove anything except

that he had not yet quite grasped the essential new direction we now recognize as Phenomenology — a direction whose essence Steiner had evidently divined in the seminal work of Brentano? Is it not more significant that Phenomenology in its turn was to run into certain difficulties when it tried to 'suspend' the natural standpoint — difficulties to which Steiner could offer new solutions if we are open to hearing them, as a result of his subtly different project of clarifying the historical and evolutionary changes of standpoint, the 'self in development,' which is the subject of his 'anthroposophy'?

INTRODUCTION

The Philosopher of Freedom

Freedom and its Perils

No philosopher has made greater claims for the scope of human freedom than Rudolf Steiner, and at no time have the issues of freedom and our responsibility for the world we inhabit been more urgently in need of clarification than they are today, as we embark upon the new millennium. It has rather belatedly been brought to the attention of unprecedented numbers of people that all human action has an ecological significance. And as a result, ethics has taken on the aspect, not so much of either rules or good intentions, as a need for awareness that reaches into the details of our lives: using unnecessary electricity, spraying with aerosols, eating commercially prepared and wrapped foods — all these have emerged as factors over which we need to exert consciousness and moral control.

It is often taken for granted, however, that such new ecological imperatives must be set over against the drives for freedom and knowledge which have inspired human development in modern times, checking our 'selfish' drives, with the implication that these must be 'curbed', or 'reined back' if we are to make a viable future. We are often asked in effect to go backwards, to relinquish the assertion of individualistic wishes to change the world and to return to older, more 'traditional' moral attitudes. The contradictory forces in the modern experience of the world are thereby exposed. But it is hard to see how we can ever un-know the things our course of direction in recent civilization has taught us. Ever since Bacon realized that 'knowledge is power,' the kind of understanding that has been sought is precisely that which enables us to intervene, to experiment, to make things happen and change the world. So knowledge — at least knowledge of the scientific-technological type — and morality seem increasingly to be on a collision course. But few have been able to offer the vision of a deeper unity by which the emergence of an ultimate resolution could be envisaged. The immense caring and goodwill that meets ecological concerns when they are raised for the most part lacks a coherent philosophy in the proper sense. Steiner's radical rethinking of the nature of human knowledge and moral action has come to seem more and more significant as the crises of modern life have unrolled.

In contrast to the materialistic exploitation of the world, he taught a spiritual philosophy which is yet in no sense an attempt to 'go backwards.' In fact, as we shall see, it has foreshadowed a good many of the most exciting and innovative tendencies in contemporary thought. He addresses us in the modern situation with increasing directness. Yet Rudolf Steiner does not propose that we need to violate our own profoundest aspirations, our path of self-realization, in order to save the world, but believes rather that we need precisely to understand our freedom and the nature of humanity more deeply. For him our knowledge and our moral freedom are from the outset intimately connected, and so for Steiner all knowledge bears a moral significance, and our relationship to the world as knowers (traditionally a somewhat academic topic) is already in the strictest sense an ecological matter. The solving of our current dilemmas, so many of which he saw looming, requires a further step in self-understanding and self-development, not a curbing of it. Despite much that has been written and thought about the contemporary crisis, only Rudolf Steiner, it may still fairly be said, was willing to go to the roots of the problem and to give us the basis for an ecology of knowing. Without such a change of attitude, our crises can be postponed at best, at worst left dangerously hanging over us.

His ideas are still best known, perhaps, for inspiring the Waldorf Education movement which now has schools across the world from Israel to Peru. But they have also fathered a startling variety of scientific, medical, agricultural, architectural and other activities that are increasingly recognized in Europe and around the world for their vitality and uniquely original approach. Born in obscurity on the outer reaches of the Austro-Hungarian Empire as long ago as 1860, he was already a controversial figure in his own lifetime. First known as a Goethe-scholar, he was subsequently associated in the popular mind with Nietzschean ideas before developing his Anthroposophy or 'spiritual science'. But although his subsequent life, after the turn of the century, was devoted to fostering the many off-shoots of his pioneering ventures in practical life, the underlying pursuit of spiritual values in religious, social and economic organizations remained true to his original bold outline of 'a modern conception of the world'.[1] Written by the young philosopher in his thirties, his philosophical testament *The Philosophy of Freedom* is still the proper starting-point for a comprehension of his subsequent, less academically orthodox line.

Not so much a set of conclusions as a liberating process in thinking, it is written in non-technical language that still has a broad appeal. Nevertheless, in the hundred years or more since Rudolf Steiner published *The Philosophy of Freedom* (1894),[2] a good deal has happened to change our ways of thinking. That was naturally something the great 'ethical individualist' would have welcomed, and which indeed he strove all his life to bring about. As we look back upon those changes, Steiner's characteristic independence from conventional assumptions makes him a refreshing as well as an admonitory voice helping us to evaluate where we have come from as well as where we are going. The tremendous perils all too evident to us today, both in the political and cultural world, and in our upsetting of the balances of nature, as well as the enormous potentialities of freedom for ourselves and for the world, were all part of his vision. As a thinker who challenged the philosophical establishment of his day, Steiner increasingly has the power to make us rethink today. Though sometimes misunderstood for his Nietzschean radicalism, Steiner was in reality concerned to put forward a far-reaching new approach to such issues as human freedom, evolution and the sources of moral value. He resisted the academicizing and compartmentalizing of philosophy, and insisted upon the interrelatedness of human knowledge, putting the human sciences firmly in the centre of his thought. In our own time, when the question of man's relationship to his environment has ceased to be a merely academic and become an ecological and vital one, the relevance of his approach and the issues he raised has never been clearer. The many practical activities, including the Waldorf or Steiner Education movement, the Camphill Communities for those with special needs, and the Anthroposophical Society thus continue to draw inspiration from his ideas. The concepts he developed open new perspectives on the nature of science and on the changing character of religious experience — perspectives that have often since found their way, rather watered down or in less far-reaching contexts, into mainstream thought. To rediscover his formulations of our struggle continues, however, to be always a challenge and sometimes a shock.

A Spiritual Philosophy

Beginning in the last decades of the nineteenth century, Rudolf Steiner wrote a considerable number of philosophical books and gave an even larger number of lecture-courses in which he applied his ideas to almost every aspect of life. In them all the keynote of freedom is sounded. Unlike many purveyors of 'spiritual' approaches to life, Steiner did not urge us to obtain freedom at the cost of rejecting the world or our place in society, however, but argued that we can be free within the tensions and contradictions of modernity, free to fulfil our own potential by meeting its challenges. Since his thought is thus in some ways different from either the naturalistic approach that sees us as determined by the forces around us, or from the usual religious — or indeed those 'alternative' movements which assert that we can find ourselves only by opting out of those forces, — it will be worth while to examine the kind of thinking which Rudolf Steiner evolved.

It is highly individualistic in emphasis — yet its goal is to engage with the forms of thinking that develop in living complexity in society as a whole. It is 'spiritual' — yet it does not suggest that we must believe in some 'metaphysical' reality beyond what we can see and know, a 'thought out' spiritual world in the 'beyond.' It seeks rather to make us aware of the spirit through our own activity, interpreting and transforming the world around us.

Now the terms of the arguments we conduct about our role in the world have inevitably shifted over time. That is something which the great exponent of freedom would not only have expected, but hoped for. A re-examination of his thought therefore seems called for, which may enable us to confront the challenging implications of his approach anew. Steiner necessarily put his case in the (largely neo-Kantian) language of his time, and sought to present his ideas in terms his contemporaries could readily understand, though he cut through many of their precious assumptions too. This introductory book however is not a full attempt to rewrite Steiner's work. It is rather a collection of observations on the continuing relevance of his thought in the modern world. We may state it as the essence of his view, however, that philosophy and freedom are inextricably intertwined. Not that one can establish the other. Freedom, for Steiner, has to be grasped in every instance by an act of individual awareness: it cannot be proved in theory, to be taken up off the shelf or not as the whim moves us. For him, therefore, it is in freedom that philosophy becomes part of life, and it is indeed this very duty of rethinking for ourselves — of 'spiritual activity' — which validates our freedom and which Steiner exhorts us to undertake. That is in fact the only commandment which his ethical individualism can contain. What that means, in the first instance, is that we establish our own moral frame of reference along with our actions, which cannot be judged in advance:

> We know
> That we have power over ourselves to do
> And suffer — what, we know not till we try.

Philosophy arises in his sense, therefore, in the immediacy of our response to life. It certainly has very broad implications, and there is a sense which obviously applies very largely to Steiner in which a man's philosophy could be taken to mean the whole sweep of his thinking across the board of life. Steiner's writings concerning man, nature, evolution, God, education, art and

almost everything else constitute an extraordinarily full statement of his philosophy in this sense, embodied in his thousands
of lectures and the array of books. But it is not for me to para-
phrase or summarize them here. Such summaries have been
attempted, but they risk losing that very essence of what I mean
by the philosophy in them. For by that I mean, as I think Steiner
meant, the sense of opening up new approaches, of freeing the
thinker and enabling him or her to see things afresh. Steiner possessed this gift of illuminating his material philosophically in
the most amazing degree. Two examples may help make the
point. One is from a scientist, Ernst Lehrs; the other, the literary
and philosophical writer, Owen Barfield.

Ernst Lehrs thus recalled his meeting and discussions with
Rudolf Steiner:

> I told him of my experimental researches in electrical high-
> frequency phenomena, briefly introducing the particular
> problem with which I was occupied. I took it for granted
> that a question from such a specialized branch of physics
> would not be of much interest to him. Judge of my
> astonishment when he at once took out of his pocket a note-
> book and a huge carpenter's pencil, made a sketch and
> proceeded to speak of the problem as one fully conversant
> with it, and in such a way that he gave me the starting-
> point for an entirely new conception of electricity ...[3]

What struck the experts was not just Steiner's extraordinarily
wide-ranging knowledge of contemporary ideas, but his ability
to seize on the point that transformed the whole discussion, to
start off a new world of discourse. Owen Barfield recalls his
impression that:

> so far as concerned the particular subject in which I was
> immersed at the time, that is the histories of verbal
> meanings and their bearing on the evolution of human
> consciousness, Steiner had obviously forgotten volumes
> more than I had ever dreamed. It is difficult to lay my
> finger on what convinced me of this. As far as I know
> there is no special treatise on semantics or semasiology

among his works. Rather it was a matter of stray remarks and casual allusions which showed that some of my most daring and (as I thought) original conclusions were *his* premises ...[4]

Behind this stands Steiner's idea of philosophy as a liberation from limiting forms of thought, rather than as a wagging moral finger or an intellectual programme. Some of his best philosophy recalls that ungainly sketch, those casual remarks which yet suggest the depth and wholeness of his vision. Those who seek from him ready-made answers to all life's problems will seek in vain, or at best make of him another idol. For those who accept his work in the spirit in which it was imparted, there are few philosophers who afford such exhilarating opportunities to consider the relation of philosophy to freedom.

Of course, Steiner came to a great many definite results, which his spoken and written works expound in some considerable detail. When I say that he left us freedom I do not mean that he fought shy of commitment to definite conclusions or lines of thought. In fact, one problem many people initially find is that Steiner is so definite and concrete on large issues where it is tempting, and where it may be morally easier, to remain vague. What it means is rather that he allows us at every point to consider why we should think about the issue in this particular way. Therefore it is not the plethora of results, still less of their applications in schools, architect's offices, on farms or in clinics and hospitals, of which I shall speak under the rubric of Steiner's 'philosophy.' What will engage us here is the kind of thinking by which Steiner brought his insight to bear on those manifold domains with such surprising success (for whether in the classroom, the clinic, or the water-purification plant, Steiner's ideas have undeniably worked). When we think about things, we must have settled on a framework within which to consider them. And within a framework many fruitful conclusions can be reached. The questions of which framework, and why, of thinking about thinking, are the questions of philosophy.

But those to whom Rudolf Steiner is primarily a guide to personal-spiritual development, or the pioneer of those several forms of life and community which still continue and flourish, should not feel that the 'philosophical' Steiner I discuss is a different figure. The medium may appear more abstract, but we must remember that the liberation which enables us to see other possibilities, other frameworks, takes place for Steiner in the thick of life, and coincides with the freedom to see things anew or in a fresh connection. What is valuable about Steiner's 'concept' of freedom is precisely that it may also be embodied in the form of a building or a room, in a gesture or a painting.[5] The kind of thinking which I shall try to identify and evoke is precisely one for which many of the conventional barriers are irrelevant.

That is perhaps also why many of Steiner's most interesting philosophical remarks are scattered through his books and lectures on so many different themes. Though I shall basically remain in the sphere of the more strictly philosophical questions which Steiner addressed, it is important to be aware that at every point their expression can be linked to the life they transform by making us see it differently, just as a building makes us experience ourselves differently in space, etc. In all this it ought to be clear, then, that there are not, in reality, two distinct approaches within Steiner's work as is sometimes supposed — an early 'philosophical' one and a later 'spiritual' or anthroposophical one.

In his anthroposophy, Steiner did, it is true, speak about direct experiences of spiritual matters. He did so, it should be added, only after long and even agonizing deliberation, as the chapter 'Must I keep silent?' in his autobiography reveals.[6] It would be quite wrong to imagine Steiner coming forward with the overwhelming conviction that he knew all the answers, or (again as is sometimes asserted) offering a new religious revelation; Steiner thought long and deeply about the problems of understanding spiritual experience in ways suited to the free individual of modern times. Anthroposophy or 'spiritual science' is something different from philosophy, but it is spiritual experience considered from the standpoint of freedom which his philosophy is concerned to propound. For one of the most difficult aspects of 'transcendent,' 'mystical' or 'spiritual' experiences has always been precisely the problem of knowing how to interpret them. It is not just the question of what they mean, but how we would know whether our interpretation was right or wrong at all. Approaches in the past can well illustrate the point about frameworks. For medieval Christendom, any such experiences were 'mystical' revelations, and as such automatically taken to confirm the doctrinal truths of the Church — if not, the only other available category, or 'damnable' magic, etc. was invoked. But for those living under Islam, or Hinduism, the validity of their faith's beliefs likewise formed the point of departure. We are left with the problem that to those of different religious persuasions, spiritual phenomena therefore suggested quite different interpretations. A healing which convinced a medieval Catholic of miracles would have persuaded others of the effects of *yoga,* and suggested to others still the potency of a nearby shrine containing the relics of a pious sheikh. Steiner did not wish to pose the question in any such monolithic way, but to investigate spirituality, even spiritual 'phenomena' scientifically — which of course is also culturally specific: it is the approach of the modern individual thinker. Indeed, what he means by 'scientific' in this spiritual context is firstly that he does not ask for a prior act of belief. If he adopts a point of view in advance, it is that of the modern free individual with a desire to see for himself or herself, that is, to put to the test both the facts *and* the frame of reference, the assumptions we make about how to explain them. It was in that sense, clearly, that he thought of his 'spiritual science' as appropriate to the modern day — and not as some kind of algebra of the soul.

We may contrast his approach with that based on so-called scientific frameworks which turn out to be equally monolithic as those of the past. Much of the research which still continues into 'psychical research,' for example, has been bedevilled by just such conceptual issues, and a failure to break out of either-or terms. Either we can conclusively prove something which breaks all the known laws, or we fail to do so; either the accepted framework of material-scientific thought holds, or we have to admit something utterly outside and beyond it. 'Science' is in danger of becoming a sort of idol here, a fixed set of results from the past which nothing can challenge rather than a method of free investigation. The aim is not so much to find a scientific method appropriate to the subject-matter as to attach to occult or psychic matters the prestige of established areas of thought.

Steiner rightly objects that the successes of science in the material domain do not at all mean that it can only be applied there. There is a kind of illusion involved in the notion that we can accept the materialist's framework, and force him to see that there is something beyond it. Steiner resists this, as he resisted many of the false choices which have been thrust upon twentieth-century humanity (Darwinism *or* fundamentalist creationism, science *or* religious truth, holistic versus analytic thought, collective versus individualist emphases in society). For him, if we accept spiritual reality into our world-picture it cannot be as a wild, rule-breaking additional 'something-or-other.' To be truly 'scientific,' and make spiritual thinking scientifically useful, we must rework the whole picture, the 'material' half as well as the spiritual. Instead of fixed attitudes and attachment to large-scale blocks of ideas because they have proved useful in some domain, Steiner advocates an openness which need not threaten the successes of science in the past, or the genuine insights of religion.

It is when this is not understood that highly misleading assumptions about Steiner can sometimes be made. It is often taken for granted that because he spoke about 'spiritual' entities that he must have imported with that idea the whole apparatus of metaphysics which has in times past been used to uphold a spiritual world-view — that he must have been a sort of Neoplatonist! But his stance is far removed from that of a Plotinus. Spiritual experience, mystical intimations of union with the cosmos, etc. were of interest to the Neoplatonists primarily because they seemed to corroborate their idea of 'the One,' the all-explaining concept at the summit of their intellectual system. Whatever else it may have meant to them, it was grist to the mill of a speculation, worked out on their philosophy, that the basis of the universe must be One, must be Mind. But Steiner had cut his ties with 'speculative' philosophy, along with the German Idealism which was the last great system-constructing philosophy along similar lines. Thus he declined to think of the fundamental 'Ideas' — the controlling principles of thought — in their sense as higher-order truths belonging to a superior faculty of Reason, conceived as different in kind from ordinary Understanding. 'Ideas,' he insisted, 'do not differ qualitatively from concepts. They are only fuller, more saturated, more comprehensive concepts.[7] Steiner's perspective in his anthroposophy — as I shall try to bring out, in the face of wide-spread assumptions to the contrary — is anti-metaphysical. In fact, he thinks about spiritual experience in highly modern, sci-entific, evolutionary and critical ways that are more familiar in the twentieth century in areas such as biology and physics. But he did not therefore limit science to its successes there, and carry over their particular limitations with them into other domains. Nor was he tempted to suppose that because we adopt those 'modern' kinds of thinking we must therefore deny God. Quite the reverse. New ways of thinking may then suggest new ways of understanding God. A developing universe, if one thinks about it, does not carry any necessary connotation of a materi-alistic universe. Indeed to suppose so is to fall victim to history through failing to confront it squarely, mistaking the circum-stance of the emergence of evolution, as a replacement to older, God- and creation-orientated views, for a proper, in-depth investigation of the scope of the concept itself.

Characteristically, Steiner's philosophy makes us aware of our own presuppositions and the historical situation which determines them, and so is able to set us free. He turns our awareness back upon itself. 'Anyone pondering the significance of natural science in human life,' he observes,

> will find that its significance is by no means limited to the acquisition of so much detailed knowledge of nature. The detailed items of knowledge can, in effect, only lead to an experience of what the human psyche is not. The soul lives, not in the finished propositions about nature but in the process of knowing scientifically about nature. In working upon nature, that soul becomes conscious of its own life and being.[8]

Scientific knowing is the way in which *we* can relate to the world through developing our inner activity. Through it we are estab-lishing a particular relationship to nature and defining our own stance. As we enter Rudolf Steiner's thought more deeply we will find to our surprise, perhaps, that scientific activity does not reveal our passivity before fixed 'facts' of nature, but our own living process of knowledge, the free development of our self.

Naïve accounts of science might tend to present the case differently, implying that the natural-scientific way of thinking has been discovered to 'fit' the world, and that previous ways of thinking were incorrect or pre-scientific. But this is precisely because we project our own attitudes and viewpoint back upon others in the past. To them, their own interpretation seemed as natural, as transparent as our scientific one does to us. In fact neither is transparent, but the result of our positioning ourselves in a certain way toward the world. Steiner's awareness of the lack of transparency of the framework, of our own implication in the process, anticipates much more recent ideas. And so we come to one of his central insights, and one crucial to his concept of freedom. 'Thinking,' Steiner notes, 'is the unobserved element in our ordinary mental and spiritual life.'[9] This more than anything else defines the essential modernity of Steiner's thought, in contrast to the search for definitive 'answers' which preceded the modern self-awareness. It is philosophy's task constantly to remind us of that fact, putting us back, as thinking beings, into the picture of our knowledge of the world. His sensitivity to history dissolves the illusion of the fixed nature of the 'fit,' and opens our minds to further possibilities of scientific thinking, as well as to an understanding of the changes in consciousness that enables us to have a more realistic view of thought in the past.

It is worth continuing to examine some fundamental aspects of modern thought, and attempting to put them in a philosophical perspective such as Steiner adopts. Consider the way that Darwinian evolution has replaced 'theological' interpretations of purpose and goal in the widely accepted view of the world. Is this because evolution has been found to 'fit,' and pushed out the misguided or confused ideas which preceded it? In fact, prior to the sharpening of the debate into the Genesis *versus* Geology, religion *or* science debates of the later nineteenth century, some of the most exciting developments in thought suggested that a more dynamic interpretation of the universe might link on to theology at the climax of its creative vision. When Darwin's book came out, evolution was actually hailed by some as a contribution to understanding purpose and design in nature. And going back only a little earlier, much of what we call Romanticism was a comprehensive attempt to come to terms with the implications, in every sphere, of process, development and change. Steiner surveyed some of those developments in his *Riddles of Philosophy*, and Owen Barfield in particular has been an advocate of Steiner's links to the kind of thinking that was developed in the Romantic period. Goethe, the great discoverer of 'metamorphosis' and developmentalism in biology, belongs centrally in that context of ideas, which Steiner believed had been sidetracked in the drive to emphasise the materialistic version of evolution.[10] In his own thinking, he took up the possibilities he perceived to be still unrealized in their thought. Far from rendering outmoded the 'theological' dimension of life, Christianity's vision of God's becoming human, Steiner saw, might turn out to be only the more relevant in an evolving, ever-becoming cosmos.

The reason that most of the modern world may have passed these ideas by, we may reflect, is not because their case has been examined and found wanting, but rather because a defensive atmosphere has poisoned and polarized the arguments. Theology became defensive once the substantial scale of the reinterpretation demanded by evolution became apparent. Evidently the risk seemed to many theologians too great to take. Religion clammed up, seeking to hold on to traditional certainties and limit the area of scientific knowledge. But the results have scarcely been successful: erosion of religious belief has followed, and the defensive circle has proved hard to break. Fundamentalism is a last desperate gesture; while in relation to practical, scientific-technological and economic life, spiritual values were made to seem increasingly irrelevant and outmoded. But once more it would be quite erroneous to see this as resulting from the 'nature of things,' as though we had found out that life is 'really' a Darwinian struggle for survival of the fittest (itself a notoriously vacuous idea).[11] It is more a historical and cultural failure of nerve.

Modern historiography has begun to understand what happened, in a way that shows up the naïvety of the 'as we now know' conception of scientific progress. As a matter of fact, God long maintained his position as an integral part of science, and even improved it in the later eighteenth century; it was religion which faltered, and began to swing between a rationalized deity, who evoked no real religious devotion, and a fundamentalist, naïve-realistic God who could play no part in the cosmological and scientific arguments of the eighteenth-to-nineteenth centuries. 'No one thought that Christianity might give way to rationalism,' concludes a historian of the Enlightenment, 'until Christians tried to prove that Christianity was reasonable.'[12] It was spiritual thought which failed to keep up, and played into the hands of materialism. In Darwinism, evolution fell victim to the rift that had been opened. Steiner, with his devotion to Haeckel and the evolutionists of his day, thus stands as a unique figure — or nearly so — in following through his contrary judgment that spiritual thinking could survive and be enriched by the evolutionary universe. (Christianity had persisted in fact through several similar reinterpretations in the course of its centuries-long previous career.) We may now be beginning to recover from the failure of nerve which has got us into what seems increasingly like a blind alley. Rudolf Steiner offers a reminder of what it might be like to think things through holistically. Instead of being trapped in a situation that remains unacknowledged, he gives us the philosophical path to the awareness of how we got here, and frees us to move on.

Certainly science like all human knowledge, according to Steiner, needs an awareness of its history. We need constantly to be reminded for example that the way questions are first asked necessarily determines a good deal of the direction taken by subsequent thought. Seen thus, history is not only orientated to the past, but to the future in that it prevents our being trapped into supposing that only one way of thinking is possible. That does not mean that we reject the actual achievements of thought that have since emerged. We are made free in relation to them.

Rethinking the Past

We can see however why Steiner was frequently misunderstood here, as happened for example when an organization which held itself to be following the liberal, modernizing direction inspired by Giordano Bruno (a pioneer of naturalistic ideas who was burned by the Inquisition) expelled him for suggesting that there was much of philosophical value in Thomas Aquinas.[13] The ironies are striking. Behind the event lies Steiner's perception of an important older thinker eclipsed and denigrated by the exponents of ideas only interested in spotting forerunners of nineteenth-century science. As a result Bruno's own work was itself distorted — he was not actually a modern-style liberal; and, as ideas have altered, the twentieth-century revival of serious interest in Thomism has amply borne out Steiner's estimate of the importance of the great Dominican's thought.

Steiner's ability to reappraise the thought of the past while remaining essentially modern in spirit is in fact one of his most remarkable facets, and draws attention in a special way to the historicity of thought. At the same time misunderstandings have sprung from his consequent use of mythological and other terms, for example. He himself found that his critics seized simplistically upon these. 'Paying little heed to the real direction and content of my descriptions, they focussed attention on the words.' But Steiner never merely sought to revive an antiquated idea. The reader should have noticed that the account in its substance appealed only to his own observation and thought. If he used terms from traditional literature, he pointed out, 'I used them quite freely. In the way I apply them, scarcely one of them coincides exactly with its connotation in the source from which I took it.'[14] We may take an instance with some considerable modern interest, and also showing how frameworks and perspectives change.

It was the great physician and chemical genius Paracelsus (1493–1541) who brought about a modernizing revolution in medicine. This, points out Charles Nicholl, was his 'recognition of specific treatment. Orthodox "Galenist" therapy' — the basis of medieval medical practice — 'was non-specific. All disease was interpreted as an upset in the balance of the four physiological "humours" — blood, choler, phlegm and black bile — and all remedy sought to restore that balance, by counteraction or by evacuations such as blood-letting, sweating and vomiting. To Paracelsus, however, each disease was a specific entity — a "living thing, a seed" — within the body ... and healed by a specific *arcanum.*'[15] The breakthrough he brought to medical science is clearly of fundamental importance. But in retrospect we are also aware of something else. The 'Galenist' notion which he successfully displaced nowadays regains a certain attractiveness, since the pursuit of specific chemical remedies has been carried to astonishing lengths in modern interventionism; the realization that over and above the remedy and disease alike there is a person with a particular balance, physiological and psychological, that needs to be restored and harmonized in order to regain health — that now sounds like an anticipation of the holistic approach that is important in anthroposophical medicine and in many of the developments that have run parallel to it in modern times!

Now, by insisting upon a 'holistic' approach when he pioneered, along with Dr Ita Wegman, the groundwork of his contribution to medicine, Steiner was not reviving the medieval mentality which attributed everything in the body to four basic fluids, any more than he was recommending a return to 'blood-letting, sweating and vomiting'! He formulated his ideas anew, while recognizing that he was restoring something that had been understood in older times, and suggesting that it need not have been lost in the one-sided quest for specific remedies, the value of which he completely acknowledged too. Seen from this perspective, understanding history does not tie us to the past, but liberates us to work with it. (Note in passing the further irony concerning Paracelsus: failure to understand his modernizing role gradually led to a radical misconception. His work was merged in the vague mist of 'medieval superstition,' because later times noted the lack of what had since come to constitute the only acceptable and 'scientific' criteria. A pioneer of modern science in one central respect, Paracelsus' true role was soon lost to sight precisely among those who had reaped the harvest of his discoveries.)

We may take the case a stage further. Steiner took up the idea of four 'temperaments' — the psychological aspect of the 'humours' — in his educational method. It is not enough, he argues, for us to suppose that a child ought to develop in such-and-such a way, or have mastered certain ideas and subjects by a certain age. Different children enter into knowledge in different ways. A presentation that is a stimulating challenge to one will be a depressing obstacle that defeats another. The four traditional types (sanguine, choleric, phlegmatic and melancholic) showed that medieval psychology had understood the different attitudes which certainly do have a psycho-physiological basis. Yet a comparison of Steiner's characterizations with the medieval meaning of the terms soon shows that there is little direct relationship in detail. Steiner's concept is grounded in educational experience and a fresh classification of psychological phenomena. Nor should one fail to note that Steiner is a pioneer developmentalist. More orthodox developmental psychology has come groping along in his train. Against the widespread modern notion that everything can be accounted for developmentally as the child engages with the world, Jerome Kagan notes that children at similar stages of development do not in fact always react to a stimulus or challenge in the same way. He arrives by his own route at the insight that 'temperamental variations among young children imply that there will be few uniform consequences of a particular class of experience. Each child's temperament leads him or her to impose a special frame on experience ...'[16]

The details of the case are less important than the way we can see how Steiner's philosophy provides a deeper backdrop to their understanding. The results can certainly not be decided *a priori*, but from concrete investigation into human development and characteristic behaviour. Yet Steiner's way of thinking makes him aware of underlying tendency, by which a new way of understanding a subject leads to a polarization — often to a false dichotomy or to a choice between alternatives which ought really both to be given their due: holistics-specifics, evolution-religion, development-temperament. Where nineteenth-century science saw 'discovery' of 'what is really there' sweeping away 'ignorance' and 'superstition,' Steiner was aware of the complicity of thinking — of the 'unobserved element' in experience. In fact, he came to see the tendency toward polarization as fundamental in the evolutionary account he gave of meaning. Analytical thought leads to highly focussed insights: but if we mistake them for what is alone 'really there' we forget that we have isolated them out of what is by definition a larger whole. Steiner does not therefore reject analytical thought, but calls upon us to be aware of our own thinking processes, and to be always balancing the tendency to polarization which, if allowed free rein, inevitably leads us into viewpoints which are one-sided and unreal, perhaps above all humanly destructive. The need to be constantly rethinking is thus at the heart of Steiner's philosophy. For in the balance between the opposing tendencies inherent in our own thought is the relationship he called knowledge and freedom.

Steiner is potentially so exciting, then, because he does more than offer a 'complementary' view on the major developments of ideas in our time, pleading for some kind of residual role for spiritual ideas. Rather, he makes us aware of dimensions of meaning in the very ideas which constitute the framework of the modern world, whose consequences we have all too often failed to face up to, at least until the situation becomes too critical to shirk any longer. He shows our culture not an 'alternative' but a challenging version of itself.

Here then is the basic paradox of the simultaneous familiarity and strangeness of Steiner's thought. To a surprising extent, indeed, the kind of thinking for which he contended is appearing all around us, or at least is now being urged and discussed on every side. The need for 'holistic' explanations in science, for a developmental psychology as an approach to the understanding of man, and for a child-centred education based on its insights into changing human needs rather than the abstract map of knowledge — Steiner is still far ahead in many respects over even the most recent reforms. In view of the changes now sweeping through Eastern Europe and beyond, one might add his recognition of the need for social forms to be based on an absolute respect for free-thinking individuals. He did not superficially oppose the individual and the demands of society; such opposition is, however, the common feature in the great opposing myths of Communist collectivism and Western liberalism. For him the individual was a creative force in society, an agent of necessary change, and a constant test of the validity of social forms, but neither an end in himself nor an 'enemy of the people.' Now that the myths of East and West have played out their extraordinary history on the stage of the twentieth century, it may be that the signs of a more balanced reappraisal of values may also draw inspiration from Steiner's proposals, formulated for thoroughly practical reasons after the First World War. They suggest a more dynamically conceived 'threefold social order' — his framework designed to obviate the unproductive dualistic tensions built into the assumptions of the-individual-*versus*-the-State.[17]

In many other ways, Steiner could be claimed as the great forerunner of many of the best and most exciting elements in modern thought. We will see how it is possible, and indeed necessary to connect him with the influential Phenomenological movement in philosophy which has overturned many of the classical assumptions about knowledge and human existential values; and more generally with the great shift in all of modern thinking from categories based on inert 'things' to generative ideas of structure, system and form. Yet such an approach would be as inadequate in its way as the more common one which seeks to relegate him to the underworld of the 'alternative' or the 'counter-culture.' To read Steiner's philosophy, still now a century or so after he began to expound it, is to meet a radical challenge. For all the significant accommodations which have certainly been made by modernity to the letter of what he asked, to revisit Steiner's thought is to become aware of a deeper, less familiar dimension of the ideas he addressed to those 'free spirits' he asked to embark upon his 'path of knowledge.'

CHAPTER 1

An Ecology of Knowing: Steiner's Thought in Origin and Outline

Steiner's thought is based on awakening a new awareness of our own activity of thought. Most of modern thinking has either tried to reduce human beings to nature — to the world we know — and thereby overlooked the significant fact that we ourselves produce this knowledge. Or, when it does draw attention to the human dimension which such an inconsistent and one-sided reductive approach so signally leaves out, it has portrayed us as cut off in our uniqueness — depicted human awareness perilously exposed, so to speak, on the existential brink, left without inner content and estranged from nature, facing nothingness.

Steiner's thought confronts the forces which have produced this situation, but in doing so he turns the process of modernity back upon itself. The polarizations of modern thought do not so much need undoing, from his point of view, as grounding in an awareness of our own responsibility in the act of creating them. His philosophy goes along with the thrust of science: he puts us indeed *inside* the world we know, not however in a passive, reductive sense — but in an active, ecological sense; and conversely the existential freedom he offers is not the heroism of alienation and despair, but a way of learning creatively and freely how to belong. To understand his thought in outline we first of all need to see its roots in the origins of the modern attitudes, to which it stands not as an 'alternative,' but as a new understanding. We shall be exploring the background of Steiner's thought and of our own cultural position.

Steiner-Nietzsche or, A Refusal to Panic

The polarizations of the modern world are rooted in assumptions that reach back to the beginnings of the last century, and a little beyond. By the time of Steiner's student days, they were far advanced in their influence on modern life. Already towards the end of the nineteenth century, as a modern commentator has pointed out, 'the intellectual scene was dominated by two great hostile schools of thought. The one, an idealistic philosophy, traced its origin back to Immanuel Kant ...: the other, an embodiment of the materialistic world-view, had come down from Jeremy Bentham and had gained considerable influence through the much-read and much-appreciated writings of John Stuart Mill. The choice before a young philosopher seemed simple enough: he could turn either to the right, or to the left. There was, apparently, no middle way.'[1] The situation has not entirely changed to this day. Philosophical discussions, especially in the sphere of ethics, tend to take their point of departure from these same dominant traditions. Much more is at stake than the arguments advanced by Kant or by Jeremy Bentham. These philosophies focus assumptions and half-conscious principles on which lives have been lived and societies founded. Their clash in the nineteenth century prefigures some of the terrible struggles subsequently enacted in the twentieth: the struggles above all concerning the value of the individual in East and West. Kant's philosophy places the individual before a world on which he must somehow impose a meaning, and in which he must overcome himself in order to find out and to do the good in a reality that contradicts his very being. Bentham's utilitarian view subordinates the individual to the needs and happiness of society collectively, denying any larger meaning to our personality and the struggle it entails.

In many ways neither dominant tradition assigns much intrinsic value to the individual as such. For both of them the moral life is something imposed on the self rather than a source of fulfilment. Kant held that moral directives come to us with absolute, binding force as 'categorical imperatives.' For him the significance of the moral individual is exhausted in the act of coming to know what is right, in expressing the moral idea, just as the knowing individual in Kant's view has only the function of recognizing the necessary laws of all existence, without which the world would not be intelligible to us at all. And if in Kant the individual is called upon to abnegate himself totally before duty and truth, in Bentham the mortal individuality never really emerges at all. Deep down, Bentham evidently believes that our only fulfilment lies in the values of the whole, the society, the tribe or the race. It is assertions of individuality which rock the collective boat. His attitude to the individual is given almost symbolic presentation in his celebrated project for reform and rehabilitation: the Panopticon. The erring subject of his benevolent prison-house is to be under constant surveillance, under the unrelenting pressure of approval or disapproval from the representative of social norms who watches over him. The Panopticon is designed to afford no privacy. Bentham's idea was for a house of correction; but it is clearly no great step to the world of *Nineteen-Eighty-Four*. Application of his principle, and not only in the former Eastern-bloc countries, has been more widespread than Bentham could have foreseen.[2]

The warring systems left no middle way. The individual self seems doomed to a kind of grandeur in despair as it tries to fulfil the rigorous demands of Kantian law, or to be submerged in the claims of nature and society. In this situation, if the young philosopher were Rudolf Steiner as the nineteenth century drew to a close, he might well be attracted to a figure who proposed to break the Gordian knot, the iconoclastic and revolutionary thinker Friedrich Nietzsche. Indeed Steiner's path brought him into direct contact with the founder of modern nihilism. Yet his response to Nietzsche's genius was a complex one. Steiner regarded him at once as a 'fighter for freedom' and 'a tragic figure,' by whose writings he was 'simultaneously fascinated and repelled.'

Nietzsche proclaimed man's liberation from all repressive codes of morality. He was only too aware that deep-seated unconscious attitudes and social pressures manifest themselves in apparently rational systems of thought. He analysed the historical origins of ideas of good and evil, and found all of them very inadequate evidence for a metaphysical reality. Under his brilliant cross-examination they turned out to be 'human, all too

human.' He announced the death of God, and the 'transvalua-
tion of all values' at the hands of his individualistic hero, the
Superman. Certainly this Nietzschean protagonist was not worried about rocking the boat and disturbing the repose of happy
society — the 'country of good sleep' as he satirized it. In the
eyes of some, however, the extraordinary medley of philosophy
and imagination in which he brings back Zarathustra, the original prophet of good and evil, to unsay all that he had originated,
already hints at the subsequent derangement of his mind.

Steiner was likewise interested in a breakthrough to a new
moral vision. He had mixed since his student days with anar-
chists in Vienna and Berlin, and perhaps found much of this not
unfamiliar. It corresponded to ideas he himself had been developing. 'I had already formed ideas which were similar to his,' he
later wrote, 'when I became acquainted with Nietzsche's
works ... Independently, and from quite different directions, I
came to concepts which were in harmony with those Nietzsche
expressed in his writings.'[3] But the strangest thing about
Steiner's book *Friedrich Nietzsche: A Fighter against his Time*
(1895) is the complete absence of any reference to the shadow-
side of Nietzsche's character — of which Steiner was certainly
aware, for he had discussed it elsewhere, even before he met the
man himself far advanced in mental illness when Nietzsche's
sister invited Steiner to his home. He was subsequently invited
to undertake the prestigious task of editing Nietzsche's posthu-
mous papers. He declined, probably because his own position
as a thinker was being increasingly misunderstood as that of a
Nietzschean radical pure and simple.[4] His book on Nietzsche,
characteristically, does not aim to sum up and pass judgment on
another thinker's work, but to bring forward whatever is valuable and capable of being brought to clear expression.

Steiner divined in Nietzsche's outpourings the very 'liberating knowledge' he had tried himself to convey in *The Philosophy
of Freedom*: liberation from the metaphysical absolutes upon
which, in one guise or another, the nineteenth-century philosophies had insisted. He is at one with Nietzsche in the philosophical gesture which marked a distinct break with the past,
and fathered the twentieth century. At the same time, Steiner
clearly does not share what we may call the panic reaction

implicit in Nietzschean nihilism. If human thinking does not have a foundation in metaphysically necessary truths, if there are no duties which make an absolute demand on man transcending whatever seems right to his personal moral sense, then it seems to Nietzsche that there can be no right or wrong, no ultimate truth (God) but only nothingness. If man's thinking cannot be grounded on timeless, logical principles which *must* be true, it has only changing, historically varying principles which are no foundation at all. And so Nietzsche accepts nothingness, and pits against it the idea of the Superman who is strong enough to face nothingness in naked self-assertion.

Steiner also faces that nothingness, and regards it as a condition of modern consciousness itself that we do so. In his theory of knowledge, however, he questions the underlying assumptions more deeply. It is true, for him as for Nietzsche, that human knowledge cannot be given metaphysical foundations; for him as for Nietzsche, man's attempt to rest the meaning of his life on something outside himself is a shirking of the existential burdens laid upon man by the nature of his consciousness — but then, why hanker for foundations beyond human thinking itself at all? The epistemological part of *The Philosophy of Freedom* argues in effect that knowledge neither has nor needs 'foundations': thinking establishes connections between things, ideal connections whose validity does not need to be backed up by quasi-'real' metaphysical foundations or forces, or any other hypothetical entity such as the 'thing-in-itself.' Such assumptions create a dualistic philosophy, whose psychology is all too clear. 'The dualist believes that he would dissolve away the whole world into airy concepts, did he not insist upon real connections between the objects besides the conceptual ones. In other words, the ideal principles which thinking discovers seem too airy for the dualist, and he seeks, in addition, real principles with which to support them.'[5] It was for similar reasons that Gilbert Ryle made his celebrated assertion that if we ask why I am having a sensation which someone else is unable to feel, that is 'because it would make no sense to say that he was in my pain, and no sense, therefore, to say that he was noticing the tweak that I was having.'[6] Both Steiner and Ryle are concerned to reject the notion of some mysterious entity which *makes* me have the experience; the explanation that I was having it is sufficient, and we do not need to make of my sensation a quasi-real entity hovering around in a private world of mine to prop up the theory. 'Our exposition has shown,' says Steiner, 'that the hypothesizing of some reason why a judgment is true, beyond the fact that we recognize it as true, is a nonsense.'[7] (Whether Ryle's appeal to the principle of tautology is sufficient here remains more dubious.)

At any rate, the anti-metaphysical thrust of Steiner's argument is clear. By rejecting the idea that knowledge needs holding up as though it were a solid edifice, he wishes to show that there is no need for the desperate reaction that thinking needs a foundation yet has none; and no moral need for the hysterical gestures in the face of nothingness, or the Superman. Steiner was always to distrust the kind of polarization, the flying to extremes into which Nietzsche ran headlong. History has proved him right. The fashionable bravado of the Superman proved impossible to sustain, and has dwindled into what has been called the 'armchair nihilism' of Nietzsche's successors today.

Against Nietzschean nihilism Steiner posed the 'spiritual certainty' of knowledge, against the Superman the ideal of the 'free spirit' meeting new situations with new moral ideas. But his connection with Nietzsche remained important, if finally unproductive. His connections with the Nietzsche Archives, and the association of his name with Nietzsche's in the public mind generally was a potential source of confusion that would probably have determined him to adopt another tack, even if he had not found the influence of Lou-Andreas Salomé 'downright disagreeable' and Frau Foerster-Nietzsche totally impossible, yet both of them all too likely to shape the way Nietzsche was to be seen by posterity. Steiner's book on Nietzsche remains a remarkably positive assessment of the philosophical possibilities he himself saw.

Philosophical Riddles

Steiner's next main philosophical work expanded on his historical approach to knowledge: *The Riddles of Philosophy* (1900; much enlarged edition 1914) concentrated on the period since

Kant, but also included the whole sweep of the history of thought, essentially developing the idea of an 'evolution of consciousness.' Philosophical questions are not treated as questions with straightforward answers but as 'riddles,' to which the key is the unfamiliar standpoint or perspective of the riddler.[8] To put it another way, we understand the perplexities of a Descartes or a Kant when we see why, at a particular moment, particular issues became problematic for them, the angle at which they were seeing them. A brilliant example of this approach is given in Steiner's treatment of Kant and the hundred thalers. For in the *Critique of Pure Reason*, Kant had maintained against the empiricists that an imaginary hundred thalers were in every way the same as a real hundred thalers. Steiner cuts through the strange philosophical perplexities, which are rooted in the established empiricist arguments that perceived things are somehow, clearer, more definite, stronger and more distinct. Instead of entering into the whirlpool, he asks: from what standpoint is Kant's perspective valid? From that of someone for whom *using* the hundred thalers does not arise — for then of course the difference would most certainly emerge! Kant's perspective is that of the outsider, the pure onlooker. 'When a person cannot have them, then a hundred actual and a hundred possible thalers are in fact of exactly the same value.' And at once we see deeply into the kind of attitude which underlies the Kantian mentality, and the sense of explanatory power as well as the oddity that goes with the decision to stand outside reality, making it apparently unknowable 'in itself.'[9] For then we have the possibility of making the world pure idea, pure contemplation as if from a God-like elevation. Once we comprehend their particular slant on reality, the unfamiliar questions asked of it — then the situation becomes transparent. For Steiner, the starting-point of any philosophy is always an existing but changing state of ideas and interpretation. As in a riddle, the point is not the odd things being said, but we need to know from what unfamiliar perspective the question has been asked.

Questions become riddles because knowledge needs to change. Questions become 'metaphysical' when the thinker fails to realize that the framework to which they belong is a particular viewpoint. A changed perspective then continues to be confronted with ideas that no longer correspond to the living relationship that evolves between a thinker and his world. But Steiner does not offer in the conventional sense a refutation. He strives to help us understand the kind of awareness which gave rise to the way of thought. Becoming aware of our own thought-process, the 'unobserved element,' will then restore our perception of its real meaning. Steiner had already illustrated this approach in *The Philosophy of Freedom*. Philosophies — or at any rate, all philosophies worth studying — can bring a liberating insight when we cease to argue for or against them as such. For the philosopher is one who questions the naïve assumption that his own view is equally reality's view of itself. 'When the philosopher thus begins to reflect upon his relation to the world,' says Steiner, 'he finds himself caught in a system of thoughts which dissolves for him as fast as he frames it. The thought process is such that it requires something more than theoretical refutation. We have to live through it in order to understand the aberration into which it leads us and thence to find the way out.'[10] A picture held us captive, as in the famous dictum of Wittgenstein's *Philosophical Investigations:* but Steiner's account is less directed than Wittgenstein's toward disentangling a web of thoughts, more to placing for us the original insight that will suddenly make them all clear, and enriching our own consciousness through awareness of our changing historical relationship to the universe around us. Recognizing the picture as a picture liberates us to imagine new possibilities, not just to recognize our captivity.

By drawing attention to our own activity in this way, Steiner evades the seductive but ever elusive idea of a simple encounter between mind and matter, of just finding things, which makes of man a perpetual stranger — always opening the door, so to speak, on a totally unfamiliar situation. For such an onlooker-perspective, man inevitably remains always an outsider, and knowledge is necessarily something imposed upon the mind. But for Steiner, our consciousness is always adopting new viewpoints and encountering as a result new problems of interpreting things. The recognition of the problem is philosophy; the solution to these problems is knowledge. But the knowledge of one age is never the same as the knowledge of another, because man himself grows and changes.

At this juncture the Nietzschean panic-symptoms threaten once more: Steiner leads us to the brink of a frightening relativism. Becoming aware of our thinking, rather than perpetuating the happy assumption of its total transparency to the world it interprets, places us on the edge of the abyss. How, we ask, can knowledge be knowledge at all if it is always changing? But Steiner refuses to panic. Knowledge arises, and changes, when ideas are applied or modified according to the demands made upon them. We step into a new framework: but that does not mean that the moment before we were standing upon nothingness. We were standing within the world of understanding and interpretation that had then been reached. For Steiner this spiritual dimension — consciousness and its ever changing perspective — is an irreducible part of the picture. Knowledge is always somebody's knowledge from somebody's determinate point of view.

The great philosophers offered quite radically varying starting-points and systems for philosophy. Each of them was working with the ideas available at the time, however, and it was to the riddles posed by the thought of their time that they proposed the novel answers which have rendered them important thinkers. Steiner convincingly avoids the false perspective — which has nevertheless gained great prevalence today — which surveys the various systems alongside one another, and attributes the special emphasis on particular ideas to an arbitrary 'privileging' based on the interests of a special group. The implication is that there is nothing in the nature of things to compel us to make those ideas central to our interpretation, except perhaps in the power structures and self-interest of society or a group within it. Invoking the arbitrariness of 'privileged meanings' is an attempt to evade history. It forgets that earlier philosophers could not have our perspective. Yet all it succeeds in doing is to project modern intellectual pluralism (our awareness of different but co-existing systems of truth and moral value) inappropriately back onto historical subjects, treating Plato or Spinoza in effect as though they were dons on a modern American campus. It is to forget that awareness of plural possibilities is itself a particular historical phase which we have reached. But in reality the differing emphases in the great philosophers' ideas resulted from the different historical constraints upon them. The 'evolution of consciousness' means that we must see why people of the past were not able to ask questions which we can ask — much in the same way, as Steiner also saw, as children are constrained by their developmental stage. Nor are we different. Least of all can we exempt the modern relativists. Modern pluralism has itself arisen by a historical process — largely in recent American history, which is the story of people from diverse cultural backgrounds trying to live together. It is no more free from the given starting-points of history than any other view.

Where much of modern relativism has chased its own tail, Steiner's acceptance of an historical continuum of knowledge offers a way of inner assurance. And where we observe historical crises in the way people have thought — scientific revolutions or other fundamental reorientations in thinking — Steiner is able to point to underlying continuities, not in a constructed timeless world-out-there, but in an evolving relationship between man and the world he knows. Knowledge changes, and man grows in knowledge. The transitions are not arbitrary, since they are constrained by our human processes of transformation, developmental processes which ensure our continuity as knowers. Relativism however has made its point that the world cannot impose on us any single, necessary way of looking at it. Steiner can accept that, without feeling cut adrift. He embraces varied perspectives. Such changes are rather a leap to a new starting-point, the start of a new construction that changes the meaning of things. Steiner sees this not as arbitrary but as compelled by man's inherent development, his changing consciousness, his will to evolve. It is our presence on the scene which raises the questions, and the resolution of them is a matter of our doing. 'Knowledge,' as he put it, 'is not a concern of the world as such, but an affair man must settle for himself. *Things* demand no explanation.'[11] His philosophical theory is a working out of this basic idea, with its freeing consequences: knowledge as relationship. Steiner's anti-metaphysical starting-point is the restoration to the picture of this spiritual dynamic in its human-centredness. It brings with it the implication that meaning, or man's existence, can never be dictated from outside, and so cannot be limited or prescribed. And that, with its potential for terror and for transformation, is freedom.

The Outlines of Steiner's Thought

> In explaining our ideas, philosophers have found the greatest difficulty in the fact that we ourselves are not the external things, and yet the form of our ideas must correspond to the things. But on closer inspection it turns out that this difficulty does not really exist. We certainly are not the external things, but we belong together with them to one and the same world ... To my perception I am, in the first instance, confined within the limits bounded by my skin. But all that is included within this skin belongs to the world as a whole. Hence, for a relation to subsist between my organism and an object external to me, it is by no means necessary that something of that object should enter into me, or make an impress upon my mind like a signet-ring on wax ... The forces which are at work within my body are the same as those which exist outside. Therefore I really am the things — not, however, 'I' in so far as I perceive myself as subject, but 'I,' in so far as I am a part of the cosmic world-process. *Rudolf Steiner*

In his philosophical writings, Rudolf Steiner set out to challenge many of the false assumptions which he believed prevent us from realizing our place in the great stream, as he often put it, of the world-process. He objected profoundly to the mechanical treatment of the problem of knowledge, as though it could be solved in terms like those of a camera taking a snapshot of the world without being involved in it. Knowledge for him was an essentially living complex, a human activity. And it betokened our engagement with a world to which on a deeper level we ourselves profoundly belong: the world which has given us our organization as knowing beings. Our consciousness of a world 'out there' is for him not a strange contradiction in the

constitution of things, but an enigmatic feature of our to relationship to our environment, to be solved with the help of concepts of form, development and a deeper idea of evolution.

From the time of his pioneering work on the scientific writings of Goethe, advocating different interpretations of colour
and of biological growth to the materialistic theories of his time,
Steiner found himself in the *avant garde* of many of the developments in the understanding of structure and form, so important
in modern thought. Early on in his work he saw the need to
establish the epistemological basis on which Goethe's science
rested, and in his *Theory of Knowledge Implicit in Goethe's World
Conception* he sketched the implications of these ideas for the
physical, biological and the human sciences in a way which
already offers a glimpse of the direction his own work was to
take after the turn of the century.[12] Nowadays when the classical
scientific structures of the nineteenth century are increasingly
questioned, Goethe's ideas are once again attracting attention,
and much of what Steiner had to say is strikingly relevant to
modern discussions of the nature of science, especially those
which stress the developmental processes underlying the
'growth of knowledge' and the historical setting in which
knowledge is generated. Steiner's great concept of the evolution
of consciousness, and the changing conditions of knowledge as
an expression of man's changing relationship with the world, is
perhaps becoming easier to grasp in the age of developmental
psychology (such as the child-psychology of Piaget).
Knowledge is described by Steiner as process and relationship.
As we have seen, he rejected any kind of 'metaphysical' view of
knowledge, based on the notion that we can somehow step outside our own position of involvement with the world. Putting it
simply, we attain objectivity not by stepping outside our perspective as knowers to see what things are 'really like,' but by
understanding the angle of our vision from within, and the conditions it entails.

It is often held against Steiner that he thereby still somehow
wanted to extend science beyond the observable, or externally
representable. His use in this connection of the old term 'occult'
for the component in our knowledge which cannot be reified or
attributed to objective reality, which Descartes had tried to

expunge,[13] led to further misconceptions. But developments in the conceptual language of science, as much as philosophical understanding, have put him back in the forefront of scientific debate. For modern physics has had to take the leap into the non-representable which raises all these issues in acute form. Very many of the entities and processes which physics uses to explain the world cannot be pictured in terms of the world we experience, or behave, in its terms, in self-contradictory ways. Nor is it just, as is often assumed, just a matter of events too small to be perceived which create problems. As we shall see, the astronomer Norman Davidson gives the telling example of our solar system, which the textbooks so often invite us to picture, with the sun like a football, and pea-sized planets a football-pitch or two away, and so on. Yet the exercise cannot be done. For if we make the objects to scale for the distances involved, we will not be able to see them at all![14] In other words, the attempt to construct a concept of how the world is which puts the observer outside, merely looking at it, cannot be fulfilled. The picture, in this case the celestial 'model' cannot be made self-standing. If the model is valid, and unless we want to go back to attributing some sort of metaphysical power to thinking, beyond the range of what we can perceive, we must suppose that the 'unrepresentable' relates rather to our particular perspective. The model becomes functional when we specify where we are in the picture, and so the particular aspects we would be able to see; if it is to connect with reality, therefore, the relation of the model to the world must include an account of our own involvement. In crossing the threshold of the unrepresentable, in becoming 'occult' science, as we shall see, advanced science itself has come to need the concepts of knowledge formulated by Steiner independently decades before.

Steiner believed that such a view of knowledge might have saved Western thought from the crisis of relativism and all-encompassing doubt which has beset it in the twentieth century. Instead, the effort to construct knowledge as a self-standing edifice, concerning which everyone would have to agree, actually led to deep anxieties, and a sense of inner contradiction across the range of our culture. The collapse of traditional certainties led to an unhealthy polarization between reductive, sceptical science and a defensive religion that has become progressively less sure of its foundations. The celebrated 'Evolution versus Creation' debates which Darwinism afterwards claimed to have 'won' had in effect already conceded the ground on which the arguments were fought, leaving the impression that there was no choice except between the monolithic alternatives of materialism or fundamentalism; thinkers who, like Steiner, questioned whether an evolving universe must necessarily be a Godless universe were already crowded out of the arguments, denied a chance to question the presuppositions made. But in retrospect we may notice that the drive behind all this to reduce all experience to its supposed foundations was the expression, not of confidence but of inner uncertainty, of the need to prop up the edifice of abstractions in what Steiner called 'a convulsive effort to attach oneself to reality.'[15] Despite all the achievements of materialistically orientated science and technology, the inner uncertainty has not gone away, however. If Steiner is right, what is needed is a deeper concept of knowledge itself.

He certainly found much to approve in the emerging philosophical movement of Phenomenology, built on the pioneering work of Franz Brentano whose lectures Steiner had attended as a student in Vienna. There are many parallels to Steiner's ideas in the work of the great Phenomenologists, most especially perhaps in that of Max Scheler.[16] Yet he felt that they had not tackled the crisis of knowledge in a sufficiently radical way — a crisis which required for its solution nothing less than a new vision of man's place in the universe. Phenomenology suspended judgment, putting the act of knowledge in brackets in order to examine it, but cast little light on how the mind and the world came to be confronting each other in the first place. Evolution furnished the starting-point for such a vision, and Steiner's thought is the most thorough-going response of which I am aware to the possibilities of an evolutionary kind of thinking. Instead of a desperate search for foundations, knowledge might be grounded in the growing, changing being of Man. That would mean abandoning the notion of the impassive onlooker, and including the seeking, striving human self in the picture we form of the cognitive process. Steiner is at his most modern, perhaps, in recognizing that knowledge has ceased to be the kind of inherited, stable set of opinions which used to be able to unite a culture in a view of the world. The epistemology of science has shifted the emphasis to the areas of new potential, with their uncertainty and their ability to relativize what we already know. The official account of our relation to truth had not kept pace, however: in a sense Steiner's human-centred philosophy is designed simply to help us relate to the changed conditions of knowledge.

It is the exact opposite of what may be seen as another attempt to resolve those same tensions, namely the giving to science of a quasi-religious status (a mix-up of categories Steiner always deplored), receiving a kind of spurious worship. Contrary to some crude misunderstandings, Steiner does not simply divinize man either; but he does explore in his 'spiritual science' our own engagement in the cognitive encounter, inserting ourselves into the world-process and being changed in our turn.

He rejected the empiricist philosophical fiction of the mind just discovering what is there, having a completely fresh impression, just as he did that other fiction of the mind filtering everything so as to be cognisant only of its own pre-ordained ordering capacities. He arrives at a picture that is neither the blank sheet of empiricism, nor the mind locked up in its own categories of Kant. Once again it is in the sphere of actual scientific development that he proves most relevant. His evolutionary view is actually strikingly akin to recent 'anthropic' ideas that have played a controversial role in the new cosmology of science.[17] For Steiner, the world is not just a spectacle which, in some odd way, simply present itself to us in so far as we have eyes to see it, organs to touch, hear or smell it, or minds to grasp it in particular ways. What we know of the world depends on the fact that we are part of the world and have been shaped by it, so that from the beginning our nature and organization become not a limit, but the actual key to the nature of the universe to which we belong and which brought us into being.

In his fragmentary sketch of the ideas for his *Anthroposophy* (1910), Steiner tackled in a novel way the question of the apparent impasse that results from the way our sense-impressions are determined by the organization of our eyes, ears, etc. It seems as though this means we can never escape from the charmed circle, or find any element of real force, of actual power, in what meets us experientially. It is just the reflection of our own perceptual instruments. It might seem therefore that we can only infer a reality that is the cause of it. But Steiner turns the argument on its head. The active, real element is not to be sought in such a metaphysical inference, but in the way that perceptual forces have brought about the evolution of the eye, nose or ear. He turns the argument back upon the *real* processes, i.e. the evolutionary shaping of the sense-organs, as the key to understanding the forces that bring about perception.[18] We ourselves become the record of their activity. And this way of arriving at the forces that bring about our actual situation through analysing our own organization is certainly close to the modern 'anthropic' principle, which basically means drawing conclusions about the world we are observing from the fact of our being there to observe it. Rather than collapsing the mind into solipsism (the older idea of the limiting 'selection effect'), this approach is leading toward a surprisingly integrated view of science, showing the far-reaching basis of our knowledge in cosmic conditions needed for it to arise.[19] At the same time, however, it has not been enough to overthrow many of the 'empirical' assumptions of modern science, which often continues to assert that we live in a random universe, etc. Steiner made the principle more integral to his thought. The resulting philosophy broke out of the older traditions of idealism and materialism alike to arrive at a new way of thinking, a new, 'anthroposophical' vision of human nature in the setting of an interrelated world.

In this perspective, knowledge ceases to be a mirroring, passive affair and becomes a process whereby we insert ourselves actively in the given setting of our lives, which therefore always carries a moral significance. No one can claim to stand outside and remain morally neutral, staying 'objective' and leaving the moral issues to others. The fantasy of many scientists that they are able to 'discover' things, and present them in a 'value free' way remains dangerous and unfounded. It is hard to see how an intelligent man, as is Professor Lewis Wolpert whom I take, almost at random, as a spokesman for such views, can write that 'Scientific knowledge is value-free and in itself carries no ethical implications' on the basis that 'knowing how to carry out an abortion is not the same as performing one.'[20] Finding out how to perform an abortion, or to build an atom bomb, are simply not commensurate with the Professor's guidance that scientists 'should not be allowed on their own to take decisions about applications of their work that may affect us all.' But few have taken the radical step of recognizing that, since knowledge presupposes a particular relation to reality from which it is true, we carry a moral perspective into every act of relating to the world. That is in fact what we mean by morals: our relation to the world is not completed in our acknowledgment of what is there, but is made by our very human presence into the basis of change, action. Knowledge does affect the situation it creates, for good or ill, and the knower is the one on the spot. Steiner's view is that we need to accept the responsibility for the way that, as knowers, we change the potential and actual course of the world.

The moral value of our knowledge and actions can never be imposed from outside but is intrinsic and derives from our own free engagement with the world around us through knowing. Hence for Steiner there can never be a normative science of ethics — a science of telling people what to do, so that the committee set up to tell scientists what to do about their discoveries would in no way be able to relieve the scientists of their apparent uncomfortable moral awareness, though there can be in Nietzsche's sense a 'natural history of morality,' in which knowledge itself becomes an account of our historically changing relationship with the world, and evolving moral attitudes. The Kantian conception of the mind imposing its own order on the things we know, on the other hand, is echoed by the idea of controlling, manipulative knowledge which many of the sciences seek. Steiner's idea of knowledge as relationship stresses instead our own need to be transformed, to learn and grow through cognitive encounter and allow reality to reveal itself in ever new aspects. We neither have nor need any standards beyond that of our self as it becomes free to tell us what to do. But Steiner argues that this is not, or not ultimately morally dangerous. For the self is that paradoxical self-transcending self which learns and deepens by encounter. There is a place in this vision for the recognition of the intrinsic *value* of the other, which we may call the spiritual — for a moral-cognitive relationship that includes not only dominance and control but also love.

The self attains to freedom through knowledge of its situation and its moral role; or rather, freedom and real self-knowledge become the same. Steiner's modern world-view accepts that we need a complex and sophisticated conception of human identity — though he does not agree that the complexity of the pressures, cognitive and ethical, brought to bear need rule out the possibility of coherent self-existence. On the contrary, they serve to differentiate it from any kind of existence as 'thing,' playing a fixed role in relation to other things. For the self cannot be defined by any past stage of its development or fixed structure of ideas, but is quintessentially a learning and growing self. It is 'free' in the real and unequivocal sense that in responding with knowledge to the demands of the world and transforming itself, the self becomes more authentic, not less. 'Man is most human,' as Steiner was later to put it, 'in the process of becoming.'[21] It is in those situations when we draw back from the encounter, and decline or remain unable to assimilate it, transforming ourselves so as to absorb what it has to teach us, that we will find ourselves determined from outside by an alien 'compulsion,' just as repression turns emotion into forces we cannot control rather than ones we can integrate into our personality. Conventional thought tries to invert the true state of affairs, and to ground our knowledge in some external framework of truth 'imposed' upon us rather than in our freedom to interpret, to discover and to deepen our given experience. An approach like Steiner's feels dangerously open-ended, lacking the external guarantees which many still seek. But Steiner argues that we do not need more than the spiritual, inner grounds of knowledge — and indeed, we never can have any others. Many of the traditional philosophical problems are turned on their head, as they have been in so much of twentieth-century thought, but Steiner is able to project a creative and even a cosmic role for the free spirit which reveals in its activity the deeper truth about the world that has brought it into being. Knowledge is actually not a reflecting of the world as it already is, but the work of the developing free self and so a further step in the world's evolving. Already in perceiving the moral dimension of a situation, we take the first step in 'higher knowledge,' of the supersensible nature of the world.

As Rudolf Steiner once summed it up:

> The result of these investigations is that truth is not, in the way that is commonly supposed, the reflection in idea-form of some real object, but something freely engendered by the human mind, and would not exist at all if we did not bring it forth. The task of knowledge is not to recapitulate in the form of concepts what is given to us in some other way. It is rather to create an entirely new domain which, when taken together with the world presented through sense-perception, yields for the first time the full reality. From this point of view the highest mode of human activity — the creative activity of the mind — fits organically into the whole process of cosmic events. Without this activity, the world-process could not be conceived of as something whole and complete in itself. The human being is not an idle onlooker before the pageant of the world, mirroring back in his spirit what is going on in the universe without involving him; he is an active participant in a cosmic creative process, and his knowledge is actually the most highly evolved part of the organism of the universe.[22]

Such words seemed to most of Steiner's philosophical contemporaries to ask for too complete a rethinking of the role of knowledge, or they thought perhaps that it pointed back to older notions of a divine Logos, the divine-creative power of meaning, which had never been put in satisfactory conceptual form. Steiner insisted rather that it arose out of the modern theory of evolution, and that it was simply spelling out the philosophical consequences of taking evolution seriously. There is growing evidence that he was right. The development of the sciences of meaning in recent times, for instance, has brought us according to one expert in the field, to face a stark choice. For they seem to show that language conceived as an onlooker imposing significance on a world that is 'other' can never explain real meaning, or give us real identity. If we do not follow the route of seeing knowledge as part of the evolving universe, we may have no other choice than to accept that we know no meanings and can find no identity — only 'meaning-effects,' and 'ultimate *aporia*,' that is, being radically at a loss before the world we inhabit. That is the cross-roads we face: we must be prepared to accept that man is indeed the utter outsider, forever unable to attach himself to the world or to be himself, or, if there is meaning at all, that we share in a God-given meaning, or logos-structure of the world. Steiner's philosophy offers to demonstrate that the latter alternative need not be a backward-looking one: indeed it is demanded by the critical situation to which development of thought has now brought us.

This introductory book is not an attempt to give a technical account of Steiner's achievement in philosophy; still less does it offer any sort of detailed guide through his fundamental texts. It is more a work about the relevance of his philosophy than a philosophical argument, and its aim is to orientate the modern reader in the direction and general significance of Steiner's thought — so often misjudged — and to point him or her to discussions that are relevant to issues perennially important or to matters that seem crucial today. The detailed work of establishing his position Steiner undertook fitfully, though often with telling brilliance. He himself offered no closed circle of arguments but suggested new ways forward where Western thought seemed to him to have a kind of intellectual species of 'blind spot.' The mesmeric effect of Kantian ideas on his own time led him into a rather Wittgensteinian exercise of entering the metaphysical maze, gently disentangling from their delusion those of his contemporaries who had become so strangely convinced that reality was always there but out-of-reach, unknowable but morally incumbent upon us in inexorable duty, the more intense because inscrutable. One sometimes feels in reading Steiner (or certain of his followers) that one almost ought first to become a Kantian in order to be liberated from his bonds. But to make Steiner's great achievement the overcoming of Kant's seductive metaphysics is both to exaggerate and to trivialize it: for one thing there is nothing like a detailed refutation, nor was that Steiner's aim. And the obsession with Kant obscures the real focus of Steiner's struggle — against materialism: the problem with Kant was that he claimed to have resolved the issue of materialism, but in fact left it increased in power. Moreover the deeper meaning of Steiner's anarchic notion of philosophy as liberating the free self is in truth transportable into modern arguments just as effectively. In other ways today we are under pressure to accept that we are up against inexorable scientific 'truths,' for instance, of genetics, which limit or more often deny our freedom outright. It is easy to overlook the fact that we decide that the aspects of human nature treated by genetics are the 'essential' ones, when genetics claims that human nature is essentially determined by our genes. In reality, quite other factors can, and do, play a part in what we are. Steiner's method, revealing our own complicity in these constructions, interpretations based on a particular relationship to the world but imprisoning us if we do not understand the forces behind their construction, can still lead us to envision new and other relationships, new and creative reinterpretations that liberate us to reassume our threatened humanity once more.[23]

In the present book, then, Kant is accordingly relegated to an appendix (see Appendix 2). What is important here is Steiner's notion that philosophy does not merely serve to describe, or even to evaluate his or anyone else's view of our situation, but is itself the source of freedom within it. The philosopher is 'an artist in the realm of concepts' — according to a metaphor which actually provides a far-reaching key to his thought. The philosophical moment is one in which we look upon our experience, or raw material of our lives, with an eye to its creative possibilities. It includes the freedom of detachment, not in order to separate us from life, but to envision it anew and reaffirm it in the light of some wider context, some new idea, some previously hidden resource.

Steiner needs rethinking, then, in terms of our contemporary world with the power of its ideas to enslave or imprison, to liberate or humanize us. An awareness of areas in which Steiner's kind of thinking is now bearing fruit can return us to his work with a sense of freshness and continuing relevance. At the same time, the force of Steiner's critique of established thought will also be borne in upon us, despite the strange half-familiarity often felt in reading what he wrote today. His spiritual response to the implications of relativism, of change, of the loss of that assured identity for man himself which marks off our era from almost all that preceded it, is finally different from those which have shaped our own restless and uncertain, distracted and distracting modern life. Perhaps that is why after all, in a manner he would certainly not have wished, Steiner's ideas have remained knowledge for the few. The sense of inner freedom which he derived from his philosophical vision contrasts with the alarming sense of constriction, of inner helplessness, felt by so many in our civilization. Steiner's thought can help us in the dilemmas of modern life, to which it remains a continuing challenge and a proffered balm.

CHAPTER 2

Knowledge as Relationship

Phenomenology

The young Rudolf Steiner grounded his thesis, later published as the short book *Truth and Knowledge,* on the call for a theory of knowledge that would be 'free from presuppositions.' The language of that call now sounds familiar to us, since it was the cry of what became known as the Phenomenological Movement, associated with the names of Husserl, Scheler, Heidegger and others whose philosophical background had much in common with Steiner's.[1] They too wished to study the act of knowing on its own terms. Yet it is worth making the effort of reconstructing the situation in which Steiner wrote, in order to realize just how strange that call must have seemed to the philosophically trained readers he was attempting to reach. For epistemology, the science of knowledge as such, had hitherto been called upon to fulfil the role almost exclusively of backing up a proposed metaphysic. Supposing one wished to prove that reality is 'ultimately' material particles: one's epistemology had to establish that knowledge could be understood in terms of impacts and impressions from without upon a material-physical nervous system. Supposing one wished to prove that reality is spiritual, or akin in nature to the human mind: one's theory of knowledge had naturally to establish that knowledge is only possible on the assumption that the mind essentially contributes to, or in some degree makes what it knows. Or, one might argue the reverse. But it would have seemed apparent to almost everyone that a theory with no assumptions was *ipso facto* a theory with nothing to prove and perhaps nothing to say.

Steiner, however, believed that epistemology had suffered many distortions and setbacks by being treated in this way as a battle-ground for contending philosophical postulates. It had led in the nineteenth century especially to an obsession with objectivity, i.e. with one aspect of the cognitive process — an obsession that has survived almost intact in many circles today, many of whom claim it as the only 'scientific' approach. Their implication is that the sole alternative would be illusory, subjective. But the philosophical problems raised by the continuing attempt to isolate some elements of experience as alone absolutely true, whilst ejecting all the others into the dustbin of the merely subjective, return with equal obstinacy. After analysing in depth the 'physicalist' approach to our perception of colours, for example, which tries to reduce all colour to physics and especially to wave-lengths of light, the philosopher Jonathan Westphal has recently concluded that it is not just the detail of this theory that is wrong, but the fundamental approach. Much that is 'real' in our colour perception does not correspond to physical properties in the object at all. Yet that does not mean that it is meaningless, or that it has no significant structure, or that it does not belong in a unified description of what actually happens when we see a coloured object in the real world. Even when we set aside the important question of whether 'physicalist' science is giving a correct description on its own level, there remains the still more fundamental issue of the misguided notion, the philosophical confusion which informs the underlying aim. 'In fields where there is still much to be learned,' comments Westphal, 'as in the physiology and psychology of colour perception, what is needed is not a reduction which so to speak polarizes our knowledge into the primary and physical, and the secondary or derivative or illusory, but clearer and more imaginative theory.'[2] He argues that a premature synthesis has actually blocked the way to a more dynamic understanding of what colour means in our experience. And it is not just a matter of clearing the way for a reappraisal of Goethe's colour-science, which was based on the relationship between the seer, light and darkness. But rather, if Rudolf Steiner was right, similar considerations need to be applied to many other basic areas of human experience as commonly treated by the analytic sciences. A part of his significance as a philosopher of freedom who refused to bracket freedom out of epistemological discussion is that he resisted the premature importation of physical and all other such ontological absolutes into the account of knowledge, and held that this had for too long obscured the nature of knowledge as engagement and as transformation. Knowledge is not so much a way that we reproduce an 'objective' world, but a relationship into which we place ourselves. It is a dimension not of subjection but of freedom.

Instead of running headlong into theories of what alone is real, Steiner argued in that philosophical sketch of *Truth and Knowledge* (later given the subtitle 'Prelude to a Philosophy of Freedom'), we need first to understand what is happening in our own processes of knowledge. Not 'what is happening in so far as it tends to prove this or that,' but simply, without presuppositions, what constitutes knowing. The human knower might then be able to take an acknowledged place in the world he knows without being necessarily intimidated, reduced to unfreedom, by the seemingly absolute nature of the known. Conventional wisdom might hold that a theory of knowledge on such terms would turn out to be vacuous. But Steiner, like Nietzsche, knew that the alternatives themselves always turned out to be 'all too human.' Once freed from metaphysical assumptions about the content of knowledge, epistemology might in a more positive sense restore to us the genuinely human content those assumptions had disguised and rendered unreal.

Those who are at all familiar with the Phenomenological Movement will find many points of similarity here. Steiner had in effect called for a pure phenomenology of knowledge, and some of his subsequent thought finds fascinating analogies in the work of Husserl, and perhaps even more in that of Max Scheler. Steiner has in common with Scheler not just an awareness of the religious implications inherent in his liberation of the human spirit, but many parallel movements of thought: his idea of values, or moral qualities as concretely perceived by a kind of higher act of seeing, his understanding of evolution, his distinction between the soul, or psychic life of man held in common with the animals, and spirit, which belongs to a different order, his Christian vision of the way that man can be freed from the past and the determined by his creative ability to change its meaning by acting in the present.[3] I mention this here rather in passing because it serves to refute the idea that Steiner somehow deviated fundamentally from the mainstream of philosophical thought, and therefore has no constructive points of contact with it. Steiner was working at problems that were to be resolved in similar ways by other important thinkers in the twentieth century. The radicalism of his approach in certain respects should not prevent us from recognizing his place in philosophical history. At the same time he certainly remained independent: his analysis of feeling, for instance, departs wholly from the approach of the Phenomenological School.[4]

One thing that Steiner had in common with the Phenomenologists is an admiration for the pioneering work of Franz Brentano, whose lectures Steiner had attended in Vienna. Brentano's concern was to develop a philosophical psychology, and Steiner subsequently hailed his famous concept of 'intentionality' as at least a first step toward the kind of 'spiritual science' he himself was subsequently to develop.[5] Intentionality goes back to a root meaning of 'pointing,' and was already understood in late medieval thought — of the kind so despised by the *Giordano Bruno Society* and their ilk. It was used by Brentano to characterize the quality of 'directedness' in such activities as intending, meaning, etc. It was a quality, he argued, that could only be understood from within: when I use a gesture to indicate the colour on the cover of a book, for instance, it cannot be distinguished outwardly whether I mean to indicate the texture of the binding, or the writing on its surface, rather than the colour. Yet this kind of understanding seems evidently prior to linguistic explanations, which indeed depend upon it since I could not learn how to apply the word 'blue' if I could not understand how to recognize it being pointed out. For Brentano, such directedness belongs to all acts of meaning and is 'existentially psychic,' that is, it can never be reduced to external configurations: there is no outward difference between pointing at the colour and pointing at the texture. It can be argued that intentionality provides the key to many activities such as reading a text, which the more usual cause-and-effect explanations bog down in bizarre complexities or seem to distort altogether. It is very hard to explain how the impact of shapes and letters 'causes' meaning to arise in the reader's mind, and the approach arguably fails to describe the reading-phenomenon completely. (We do not in fact, for example, simply allow the sequence of meanings to unroll when we read, but perform complex and active correlations, looking backward, forward and assessing blocks of material at a time.) An actively directed engagement which is brought to bear on the printed page, involving expectation, anticipation and other 'intentional' processes, seems much more fruitful an approach. And a good deal of our experience in understanding the world, picturing the world, remembering, and so on, makes considerably more sense when understood in this way. A 'mental image' is drastically misrepresented if we suppose it to be like a projection onto a screen 'somewhere' inside us; a phenomenological account of mental images more helpfully shows them as targets of directed activity, 'seeing something as,' based on intention or reference, rather than quasi-physical reproductions of the world around us, or curious, elusive entities which have to invented to supposedly 'cause' our mental states. When we represent something to ourselves as being the case, for Steiner, the relevant question is not a 'Whence?' a where lies the cause of our doing so, but a 'Whither' our reasoning process is directed. It is this which enables him to distinguish the psychic reality involved from 'love and hate,' in contrast to some philosophers who have confused knowledge with our affirming or rejecting something represented in the mind, as if its truth depended on the intensity with which we feel it. Steiner is clear that something different, something intentional in Brentano's sense is involved: 'Experiences of love and hate ... do not give rise to the question of how they converge, but rather a Whence? they arise. In the case of reasoning (judgment), the question is Whither? and the answer is, Toward the representation.'[6]

The representing to ourselves of what something is does not mean we have a picture of it inside our head. Such a notion actually fails to explain what it sets out to show. For once we turn our attention upon the mental image, the question of how to bridge the gap between the onlooking consciousness and the image is simply repeated on a more inward level: we would need to make an image of the image, and so on *ad infinitum* in a desperate attempt to reach an inner correspondence. Or to put it another way, such a 'camera'-like notion of what happens in knowing something can never deliver to us the observing self which is supposed to acquire the knowledge, since it recedes in an infinite regress. Something seems to be wrong with the whole idea. Yet strange to say, many would prefer to keep the theory, and conclude that in accordance with its outcome we must therefore abandon the observing self. They conclude that there is no such thing as the self/subject, which becomes a fathomless abyss or hall of mirrors when we try to lay hold of it. Here we have another example of the way in which philosophy serves to remind us of our own complicity in creating the situation. Steiner's philosophical method draws attention to the 'unobserved element,' our own thinking, and — as we shall see — asks us to halt the spiralling regression which estranges us from our self and from the world.

Knowing something in perception for Steiner is more usefully described as like reading-activity, rather than reproducing an image-copy of the world. A then-neglected medieval philosophy had given Brentano his basic concept, and it is there in premodern open-minded ideas (in this case in the 'medieval mystic' Valentin Weigel) that Steiner finds an account whose simplicity and directness appeals to him by cutting through the post-Kantian morass. For him, Steiner explains, perception is like reading a book:

> If the book did not exist of course I could not read it; but it could be there, and I would still not be able to read anything in it if I did not know the art of reading. Thus the book must be there, but of itself it cannot give me anything at all. Everything that I read I must bring forth out of myself. This is also the nature of natural (sensory) perception. Colour exists as the intended object, but of itself it can give the eye nothing ... The colour is no more in the eye than the content of the book is in the reader. If the content of the book were in the reader, he would not need to read it at all. Nevertheless, in reading, this content

does not flow out of the book but out of the reader. It is
the same with the sensory object. What this sensory object
is, externally, does not flow into man from outside but
rather from inside.

The late nineteenth century had painted itself into a corner with
its Kantian theory of mental images, taking man's role in their
production in a very one-sided way to mean that we can never
know anything except our own mental world. 'With this simple,
straightforward way of thinking,' comments Steiner, 'Valentin
Weigel stands on a much higher level than Kant':

> Although perception flows from man, yet it is solely the
> content of the intended object which emerges from it by
> way of man. As it is the content of the book which I
> discover from reading, not my own, so it is the colour of
> the intended object which I discover through the eye, not
> a colour which is in the eye or in myself ... Man cannot
> remain passive if he wants to perceive the things of the
> senses, and simply allow them to act upon him; he must
> be active, and bring this perception out of himself.[7]

Steiner was thus following in some of the same intellectual
paths, and in general responded creatively to Brentano's work.
He used the occasion of an obituary essay on Brentano in his
book *Riddles of the Soul* (1917) to announce the principles of his
own threefold conception of man, central to all his later work
and the spiritual psychology underlying Waldorf education.

In the same book he included a substantial appended note
'On the real nature of the intentional relation.' In this, he reaf-
firms, the soul-life is opened to something that Steiner and some
of the phenomenologists distinguished from the psychical as the
spirit, taking us into domains beyond our own subjectivity.
Earlier lectures had meanwhile developed Steiner's own thinking about directedness, mental images and psychic life, and
Brentano was also sharply criticized for falling back at a crucial
point upon outmoded Aristotelian ideas, rather than pushing
forward to the conception of spirit in a modern way.[8] But techniques of analysis like those of Phenomenology certainly helped

him articulate his account of human interaction with the world on many levels, physical, psychic and spiritual, when he came to write his anthroposophical works. A passage from his fundamental book *Theosophy* may serve to indicate this — it is also a reminder that the 'seer' Steiner did not forget his philosophy when he came to render the results of his fascinating 'spiritual research.'

Steiner characterizes a threefold relationship which we have to our world by means of the following example:

> I cross a meadow covered with flowers. The flowers make known their colours to me through my eyes. This is fact, which I accept as given. I rejoice in the colours of the flowers. Through this, I turn the fact into a matter of my own. Through my feelings, I connect the flowers with my own existence. Then a year later I cross the same meadow again. Other flowers are there, and new pleasure arises in me through them. My joy of the previous year will still be there, as a memory. It is within me, though the object which aroused it in me is gone. But the flowers which I now see are of the same kind as those I saw the previous year; they have grown up in accordance with the same laws as did the other ones. If I have found out about this species and the laws which govern it, I will rediscover them in the flowers of this year just as I found them in those of the last. And then, perhaps, I shall reflect: Last year's flowers have passed away, and my delight in them is only a memory. It exists only in connection with my own being. But what I recognized in last year's flowers and again this year will be there as long as such flowers grow. In that something has revealed itself to me that is not dependent on my existence, in the way my joy is. My feelings of joy remain in myself; the laws, or essential characteristics of the flowers, remain outside me in the world.

> Thus man links himself continually in a threefold way with the things of the world. For the time being let us not read anything into this fact, but merely take it as it stands. It follows that man has three sides to his nature. This —

and nothing else — will for the present be indicated here by the three terms 'body,' 'soul' and 'spirit.' Anyone who connects any pre-conceived ideas or even suppositions with these three terms will of necessity misunderstand the explanations which follow. By 'body' is meant that through which the things in man's environment, as in the example the flowers in the meadow, reveal their presence to him. By 'soul' is meant that by which he connects the things to his own being, and through which he experiences joy or dislike, desire and aversion, pleasure and pain in connection with them. By 'spirit' is meant that which becomes manifest in him so that, in the words of Goethe, he looks upon things 'like a divine being.'

This is the sense in which a human being consists of body, soul and spirit. Through his body, man is able to place himself for the present in connection with things. Through his soul, he retains within him the impressions which they make on him. Through his spirit is revealed what the things retain in their own nature.[9]

Steiner's account has considerable philosophical cutting-edge. Instead of focussing on the obsessive issue of objectivity, he draws attention to the uniqueness of the several dimensions of relationship implicit in a human experience. Instead of the unrealistically simplified instances often found in textbooks, his example involves somewhat complex feelings and comparisons, awareness of one's own involvement through memory and regret. The element in the experiences that transcends self is also a part of the complex whole, not treated as though it could be hypostatized in a metaphysical way as the only 'real' feature. In fact, it exists in the special dimension of relationship which Steiner calls 'spirit,' although the fact that we cannot take it to have some absolute, detachable significance does not mean any the less that it is not true, nor does it reduce it to anything merely subjective.

Many observations could profitably be made here. Firstly, Steiner does not regard the spirit in man as something whose existence has got to be proved, or inferred by any kind of deduction. It is a dimension of our experience, rather, which we must be careful not to analyse away by too crude a reduction of experience in the one-sided pursuit of our particular, 'scientific' or other purposes. Nor is the 'spiritual world' of which Steiner speaks something of which we ordinary mortals have no experience or which he asks us to take as a postulate. We can become aware of it by virtue of our qualities as human beings as we strive to understand the world, even in the experience of a flowery meadow on a spring afternoon. Steiner does assert that our awareness of that dimension can be vastly deepened, indeed infinitely so: in fact, each of the three sides of experience, since they are conceived as relationship, are capable of infinite enrichment, or are in themselves inexhaustibly rich in potential significance. That includes, as we shall see, the connection through the senses or bodily aspect of the world.[10]

It need hardly be said that on this phenomenological model there is no question of a 'dualism' of spirit and matter. Steiner's is the most monistic philosophy conceivable. Therefore there is no reason for the alarm sometimes felt at the term 'spirit,' as though a spiritual world-view must mean the denial of other domains of life. That would be to import the false assumptions Steiner is so anxious in his exposition to exclude. The meaning of the world may only emerge on a higher, spiritual level — and there is a sense in which that introduces a rift into the world — but ultimately we are able to unfold a meaning which is that of the world, not our own, because we are ourselves thoroughly part of the whole, emerging from it and, after the crisis of rift and estrangement, returning consciously, in knowledge to our own creative source. Spiritual, Steiner's view of things must certainly be called, then — precisely in the sense that it involves the recognition of things in their own right, with intrinsic value, beyond their personal significance for ourselves, either individually or even the whole of mankind. Steiner finds that in accepting them as such we are not denying ourselves, but finding our deepest fulfilment. Materialism, on the other hand, is precisely the denial of that recognition. In the deepest sense it is the denial of relationship, seeing the world as something to be manipulated, controlled, and understood solely under those one-way aspects which lead us to dominate, to use and afterwards to dispose of. Science becomes materialistic, not when it seeks to understand the laws or regularities in nature, but when it comes to regard things, beings and people as only the product of regularities, only real in so far as they can be manipulated by control of their predictable behaviour.

But in this way, as we have already found hinted, we make ourselves slaves. It would be naïve not to recognize the darker side of science's realization, going back to Bacon, that knowledge is power. Steiner is not opposed to knowledge, certainly not opposed to science: but only to the temptations which beset science. Against the materialist's one-way, slave-relationship to the world, he set a critique of the kind of assumptions that deny the interchange and mutual dependence on which all knowledge actually depends. Spirit in the world is its claim to otherness, to value on its own terms, which it would be untrue to our own knowledge-experience, among other things, to ignore.

This otherness, this claim to value, means that the world we know is demanding, even frightening. The spirit meant to Goethe a sense of seeing as a god sees — but that also brings the responsibilities attendant upon such a larger vision. Materialism may suppose that to think in this way is to mix up emotion and fact; but one of the most important implications of Steiner's ethics is that there simply is no value-free knowledge. Relationship always has a moral dimension, and knowledge, once brought down from its spurious metaphysical claims, is always knowledge from a certain point of view and for a particular context, purpose or end. The fear of the otherness of things and beings is in reality an obvious source of the need to control, and materialism is a kind of thought dominated by fear, for all its aggressively rationalistic pronouncements. That is why rationalism is so often haunted by the terror of the excluded, the unacknowledged, which thereby becomes all the more terrifying. Control over our environment constantly promises escape from fear, but in practice leads to the restless anxiety which we now see pervading our culture, and reappearing in the guise of chronic social problems.

At the same time, the kind of external-imaging knowledge which we conceive of our world has the effect, as we have seen, of removing the self into a regressive abyss. It postpones our identity as a knower to infinity. Steiner's anthroposophy is devoted above all to overcoming this situation. To do that, it must reverse the orientation of external knowledge, where we look on as if we were had no part in the world. This is the first of several reversals, which in a sense are all aspects of the same inner act of transformation, which we shall meet with in his thought. We must restore the cognitive stability which eludes us when we try to fix outer truth as the standard, and find our self in its concrete activity of interpreting, searching and indicating, entering into and loving the world. That is another way of characterizing 'inside' knowledge, of entering or penetrating into things as Steiner constantly puts it. It is certainly no capitulation to unphilosophical attitudes, therefore, but a central philosophical point in Steiner's approach that he sees knowledge, in its recognition of otherness, running its course between fear and love. The suprapersonal element in knowledge is in no way compromised. Love, after all, is our name for the acceptance of others in their own right and for their own sake, and affirmation of them above our self. We put ourselves wholly in the world, actively at the service of the world, in knowledge.

Love is also the quality of our humanity at its highest pitch, and relevant to our acts of knowing as are our other human qualities. Such is the starting-point of Steiner's human-centred spiritual vision, which is deeply rooted in his philosophical thought. 'As a result,' he concludes, 'man begins to feel himself no stranger in the universe. The universe has something to give him, and takes from him something in return ... Thus anthroposophical reflection begins by making friends with the world. We learn to know the world that repelled us at first, on external observation. And this knowledge leads us to become more human.'[11]

Many leading members of the Phenomenological Movement would have agreed with Steiner on the humanizing consequences of the method they were trying to develop. But few would have gone so far as to view the method as a reconciliation, effected by Steiner in such heartfelt terms, between man and the world with which he lives in interchange. Even Scheler, in his beautiful book *The Concept of Sympathy*, did not quite go to such lengths. On the whole they were worried, perhaps, that by making knowledge too 'human' they would run the risk of psychologism — that is to say, of confusing the mere human-psychological conditions under which we can know something with our actual knowledge. Most theories of knowledge must somehow be able to be defined independently of the mind which attained it, or at the very least in some way correspond to a reality outside it. Such theories have run into trouble in the course of the twentieth century, however, particularly in the physical sciences. And, as we shall see, Steiner's bold alternative may turn out to be more in tune with the needs of contemporary thought. By acknowledging the human status of knowledge, Steiner both restores us to ourselves and makes us part of the world we are trying to understand. By refusing to accept that we have access to a truth beyond the world we know, or aligned by correspondence with such a pure truth, Steiner leads us back by that third relation which we have to the actual phenomena, to the flowers in the meadow and the complexity of our impressions. We transcend ourselves, not through subordination to a higher model, law, etc., but in the human way of self-transcendence, through valuing the other, and in our willingness to change ourselves and to learn.

Truth and Science

It is a fundamental axiom of Rudolf Steiner's account of cognition, as Carl Unger pointed out, that 'all knowledge alters the knower.'[12] This is one of the most original and important aspects of his epistemology, and it may be possible to illustrate his point in relation to a decisive moment in the history of modern science.

We might wish to summon for our purposes an imaginary scene, as if in a fictitious conversation Rudolf Steiner were able to offer his thoughts at a 'philosophical' moment when ideas, as here about our knowledge of physical events, were stretched or had to be transformed. Though it seems a world away from Steiner's flowery meadows, the one I have in mind is the contention between the two physicists Einstein and Niels Bohr in 1927 over the status of events in a famous quantum mechanical experiment. The experiment was designed to resolve some issues in atomic physics and spectroscopy, which revolved around a problematic equation in the new quantum physics.

The equation described the phenomena in terms of spreading waves. Yet the physical impact as measured on a light-sensitive plate was extremely localized. Disturbingly therefore, to the scientists involved, the way that we record the event seemed to change the nature of the event. Issues which we have been discussing in philosophy were suddenly raised in the most immediate way on the front line of science. The question of what actually, physically took place, and the role of the observer, had become, at this advanced level of scientific dispute, the crucial issue. It is in such an attempt to isolate the workings of physical reality that the epistemological issue of our relation to the world is raised in Steiner's active sense: for here we need to decide the kind of way to interpret new discoveries which break out of the older 'classical' mould. Philosophy becomes involved in the process of knowledge — and not at all in some *ex post facto* higher level reflection upon already ascertained results.

From Steiner's point of view, it would be important to stress that the experiment already had a history before Einstein and Bohr's dispute. The experiment comes before us as part of the development of thought, not as something that just 'happened.' Interpretations of it had centred upon the way that a beam of electrons, considered as widely extended in space in accordance with a mathematical wave-function whose usefulness in solving problems was well-established, when directed upon a photographic plate must be interpreted, at the moment of impact, as a series of highly focussed, localized events. The sequence of phenomena on which the interpretation was founded basically raised the problem of the instantaneous collapse of the widely spread charge into a point on the photographic plate, in defiance of physical possibility. What were scientists to make of this physically baffling 'instantaneous' and complete transformation? At the very point where experiment seemed to be pushing toward definition of some fundamental features of physical behaviour, our knowledge of 'what is there' appeared to be forced into the form of an anomaly, a pattern that could not be physically interpreted at all.

In 1926 Max Born had already taken the step of realizing that the problem was telling us less about some 'physical' peculiarity than about our own relationship to what we know. The apparent sudden change between the widely spread state and the sharply localized state, he suggested, was more to do with what we could know at any one moment than it was to do with physically baffling alterations. He proposed that in the prior situation as we see it the probability of any of the particles being at any one spot is small, so that the wave-function is spread out over a wide area, but when the location of a particle is measured by its hitting the photographic plate, the probability of it being anywhere else suddenly drops to zero. It is not anything 'out there' which changes, concluded Born, 'but rather our knowledge of the system suddenly changes.'[13] Our method of measuring and understanding what was going on thus turned out to be essential to the description of it, and the effort to clarify the physical event was rather to be seen as an account of our changing relationship to the object of our knowledge.

It is really almost as though Steiner had been there whispering in the wings. Such realizations formed a fundamental aspect of his theory of knowledge, where the relationship to the object is conceived as producing cognitive change in just such a way as Born supposed, so that the object is known strictly as part of a process, a transformation of state which intrinsically involves the knower. On the basis of Born's interpretation, Niels Bohr formulated an extended theory (the so-called 'Copenhagen interpretation' which has come to be widely accepted) of quantum physics, while Einstein, who considered himself a realist, tried desperately hard over a decade or so to establish that it must be possible to define the physical properties involved independently of a human observer.

Despite his brilliance in many domains, Einstein had finally to admit that he was unable to devise a way of allowing us to know simultaneously all the relevant features of an object, so that it could be defined independently of specific observational circumstances. Bohr's statement of the interrelation between observer and the 'reality' of the physical events has therefore carried enormous weight in the further development of science. He summed up his view in a lecture of 1927:

> On one hand, the definition of the state of a physical
> system, as ordinarily understood, claims the elimination

of all external disturbances. But in that case, according to
the quantum postulate, any observation will be
impossible ... On the other hand, if in order to make
observation possible we permit certain interactions with
suitable agencies of measurement, not belonging to the
system, an unambiguous definition of the state of the
system is naturally no longer possible.

Thus, he added, it is in principle never possible to disentangle
completely physical phenomena ('space-time coordination')
and the interpretation of them by the observer as had been
claimed in classical physics. These must be seen instead 'as complementary but exclusive features of the description, symboliz-
ing the idealization of observation and definition respectively.'[14]

The last phrase, and indeed the whole situation again has a
very Steinerish ring. And indeed, long before scientific research
in the conceptually difficult reaches of quantum physics forced
a re-evaluation of our assumptions about knowledge, Steiner
had foreseen in their essentials the epistemological crises that
modern knowledge would inevitably make us face. Einstein, on
the other hand, for all his brilliance, seemed to be hanging on to
an outmoded kind of 'objectivism' in the definition of knowledge — though a kind that still has many, usually less critical
adherents today. Even in the 'Copenhagen' interpretation, there
is still a sense that our knowledge falls short of the fullness represented by the goal of complete objectivity. It appears that our
knowledge is limited only in cases such as this (quantum
physics). But Steiner may still seem radical in taking such
instances to represent, exposed to view where the underlying
concepts are pressed to reveal their contours, a paradigm for
human knowledge in general.

He drew instead, already on general epistemological
grounds, the conclusion which has in fact furnished the basis for
much that is good in our science: the inherent involvement of
the knower in what he, or she, knows. Looking back on his basic
philosophical books, Steiner reflected that it was precisely such
an alternative to the blatantly metaphysical interpretations of
knowledge which he had sought to inculcate in all his work. The
sense that our knowledge must somehow be inadequate, if it

lacked the absoluteness which the metaphysical (neo-Kantian) interpretation wanted to supply, he sought to assuage by reminding us that knowledge is a human affair. *Things* demand no explanation:

> These works set out to show that when we form concepts about the world, and elaborate them mentally, we are not alienating ourselves from reality ... The world, as it first appears through the senses, is for us incomplete. But this incompleteness is due not to the world but to us. And we, through our mental activity, restore it to full reality.[15]

It is because of our own nature that the world appears to us in a limited and partial way — it is not the fault of the world (e.g. for being ontologically inferior, unreal, or for being unknowable, keeping itself shut up obstinately 'in itself'). It is our own organization as perceiving and thinking beings which determines the fact that we see only a part of the nature of things. Hence there is no point, since it is our perspective that is limited not the world, in wishing to make it unlimited, nor in trying to characterize our knowledge other than in terms of our own perceiving and thinking activity — in which, indeed the truth of our knowledge resides. We see and hear and otherwise gain a partial relationship to the world around us, and the rest of the cognitive picture is made up by the realization in thought of our relation to the whole, the total situation of which our limitation as perceiving beings means that it would otherwise be only partly known. For Steiner, our knowledge is true knowledge. But the philosophical investigation of the issues involved in it tells us about our own processes and relationships, our human way of giving meaning to our experience.

We may take another instance, perhaps simpler, where we may observe the temptation to make of knowledge something standing outside the involvement of the knower. Science has formulated the concept of 'laws,' such as the conservation of matter. This basic idea underlies, in some sense the coherence of physical science as a whole, defining it in effect as a closed system that can be treated in its own terms. It is a tremendously potent and far-reaching idea. Its success makes it tempting to assume that in its formulation we have, not just a human pat-terning of experience, but an objective feature, an ontological feature as some might say, belonging to the world as such.

Let us allow the temptation to unfold. When confronted by a 'law of nature' such as this many people, including (perhaps especially including) many with a scientific training, find it hard not to suppose that its discovery must have come about when observers noticed, time and again, that processes in their envi-ronment always had the characteristic of conserving overall quantitative relationships, as given in the initial state. They were putting into thought a content which was, so to speak, thrust upon them by the nature of things, registering thereby a quality of the material universe quite independent of their own think-ing minds, their point of view. It stands indeed as an inescapable truth, which we are bound to believe because we can never find a counter-instance.

A very little reflection will serve to show, however, that such an account is a tissue of illogicalities, and even downright impossibilities. Steiner's method of dealing with knowledge will soon show a very different reality, and that we are tempted to think in such a fashion precisely because we forget our own involvement, our own participation in setting the frame of ref-erence.

A crucial component in the physical application of conserva-tion is the so-called impermeability of matter. This states in prin-ciple that matter is impermeable, which is to say that the space occupied by something cannot be occupied at the same time by anything else. Obviously, if two substances could occupy the same space, temporarily or permanently, the wider principle of conservation of quantity would be rendered unworkable. No doubt we all remember how at school we were taught how for a 'scientific' understanding of things the apparent occupying of the same space by two substances when we dissolve salt in a glass of water is really a sliding of the material particles in amongst each other, and the 'law of conservation' holds because the quantities of each substance turn out to be the same throughout. If things could keep disappearing into each other, however, we would never be able to know how much we had of anything. But in all this, Steiner points out, there is nothing that is in any way thrust upon us, forcing us to accept ineluctable facts (a 'dogma' as he puts it). What we have done is connected with the establishing of a framework, essentially the making of a definition, and to take it 'ontologically' as in the textbooks of physics would be quite misguided:

> In modern textbooks of physics you will find a statement which should really count as a definition only — but logic has not been taken into consideration. It is said that physical bodies are impermeable. Really however it should be that the definition of a physical body is that, at the place where it is, no other body can be at the same time. This should count as a definition. Instead, a dogma is created and it is said that 'physical bodies possess the property of impermeability.' Whereas the proper formulation would be that two 'bodies' cannot occupy the same space simultaneously.
> That however is a matter belonging to philosophy ...[16]

The whole notion that some ontological feature of the world has been discovered, or is even forced upon us by the facts of nature dissolves when we realize how we have been involved in defining the terms of our search. We have brought together cases which fitted into the definition we have made of a 'physical body': but were then rather oddly persuaded to be surprised when we found that all of them exhibited a certain feature, namely the one which had been the criterion for assembling them in the first place! It is less obvious but essentially no different from being surprised, after extensive research that all bachelors have in common that they are single men. We could not, it is obvious, have had the common features of 'physical objects' thrust upon us, without first knowing what we meant to designate as physical objects. The rather strange and self-deluding wish we have to make the truth external, a property of things-out-there, has made us project back a principle of our search and persuaded us that we have subsequently had it forced upon us.

The idea of conservation (impermeability of matter) is what has sometimes been called a paradigm, which guides the interpretation and investigation of nature. As a matter both of fact and logic, however, no amount of recurrent exposure to instances of conservation could ever compel us to perceive the principle itself. It is well known to researchers that younger children who are presented with observational cases, lacking in conceptual prejudice though they may be supposed to be, do not grasp conservation but will say that there is 'more' liquid when it is poured into a tall, thin jar and 'less' when it is poured into a wide one — even though they see all the liquid go from one to another. They lack the complex structures involved in compensating for changes of shape, etc. which are prerequisites in the consistent adult definition of a physical object. The situation is changed by their further mental development, — and until they attain the requisite mental age, when the complex mental operations involving the ideas of reversibility, and so on have been mastered, no amount of demonstration will furnish them with the conceptual means of interpreting what they see in the adult way, namely as the phenomenon of conservation of quantity. When they have evolved the conceptual framework, they will be able to understand the world in terms of objects and their conservation, but not until then. In recent times, these considerations have led developmental thinkers such as Piaget to reach rather similar conclusions to Steiner's, rejecting as he puts it the 'myth of the sensory origin of scientific knowledge.' Instead, they too emphasise how scientific knowledge arises out of our own activity, which cannot be reduced to the object or objects that we know.[17]

As for the other popular notion, that we must accept the principle as 'scientific' because we can never come up with a counter-example: that too is clearly based on confusion about our own mental processes. The reverse is in fact the case. For it is a familiar concept in all critical evaluations of scientific 'induction' that no amount of confirmatory instances could ever, logically, establish a principle that something is 'always' so. For however many cases do conform, there is always the possibility that the contrary instance will be found whether it be tomorrow or in a hundred years time.

The idea that a law, such as 'the law of conservation' is independent of our purposes and interests when we study nature thus turns out to be an empty one. Abstracted from the living process of knowledge, the principle ceases to tell us anything about the real world. Just so did the quantum-scientific arguments show that the attempt to push definition of the physical state of the phenomena to ultimate clarity, which would end by excluding the role of any possible observer, can then no longer tell us about anything real. It becomes an 'idealization.' Yet Steiner's point is not that the scientific use of the concept of conservation is wrong, or that the scientists are caught up in an illusion of their own minds, merely confirming their own preconceptions. While it is used in a concrete, interpretative fashion it is a highly valuable tool of thought. It has in no sense arisen merely as a postulate of the mind: it is the conceptual completion in knowledge of our encounter with certain features of the world, and as such gives us a truth about them. Indeed, Steiner restores logical clarity in place of Mill's blurring of logic and observation (induction). What is wrong-headed, according to Steiner, is not the scientific usage but the misguided assumptions involved in trying to turn one element in the cognitive process into an autonomous, 'absolute' feature ascribed to things themselves, independently of the observer. That is no longer good science but, for better or worse, it is as he says, 'a matter belonging to philosophy.'

Here once more, then, in a philosophical 'aside' to a rich and diverse lecture, we find Steiner humanizing science, and resisting those who would elevate it into some sort of absolutism of the mind. The idealization of one tendency in the cognitive process (namely, that of detachment, defining and completing) rather reaches a vanishing-point here, and loses contact with the other essential part of knowledge (involvement, modification of our assumptions, new experience). We need detachment; we need to restore the content of the other in its own right by adding conceptual wholeness to our partial, one-sided experience of it through our senses, etc. But knowledge, as Niels Bohr realized and as Steiner argued philosophically some decades before, necessarily ceases when there is either complete detachment, just as it does, contrarily, when there is no detachment, as if there could be 'pure observation.' (With Steiner's approach to the apparently exceptional case of mathematical knowledge I shall deal, at least briefly, in the next chapter.) Knowledge can only be understood from inside, as the modification of our existing presuppositions in the encounter with the world. It cannot be frozen into an abstraction, certainly not reduced to a mirroring of what we perceive.

At this juncture it has certainly become important to clarify, however, the actual content of 'observation' in Steiner's model of knowledge — and the way in which the role of the senses could actually be defined.

The clarification is needed the more urgently given the prevalence of the empiricist tradition in modern science, giving it an emphasis very different from the Kantian, rationalist one which was so influential in Steiner's own time.[18] According to the empiricist kind of approach, we have to assume that our experience is a mixture of direct information about the world around us — usually supposed to come through the senses — and interpretation, or ideas about that world. Extremely sophisticated versions of the theory in the twentieth century have attempted to show that in perception we are in possession of immediate 'sense-data,' on the basis of which we develop higher level interpretations of experience. Grouping these data together, we process the raw data so that out of a dark-coloured visual patch of a particular shape, a sensation of holding something solid and a ringing sound we construct the recurring complex of experience called the telephone we are answering. In classic form, empiricism is often presented as a theory of particular percepts being gathered together under more general ideas, and some such theory of knowledge has seemed to many to combine an account of the organizing, interpreting side of the mind with a guarantee that the resulting structures are ultimately based on something prior to any interpretation, the datum or 'given.' By recourse to an examination of what we actually see and touch, we should always be able to tell e.g. whether it really is a telephone or a child's toy.

In its virtual obsession with the isolating of 'the given,' empiricism betrays a distinct anxiety — a need to find something which makes our experience true, in terms of 'realistic' elements that are supposed to enter into its construction. If we stop to think about it there is something distinctly odd about trying to *prove* that something is yellow, rather than looking to see whether it is yellow or not.

Characteristic of empiricist theories is the key notion that I must always fundamentally be able to know what sense-data I am having, and that the content of the interpretation appears to arise wholly out of given materials. More subtle versions of the theory in modern times have attempted to grapple with the problem that it seems difficult in fact to point to anything like a patch of colour which is really different from the telephone. Practitioners have sometimes reconstituted it therefore as a theory of 'two languages,' one of sensations and one of objects. It has in common with traditional empiricism the crucial notion that one of the languages is more 'fundamental.'[19] It gives access to a level on which we can be certain of what it is we are experiencing. Therefore the interpretation must always be right if it is built up strictly on the data provided. The project of knowledge thus appears relatively simple. According to this model, it should always be possible to distinguish what is actually there, or 'given' to our observation, and our interpretation of it.

Steiner was already familiar with this type of epistemological theory, which has appealed consistently to scientists since the time of Locke — and already saw through its many misconceptions. In particular he was able to re-evaluate rather fundamentally the idea of 'the given.' Let us take an example of perception, which could be for instance that ringing telephone, which I am supposed to recognize as a recurring complex of sensory data. The hearing of the tone is supposed to impress itself upon the perceiver, and my understanding of what it means is supposed to be the result of previous patterns of such sensory data. 'Answering the telephone' is thus a sort of shorthand language for a set of impressions of this kind:

> A closer analysis shows matters to stand very differently from the way described above. When I hear a noise, I first seek for the concept which fits this observation. It is this concept which first leads me beyond the mere noise. If one thinks no further, one simply hears the noise and is content to leave it at that. But my reflecting makes it clear to me that I have to regard the noise as an effect.

Therefore not until I have connected the concept of effect with the perception of the noise do I feel the need to go beyond the isolated observation and look for the cause. The concept of effect calls up that of cause, and my next step is to look for the object which is being the cause ... But these concepts, cause and effect, I can never gain through mere observation, however many times the observation may occur. Observation evokes thinking, and it is thinking which first shows me how to link one separate experience to another.[20]

The key point is that Steiner yet once more restores to our attention that 'unnoticed element': our own thinking process. It is when we forget the role of our own interpreting, connecting, and relating in the construction of the meaningful world we experience that we begin to succumb to the errors of empiricism.

In reality my recognition of a ringing telephone in the example given depends upon my use of high-level concepts to organize my experience, to direct my attention and to integrate my act of recognition still further into my behaviour, which is throughout characterized by directedness, intention, inquiry and analysis. Ordinary life, it is true, does not usually encourage us focus upon our interpreting activity. The seeming 'transparency' of thinking is nothing other, in fact, than its coincidence with the normal purposes for which we employ it.

When Steiner asks us, rather frequently in certain of his writings, to become conscious of our mental processes, his meaning is not primarily the enrichment of our subjective life (in a psychological sense, for instance). It is primarily to liberate us from the illusion of transparency, and free our thinking. The result is equally not to add to our knowledge an assertion about what is 'really there' as the cause of our subjective experience — such as Einstein was trying to establish, when he argued that it must somehow be possible to know what the particles are really like, independent of our own relationship to the events in the experiment. In Steiner at any rate, the perspective is quite different: for the realization of our own active involvement leads, as Owen Barfield puts it, to a 'felt expansion of consciousness' that changes the experience. Unfamiliar or newly discovered knowledge requires us to extend our interpretation, consciously questioning our previous apprehension of the meaning of things. We cannot then rest content with our previous patterns of thought. The experience is transformed from within. We see more deeply into the situation and our relationship to it.

To the question of the search for ultimate external 'grounds' to our knowledge, Steiner gave a Wittgensteinian answer: explanations come to an end somewhere. Or as Steiner puts it:

> One cannot simply go on asking questions in an arbitrary manner. I once gave this example: We see tracks in the road. We can ask, Why are they there? Because a carriage has driven over the road. Why was the carriage driven? Because its occupants wanted to reach a certain destination. Why did they want to reach a certain destination? In reality, the asking of questions must come to a stop somewhere.[21]

To the metaphysical cast of mind, this appears to leave knowledge dangerously drifting, without an anchor. To Steiner, the metaphysical mind is one which thereby shows that it shrinks from the opening up to new knowledge, to the creative potential of new perspectives which becoming aware of our own thinking processes makes available. It tries to consolidate past experience, extending it illegitimately to try to limit the openness of the present. He himself drew the quite opposite, anti-metaphysical conclusion, that in knowledge we have a free relationship that is capable of deepening and expanding.

He concluded that no one element in a living experience 'grounds' all the others. It is certainly possible, and highly important to differentiate the perceptual content of an experience from the concepts which we use in order to interpret it; indeed, that is the very process of becoming aware of our thinking which he demands.[22] The result is a clarification of knowledge. But we must not confuse the analytical process with an actual reduction, as though it were possible to extract quasi-real percepts out of the interpreted complex, say, or to infer some real thing that must stand behind the experience in some mysterious way and 'make' it happen. The truth is that we can distinguish but not divide.

Still less can we infer from our percepts any sort of necessarily real something behind them, because they are themselves only a half-reality, an analytic abstraction from the interpreted whole-ness of our knowledge:

> What then is a percept? The question, asked in this general way, is absurd. A percept always emerges as something perfectly definite, as a concrete content.[23]

It is always a something recognized, related to other contents, and playing a specific role within our experience. It is never an unhighlighted, indeterminate, a merely presented, like a 'patch of colour' or a 'sense-datum,' from which our knowledge can be explained. The philosophers' house of cards tumbles down:

> To form a link between something subjective and something objective is impossible for any process that is 'real' in the naïve sense — that is, one that can be perceived. It is only possible in thinking.[24]

Owen Barfield points out how Steiner develops his important phenomenological approach to 'the given' through showing how our thinking about our experience 'keeps inserting us, as it were, into the very texture of the Given. Out for a walk, we hear a sudden whirring noise, which 'means' nothing to us; a moment later a partridge rises from the hedge near at hand ... Next time we hear the whirring noise, it carries its meaning with it.'[25]

Thus Steiner already arrived on general epistemological grounds at a formulation striking in its similarity to that subse-quently thrust upon Niels Bohr by the needs of developing physical science. The observational and interpretative aspects of knowledge cannot be ultimately separated; each is rather an ide-alization, a theoretical projection, of the observational and the conceptual aspects of cognition. Neither one of them can be regarded, as Steiner therefore concludes,

> as something finished and self-contained, but only as one side of the total reality ... Only the percept and concept together constitute the whole.[26]

Their unity is knowledge, giving us a valid account of our relationship to the phenomena under scrutiny, and at the same time showing our own relation to the situation. The attempt to isolate one or the other leads to the dissolution of relationship, and so to lack of content, a half-reality. Rather than 'real' or quasi-real elements combining, matching up so as to make our thoughts correspond to a self-sufficient physical truth, observation and definition, perceptual and conceptual truth are twin projections or idealizations of aspects of our involvement with the world. We ourselves make this separation precisely in order to become conscious of our situation, in which the truth of things becomes clear to us in a specific way.

In summary then: Steiner rejected the kind of philosophy which sees us as forming mental pictures of a world 'out there.' But from the mutual dependence of observer and observed he did not draw any kind of 'idealist' conclusions, that the world is only in our minds etc. These — materialism and idealism alike — are misguided attempts, albeit deriving from processes necessary to every act of knowing, to press one aspect of human knowledge or the other beyond what they really are.

The search for knowledge is therefore not submission to a supposed order of things we are compelled to accept — no such external compulsion to think in particular ways about the world does or can exist. No more is it the gradual approach to some grand idea, as in Hegelian-idealist thought. It is the search for our own human relationship to the world around us, changing it and being changed by it. That relationship is not given to us from without, but:

> The fact that thinking, in us, reaches out beyond our
> separate existence and relates itself to the universal world
> existence gives rise to the fundamental desire for
> knowledge in us. Beings without thinking do not have
> this desire. When they are faced by other things, no
> questions arise for them ... But in thinking beings the
> concept rises up when they confront something external.
> It is that part of the thing which we receive not from
> without but from within.[27]

And with this inner unfolding of our own activity, Rudolf Steiner finds a sufficient source of certainty. The idea that knowledge might be determined by our own desire and search for relationship gave him the clue to a path that could lead us through the perils of relativism that open up here. For if it is we who polarize the world, if we are not alien to the world but ourselves insiders to it, then the sources of the ordering of our human reality coincide with the finding of our own identity — not with standing in some impossible, paradoxical way outside it. This is the sense in which he took Goethe's phrase about the god-like ability we have to reveal the truth, in that third, spiritual relationship, without absolutes, but with the right to look upon our own world, affirming it and knowing that 'it is very good.' This is 'making friends with the world,' and the start of a developing relationship.

A Modern World-View: 'Anthroposophy' — with a Hint about Art

Steiner notably shifts the governing metaphors of knowledge that have been familiar, especially since the nineteenth century. One such metaphor spoke of the 'edifice' of knowledge, which implied that item after item could be added, as it were brick by brick, to a permanent structure. To those thinkers involved in the grandiose architectural project — as well as to ordinary mortals dazzled by the achievements of science in the last century — the individual contributors evidently seemed like bees buzzing around an ever more clearly defined honeycomb structure. A discovery once made was understood to be unalterably true, and could be treated as reliable building-matter, and those who contributed the individual blocks were dwarfed by the vastness of the projected building, which stood independent of the knower.[28] The imposing nature of the latter inspired a kind of religious awe among the secularists of the turn of the century, who often preached science, quite literally, holding Sunday gatherings and proclaiming science as rationalist redemption. (If Steiner seems sometimes unduly hard on contemporary scientists and their dogmatism, it is as well to remember such symptomatic practices and the extremist rhetoric which a dissenter such as himself had frequently to bear.) Steiner did not deny the enormity of the scientific undertaking, nor its grandeur; but he refused to be intimidated by the picture of a merely instrumental, 'building' role for the mind, realizing from the start that this simply did not characterize the process of knowing. Now that information has proliferated along with ways of transmitting it, indeed to the extent that no one can any longer even be sure what has been discovered and what has not (many 'duplicate' discoveries going long undetected), the question of what constitutes 'knowledge' as opposed to mere 'information' has emerged much more clearly. Information is indeed only to be defined by the way we process it. It is precisely this understanding which has led to the new awareness of communication. Bernardo Gut has pointed out several important ways in which Steiner's thought is confirmed by the 'information theory' that has nowadays arisen to help deal with it.[29]

Until those developments, however, the objectivism of nineteenth-century science did little to address the issues of the human significance of knowledge that had essentially been looming since the Enlightenment. For ever since then, with the 'discovery of discovery,' that knowledge, discoveries, facts, theories and hypotheses have intruded into the settled lives of ordinary people, often with unsettling results. By concentrating so exclusively on the product, rather than the processes of knowledge, philosophy long helped to prolong rather than to resolve the crisis. Steiner's significance may be seen quite simply as that he is one of the few thinkers to confront that question of knowledge in its human dimension — one of the first, and still one of the most challenging. His epistemology, as we have seen, shifts attention away from the supposed 'foundations' of knowledge and the architectural metaphor, and on to our creative role. The wall of knowledge gives way to descriptions of interchange, of emergence and development, of penetration into the network of relationships that surrounds and includes us. Here again, Steiner was far ahead of his time. He already foresaw a science that would have to renounce what even Einstein seemed unwilling to relinquish: namely, the reassuring sense of a picturable reality that could be contemplated, like that grand edifice, from a secure vantage-point outside. Steiner foresaw that we would have to learn to understand even where we cannot picture in this way, as if it could exist apart from and spread out before us.

In the resultant 'anthroposophy' or spiritual science, he certainly estranged himself from the orthodoxies of science once more by using the taboo world 'occult' to describe aspects of this relationship. But it is important to grasp that a very great deal of our science has in principle become 'occult' — and thus in significant ways fundamentally different from the classical Newtonian notion of the way things can be represented as existing in space. It has come about precisely through the acceptance of the involvement of the observer which Steiner already grasped. It is now accepted that we cannot carry the customary assumptions of relative separateness that governed the classical cosmos over into the world of particles and forces that is envisaged in modern physics. As a result they simply cannot be pictured, or imagined as if they were visible in classical space. But it would be wrong to suppose that this fact has relevance only to the minimalist world of advanced physics. The astronomer Norman Davidson points out that it applies just as much in the model of the solar system which is handed down in the textbooks:

> The modern system of planetary movement is, in fact, based on a hypothetical observer sitting in space far enough away from the planets to enable him to view them ... going round the sun. The fact is that if he were placed thus far enough away he would not see the planets at all. No one has ever seen or ever will see the suncentred system as drawn in books.[30]

The notion that the pictured system of planetary motions could actually be seen, 'out there,' turns out to be illusory. Either we can go on pretending that this does not matter, or, we can take the step across the visibility threshold with full recognition of the observer's involvement that the conventional version sweeps under the carpet.

The implications for science of the renunciation of picturable models were boldly faced by Steiner, who was very interested in mathematical (among other) analogies for the kind of under-standing involved.[31] If the term 'occult' suggested all too easily pre-modern analogies, it turned out nevertheless to be typically prophetic of the issues that would surface in advanced twenti-eth-century thought. Steiner's interpretation of science demands that we consider the complexities raised on the philo-sophical level as integral to the problem — and that we pene-trate beyond the term 'occult' to the difficult questions, however we choose to label them, to which he pointed the way. The approach to the 'occult' is perhaps connected with a further aspect of the case. For still, even in the 'Copenhagen interpreta-tion' of the involvement of the observer, the realization that we end by describing a change in our knowledge, rather than 'inde-pendent' physical events, is treated as a kind of limitation. We find ourselves unable to transcend our own perspective; our own role becomes problematic, and sets a bound to what we can find out. But in Steiner's formulation, the transformation under-gone by the knower, during the research or experimentation, is regarded much more positively: for Steiner it is the attempt to stand 'outside' the system that blocks further knowledge, while the step into the picture releases us to move forward with pre-cisely the kind of interpretation that weaves human involve-ment into the fabric of our knowing.

In Steiner, the participation of the knower is not a boundary and a limit, but a key to the nature of what happens and how we know it. The implications of his theory of knowledge thus reach even beyond the issues raised in the celebrated quantum-exper-iment. They gesture towards still more recent ideas, according to which the resolution of quantum-physical problems can only be more fully achieved through an 'anthropic' science — which is to say, one that is based on making explicit the connection between our own position, as human observers, and the world we inhabit.

For by making friends with the world we come to realize, above all, that it is a world suited to produce human life, con-sciousness, etc. Our own presence in the equation, so to speak, is therefore not a blank, a boundary-line or mere unknown: the nature of the world out there therefore does not lie in a 'given,' completely other than ourselves, but is a cypher that can potentially be filled in by an understanding of our own grounding to the wider matrix of events. Here Steiner found a key to the human-spiritual dimension, where we can find the fulfilment of our own nature in the greater world, yet without calling upon any kind of speculative principle as had the great nineteenth-century idealists. The 'anthropic' approach is in this the exact opposite of metaphysical logic which tries to deduce a reality beyond what we know. Already in his early sketch *Anthroposophy – A Fragment* Steiner was able to develop such ideas, and thereby to cut through the impasse reached by nineteenth-century idealism.

The latter had stressed the dependence of the world we know — the world of sights, sounds, smells, etc. — on our own perceptual organization. If we did not have eyes, there could be no colour in the world. Nor did it prove at all easy to say how we could ever know what was 'really' there when we have an experience of, say, red: the redness appeared to something that happened in us, not in the world, and anything beyond it was a matter of speculation, construct, metaphysics. Or, if we do not believe in metaphysical deductions, we must be content with the unknown and unknowable. Steiner held firm to the rejection of metaphysics. But Steiner challenged the notion that we do not know anything else beyond our own sensory organization. We know that the world is such as to have produced our sensory organization. As he argued in *Anthroposophy:*

> Before the world of sensory representations can come
> before us, these sense-organs themselves must have arisen
> out of it. The world would be silent, indeed, if we did not
> have the sense of hearing; it would be without warmth if
> we did not have a sense of warmth. Yet true as this is, it is
> equally true that in a world where there was nothing to
> hear no sense of hearing would ever arise; in a world
> without heat, there would never emerge a sense of
> warmth ...

Certainly more is present in our experience than mere sense — namely, our relationship to the world which has shaped us as living, perceiving beings:

One need only formulate this with absolute clarity to
realize that the world which is given to us through the
senses, and subsequently forms the basis of our own inner
world, must itself be founded upon another world. It is
the world which makes that of sense-experience possible
by virtue of the fact that it brings the senses into
existence. Moreover this world cannot itself ever fall
under the observation of the senses, being in every
respect the presupposition of their existence.[32]

The last step in the argument is particularly crucial. For to go
back on the anti-metaphysical clarification of the limits of the
senses, and so attribute to something within our world of ideas
and sensations a 'real' existence, would be throwing away the
baby with the bathwater. It would be casting away the critical
achievements of natural science along with the false metaphysical implications that had been based on them. Steiner does not
want to add something redundantly metaphysical to science in
that way. What he envisages is rather an extension of science, an
'anthropic' dimension: but this will have to recognize forces that
cannot be derived from the world revealed to the senses. It is
another way of saying that knowledge cannot be reduced to the
sensory content, to the object. It always includes the relationship
to the knower. As for the way in which this 'other' is to be envisaged as actively forming the sensory and cognitive organization
of the knower — that will be a matter we will have to consider
when we treat of knowledge as belonging essentially to
dynamic, living organisms.

Methodologically speaking Anthroposophy begins, in fact,
not in a one-sided spiritual way supplementing natural science
from above, but in an 'incarnational' way, by clarifying the
nature of our senses and the way that we inhabit the world bodily.[33] Steiner arrives subsequently at an understanding of the
spirit, very typically, in a way that is not old-fashioned but con-
troversially modern and 'anthropic.' It reaches its results concretely by examining what we ourselves are or become, just by
being in a position to know the world we perceive, in ways that
are open to scientific correlation. Here again then we have a
'hidden' element in the shape of the knower emerging into the

picture of knowledge, constituting a modern domain of the
'occult' in Steiner's exact sense. Such ideas, despite strong resistance, have been increasingly influential in recent science.

Steiner's resistance to metaphysical importations (those supposedly 'necessary' inferences) into the theory of knowledge
thus led him to views that have opened new vistas in the sciences, bringing formerly speculative areas gradually within the
jurisdiction of progressive thought. I have urged that he represents the kind of comprehensive shift in philosophical terms
which those developments require. There are also many signs
that ideas like his have produced interesting results in more
strictly philosophical areas. In the understanding of mental
images and representations, for example, his move away from
the notion that we can effect an ultimate reduction of thought or
perception, but treating each as an idealization rather of elements in experience, has been echoed by a widespread move
among philosophers, even in the empirical Anglo-Saxon tradition, away from conventional models and towards a recognition
of directed activity in our interpreting of the world, both in
thinking and perceiving. One of them, Mary Warnock, comes to
the interesting conclusion that the two may not be ultimately
distinct. She argues 'both that we must think of perception as
containing a thought-element, and perhaps that we must think
of thinking as containing a perception element.'[34]

Steiner had likewise been interested by Goethe's provocative
suggestion that the scientist was not a collector of facts, but
directed upon the world what he termed 'a perceptive power of
thought' *(anschauende Urteilskraft)*. Indeed Goethe had clearly
grasped intuitively, at least, the kind of science Steiner sought to
justify in his philosophy. 'Goethe considered the sense-organs of
man,' says Steiner,

> to be the supreme physical apparatus. For the world of
> colours, he was constrained therefore to esteem the eye as
> the highest arbiter for the observation of the laws
> governing their connection. Newton and the physicists,
> on the other hand, investigated the phenomena here in a
> way that Goethe deplored as 'the greatest disaster in
> modern physics,' consisting in the fact that the

experiments had been separated, as it were, from man ...
Newton and his followers meant to observe the processes
of light and colour as they would go on if no human eye
were there. But... according to Goethe's world-conception
... the effects that the eye perceives, taken as a whole and
shown under the law of their connection, are the very
essence of the phenomena of light and colour, not a
separate world of external processes, to be determined by
means of artificial instruments.[35]

The role of the interpreter in knowledge was the clue, for
Goethe, to what 'really happens' — in this instance the relationship of the seer to light and darkness which reveals itself as
colour. Refusing to admit the seer into the equation, the
Newtonians were led into speculative ideas that were intended
to explain the phenomena. The 'perceptive power of thought'
finds the meaning *in* the phenomena themselves. The recognition that it is actually we who polarize our experience into perception and thinking through our own relationship to things
which Steiner developed thus points to a more sensitive
description of the way that the informed scientific eye can 'see
more' in a colour, or in spotting a rare butterfly, or in a chemical
reaction. Conversely, it sheds light on the way that in an artist's
work 'blue' may be a thought — or even a range of thoughts
that can be explored over years, as with Picasso; or the way the
pale greens and blues of Cézanne are part of the 'meaning' of his
painting.[36] The role of interpretation thus brings together science
and art, highlighting the part played by creative seeing in both.
The two are not confused: but both are related to the human centre, and neither is treated as possessing a monopoly of truth to
our experience of the world and ourselves. Perception is never
the mere recognition of brute sensation, but can be deepened by
the artist or thinker at any point, with potentially infinite extension of meaning.

The idea of the polarization of our experience, clarifying to us
those factors which we assimilate to established patterns (definition, concept) and those which extend our response to the
other (observation, percept), thus inserting us as a knower into
the continuum of the world, is especially valuable here in the

area of art and its relation to knowledge. Steiner grasped the way we really find ourselves in thus clarifying our place in the continuum of the world. But he was not alone in realizing that this polarization might go too far. Indeed it is when we allow this to happen that the reduction of the perceptual part of the total experience is impoverished to the registering of minimal 'sense data,' and we allow purely abstract ideas to substitute for a real engagement with our environment. An example from everyday life will illustrate how we then become 'blind with seeing eyes' (another suggestive phrase of Goethe's). When we enter a room, it is obvious that we do not behave at all as the old empiricist philosophers would have us believe: we do not assemble sense-impressions and construct on that basis an account of the objects in the room; indeed, we usually take in only schematic categories (there was 'a clock,' 'a sofa,' and 'a portrait' on the wall), and would find it hard to give any perceptual details afterwards unless we had made a special effort of attention. In the modern world especially we have become very efficient at sorting out our experience in this schematic, practically efficient way. But we are therefore in some danger. For the conceptualizing tendency in our knowing, as the phenomenologist Scheler also appreciated, can easily run beyond the constructive interaction that gives it is value, and would ultimately become solipsistic, closing us off in our own set of expectations (once we saw that it was a clock, we took no further notice but assumed that it had all the usual features). Involvement with the rich texture of the experienced environment is curtailed; we note only enough of its qualitative density to orientate ourselves (the sofa was red, but we overlooked the faded gold fringeing, or the carving of the woodwork of its legs).

This highly polarized consciousness is essentially akin to that of the scientist who seeks to reduce everything to general 'laws,' i.e. features that will conform to expectation. He is quite consciously interested only in particular aspects of individual phenomena, reducing his concrete involvement with things so as to gain not just orientation but every increasing control. Steiner's theory of knowledge makes it clear that what we have here is not, as has so often been supposed, the starting-point of knowledge, that will help us make sense of the chaos of 'raw' sense-experience, but rather its final analysis. It is the end-product of a separating-out of the components of experience to the point where our many-sided human encounter with the world around us through activity, perception and thought has been dissected and 'benumbed': it remains with us as a pure abstraction. We have assimilated it totally. But thereby we renounce fully human response, with all its capacities of change through engagement with the unfamiliar and the new. Pursuing the clarity of knowledge leads us to a *ne plus ultra*, to the brink of dehumanization or that 'nothingness' which Nietzsche attributed, falsely, to the nature of the world. Narrowing our attention to what can be controlled, we find that we narrow ourselves to be only controllers, locked in to the empty mechanism of control.

Yet Steiner points out that the richness and depth of our primary response now reappears on another level. It reappears as the aesthetic — as beauty. It is most important to realize that in Steiner's thought art springs from the human response to the world along with knowledge, as a part of the same complex evolution of the mind. Art is not to be set in opposition to knowledge, but is fundamentally speaking the complementary, answering movement which rescues us from the reduction to nothingness, to emptiness, to which ultimate definition necessarily leads:

> The search for truth renders us ever more humble. Yet if man were merely to continue along this path, becoming more and more humble, he would eventually arrive at his own dissolution ... The peculiarity of the aesthetic life is this. It comprises truth, that is, selflessness, but it is at the same time the assertion of self-supremacy in the life of the soul, giving us back to ourselves as a spontaneous gift.[37]

Thus in art the tendencies which had come to a dead end so far as knowledge is concerned are freed once more to become part of a new wholeness. The abstracting, pattern-making tendency becomes an agent of control on a new plane in artistic creation, and is integrated once more with our perception, now intensified through the element of choice and selection which the artist introduces. The artist, according to Steiner's conception, does not ignore truth. In fact, it is out of the very elements of truth as they emerge in human experience that he or she fashions an adequate human response, showing us how to live the truth which would otherwise die into abstraction. And by thus showing us how to respond, the artist restores us to ourselves.

Steiner's deep conviction of the unity behind science, art and that sense of wholeness which is our intuition of the spiritual, was not a programmatic, still less a dogmatic assumption. It was a detailed understanding of the human needs involved in the modern search for knowledge and power, and of the sources of renewal that we need fully to live the life which that search opens to us. The beauty of art is not, as has been sometimes urged, either a protest or a consolation for the bleakness of the human situation but the other side of our drive to understand the world, and to transform it. The reversal which leads us to stop categorizing, controlling and abstracting, turning back in art to the wholeness of experience to put knowledge in its human context is another version of the reversal we saw already as 'making friends with the world.' Ultimately all these reversals will appear to us in Steiner's thought as versions of the same inner act, which is the discovery and assertion of our freedom.

The resources which the artist uses are thus the same as those which the scientist deploys — but with a different 'direction,' or intentional goal. Waldorf education attempts to foster the interplay between art and understanding throughout the curriculum, and its success shows that both can be enriched through a deeper awareness of their role. Finding the bridge from knowledge to art may have indeed been the most significant aspect of these ideas for Steiner's subsequent thought. Certainly it is important for the arts today, which are so often in danger of losing the aspect of shared truth to become one-sidedly indulgent in the personal, the exhibitionistic or the shocking. Perhaps even more importantly for our present understanding, however, they rescued Steiner from the desperate alternative espoused explicitly by a number of his contemporaries, and still experienced by many as an issue today. Thinkers such as the evolutionist Henri Bergson, and even in this respect Max Scheler, came to the conclusion that thinking inevitably leads us to abstraction and alienation: therefore, we must reject it as inadequate to our intuition of wholeness, and turn instead to emotion, or faith, or a vital *élan*, a mysterious force, to shape a living picture of the world we inhabit. That may also be why numerous artists, supposing that conscious cognition must lead to the 'dry' formulations of scientific theory, thought that art must work only from the irrational, the unconscious, the unintelligible. All these responses were predicated on suppositions about the nature of thinking (though note once again the tendency rather to blame the nature of things rather than ourselves and the way we think about things!). For Steiner, on the other hand, thinking only had this character if one separated it from the human involvement with the world which it served to articulate and clarify. In the pursuit of external 'truth,' thinking could forget its own nature and origins. Steiner drew attention constantly to the human reality. He concluded rather that one could not divorce thinking from the thinking-and-experiencing being, and that it formed an integral part of the same aspirations which motivated religion (spirituality) and art. Therefore he did not lose faith in clear thinking, giving in to intuitionism, will-philosophy, vitalism and the like. He held on to the conviction that thinking is adequate to the problems which we set it — precisely because these are our problems, not those of the world. Thinking connects us with a greater reality by fulfilling our need for clarity and at the same time for belonging, for that profoundest human way of relating which we call love. We do not need to seek this through spurious compensations; we find it in our thinking as in art or in religious devotion, expressed in a unique way that belongs to this aspect of our relation with the world.

Instead of concentrating on a one-sided notion of thinking as detachment, Steiner presented our cognitive activity therefore as 'warm, luminous and penetrating deeply into the phenomena of the world. This penetration is brought about by a power flowing through the activity of thinking itself — the power of love in its spiritual form.' He had shown the potential of his approach for redrawing the distorted intellectual map. Human knowledge was to be understood as the way we find ourselves, developing and growing through the learning-process, and insert ourselves into the world-order in a uniquely human way through an activity that overcomes the limited, partial apprehension our initial organization gives us. It is our way of restoring wholeness, of 'making friends with the world.' In the light of it, many of the metaphysical puzzles about knowledge dissolve, and many of the fears which lie behind the quest for metaphysical guarantees are exposed as groundless. They are fears that belong, not to our perilous existential situation as such but to the freedom we must face clearly and take for our own. Knowledge as relationship seemed precarious so long as the knower was thought of as an outsider, looking on: it had a new validity however in the 'anthropic,' or rather anthroposophical perspective where knowledge is the actualizing, at least in part, of our profound connectedness-in-origin with the world.

Many new questions arose, however: and Steiner had to demonstrate that his account of that spiritual 'activity' and that developing self could give knowledge something like the ability to show man his place in the universe as an ethical and spiritual being that was traditionally, if erroneously, sought from a metaphysic. Materialism, on Steiner's account, was premature in its supposition that these questions could simply be swept away, and was itself still mixed up in quasi-metaphysical confusion about what belongs to ourselves and what belongs to the world. His attention was increasingly directed, in the first decades of the twentieth century, to the inner dynamic of knowledge and the locus of its emergence: the self in development.

CHAPTER 3

The Self in Development

We are equally incapable of abiding in ourselves and in things,
and are thrown back from them to ourselves and from
ourselves to them.

Montaigne

The Self and the Other: Constituting the World?

Other philosophers in Steiner's day were certainly taking steps
toward a view of knowledge that recognized the role of the interpreter. One must not overestimate the originality of Steiner's
thought. Yet in reality, an examination of other developments
would, I think, still serve in many ways to bring out the radical
nature of the step which Rudolf Steiner took, in comparison with
the attempts of many philosophers to hold on to some of the 'certainties' of the past. The crucial understanding of the self is a case
in point, and the legacy of the fumbling steps that were taken in
rethinking our own relationship to the world that was implied by
the new picture of knowledge is even now causing some of our
profoundest modern problems. For the failure of philosophers to
move radically in order to resolve the issues which it raised has
meant that the problems Steiner tackled have repeatedly surfaced
again in twentieth century thought. Here, as so frequently, Steiner
offers us ideas which might still help us to move on.

It was above all the Phenomenologists who had taken up the
challenge of describing the world without metaphysical presuppositions, allowing it to reveal its essential structures and modes
of appearance. As a result they found themselves often confronting fundamental issues again. Phenomenology rejected

any return to unprofitable discussion of what things were in themselves, apart from our knowing them. But when seeking to give some account of the cognitive process, basic problems were once again raised which it was still tempting to resolve in some sort of idealist manner: once again though in a different manner projecting the dynamic relationship of mind and the world in its manifold forms of appearance into a convenient metaphysical absolute. For otherwise the 'psychologism' or relativization of knowledge which this entailed, seemed to many to threaten the very concepts of truth and certainty — and even more so, concepts such as human identity and moral values. The titanic gestures of the Nietzschean 'superman' had done little to reassure them.

Many thinkers were especially disturbed that the new climate of 'psychologism' threatened to engulf even the prestigious mathematical sciences, long regarded as the chief guarantee of certainty in scientific knowledge.[1] Mathematicians in particular regarded numbers as pure ideas, needing nothing to validate them except their own definitions. But recent theories about the possibility of 'transfinite' numbers had upset this certainty, as did some philosophical approaches which sought for the 'origin' of the concept of number following the lines of Brentano's descriptive-psychological approach. The work of the pioneering phenomenologist Edmund Husserl grew out of this dispute, and indeed reached its defining moment when he checked the psychologistic tendencies in his own early work and sought to clarify the issues involved generally in mental relations and mental acts.

One can easily have the impression here both of the exciting potential and the defensive reactions evoked on opposing sides. One the one side, logicians such as Frege insisted against psychologism that numbers are just there, 'part of the furniture of the world'; Husserl, coming from the other, had to construct elaborate defences to prove that he had not made mathematics merely subjective, confusing the way we learn about numbers with numbers themselves. Nevertheless, in his ideas, we come closest perhaps to the 'spiritual activity' central in Steiner's thought. The stakes were high. Perhaps it is understandable that several among the leading phenomenologists, therefore, even though they were those who had helped create the new climate, subsequently wished to keep hold, for instance, on certain of the guarantees that seemed to be offered by elements of an older idealist strain in philosophy. Husserl came by this route to his famous notion of a 'constituting subjectivity' (*leistende Subjektivität*). The place of the knower was given special status, as it were, as rising above and dominating the world, constituting it as meaningful by a sovereign act, above the welter of limited perspectives and piecemeal discoveries here below.

If philosophy had had to reject the notion that the world could tell us how to think about it, it could still hold on to the idea that it could demonstrate some kind of necessity beyond that of our own thoughts, which makes us think about it in a definite way. These must be ideas, in other words, which we do not merely think, but which we have to assume so as to make the world conceivable at all, and which therefore show us its essential features: grounded, as phenomenological analysis would undertake to show, in the very nature of our knowledge. If empiricism had failed to provide a 'given' ('a tag end of the world' as Husserl put it) which could explain the content of knowledge, they argued that we must instead have access to a conceptual reality that 'transcendentally' determines the meaningful world.

Husserl argued that philosophy must first suspend, must place in 'brackets', the operative knowledge we have of the world, running as it normally does on unreflective, certainly unformulated, principles, so as to clarify how that knowledge is constituted in the first place. Only then can its nature be understood. Unlike empiricism which looked for a determining feature of knowledge coming from without, the new phenomenological analysis stressed the determination of knowledge from within. The role of the 'object-constituting subjectivity' looked back explicitly to the *cogito ergo sum* ('the Cogito': I think therefore I am) of Descartes to justify the notion of a self-sustaining consciousness, able therefore also to define the world.[2]

The 'directedness' of thinking, its 'intentionality', provided a distinctively modern approach and a direct link to psychology as a scientific grounding. When subjected to 'transcendental' analysis it seemed to offer the key to understanding how we make our world meaningful from within: dispensing with that endlessly problematic appeal to 'real' metaphysical entities 'in themselves' as objects of thought which had still vitiated earlier thought. When we refer to something in thought it is like reaching out to something, or like pointing, an activity unfolding from within. It is not that we are reproducing a 'really existing' something 'out there,' and a meaningful gesture of pointing need not imply the truth or reality of what we point to.[3] We do not need to believe, to take the classic claim propounded by Meinong, that when we say 'The golden mountain does not exist' there really must be, in some logical-metaphysical way or other, precisely such an entity of which we can say about it that it does not exist. Nor, even though empiricism has been rejected and our thought goes beyond what we are able to experience directly through the senses, do we need to believe that there must really be shadowy entities transcending experience to which our thought must refer. Earlier thinkers had mistakenly projected the process of constituting the world beyond human experience into metaphysics, thereby confusing an underdeveloped psychology with philosophy. Husserl's phenomenological bracketing was designed to eradicate that confusion. Thus 'purified', phenomenology undertook to establish essences and meaningful knowledge without the appeal to metaphysics that meant losing contact with empirical science, and so brought to philosophy a progressive openness to methodical scientific advance.

By asserting our ability to constitute the world we know, phenomenology appeared to enhance still further our sense of the power of the mind, guaranteeing that we can wring from phenomena their 'transcendental' essence and at the same time define our own self absolutely in relation to its world. But the brilliant philosophical constructs of Husserl and his followers could not long conceal the powerful tensions and contradictory tendencies that lurked below the surface of phenomenological analysis, with its claim that we can so completely dominate our experience and attain a sort of guarantee of its validity. The continuing conviction that human experience is like looking down from a high window, detached, defining its own perspective, and able to sweep across the landscape unhindered, would not long remain unchallenged.

For fundamentally, phenomenology had arisen as an attempt to liberate the mind from the self-centred assumptions of nine-teenth-century philosophy, to open up the question of the status of the knower in such a way as to be challenged by the sense of a greater reality. It was the sense of a world that challenged and transformed us which the young Rudolf Steiner had found exciting in the science of Goethe. It was something similar in phenomenology which had suggested to the young Jean-Paul Sartre, for instance, that to know is not to dominate but to risk one's identity yet find oneself in encountering the world, is to 'burst toward' things:

> veering out there beyond oneself, out there near the tree
> and yet beyond it, for the tree escapes me and repulses
> me and I can no more lose myself in the tree than it can
> dissolve itself into me.[4]

It seemed to offer another philosopher a way out of the conventional constructs of linguistic description to a level of primary, more emotive response: in a phenomenological analysis 'it would then be found that the words, vowels, and phonemes are so many ways of singing the world'.[5] Husserl, for all his promise, seemed at least to some to have gone back on the primary drive of phenomenology, to open up the world, free us from presuppositions, to question our own involvement, and the nature of our self. Instead he had locked us once more into ourselves, into 'transcendental' certainties that pointed away from the richness and overwhelmingness of the world we seek to discover. In order to preserve the certainty of knowledge against the taint of psychologism, and to preserve the knower as a sovereign self, he had erected powerful barriers once more to the very world he had sought to clarify. He had effectually reduced the world to a nothingness, waiting to be constituted as meaningful by our own cognitive act.

But for others, and even at times for Husserl himself, the whole thrust of phenomenology was that precisely by delving behind the set of assumptions on which we operate in our ordinary lives, rather than elevating us to the onlooker simplicity of the view from that high window, it would enable us to:

> reveal a world which, far from being a blank state awaiting the bestowal of significance, already had a distinctive physiognomy.[6]

Thus there are many interesting, even paradoxical aspects to the situation of early twentieth philosophy in the wake of the breakthrough undoubtedly represented by phenomenology. Rudolf Steiner's thought takes hold of many of them, but the path he followed was far different from the 'transcendental' one. We have seen that he too built upon the project of Brentano and wanted to elicit philosophical reflection from 'introspective observations according to the method of natural science',[7] and took up from the potential he saw in the direction established by 'intentional' psychology the impetus for a methodologically purified 'spiritual science'. But his concern in all this was certainly not to tailor matters so as to remove any threat to the autonomy of the rational, conscious mind. Indeed from his perspective recourse to the invocation of the Cogito could at best be treated, on this level, as a philosophical riddle in accordance with Steiner's usual approach. Much of Steiner's response was a creative unravelling of these defensive entanglements, and hints for the constructing of more open-ended, less reductive ideas and intellectual strategies. The old notion of a self that is defined by its rationality gave way to more modern, less stable ideas, which Steiner was able to resolve in the end through developmental approaches that made sense of human identity and of the human learning-process in excitingly new ways.

Husserl's account of the 'meaning-constituting self' rescued the self from nagging uncertainties, not only about the world but above all about itself. In effect the self is removed from the sphere of questions, transcendentalized. But the cost is considerable. To begin with we need only notice, at the crucial moment of bracketing, or 'suspending the natural attitude', the sudden and relatively unexamined substitution of an abstraction, a reconstitution in terms of 'what we must think', for the concrete and many-sided world which phenomenology wished to be given such a challenging and full-blooded presentation. We need to follow Steiner's advice — to become aware here of our own mental activity, the thinking behind the results of our thought. So it turns out that what we are dealing with is the world in so far as it subscribes to our way of thinking: the rest is transcendentally reduced to a blank. In one sense all the later developments in Husserl's phenomenology could be summarized in terms of a continuing (and not always very convincing) struggle to demonstrate that despite this its powerful reductive analyses it remained nevertheless rooted in the 'life-world'.

Other criticisms of the phenomenological method have likewise hinged upon this crucial moment of the shift to the 'higher attitude.' For in the end it remains a shift made, after all, by the 'natural' thinker, whom following Steiner's method we must always keep in the picture — and so its role in distinguishing sharply the science of essences from mere contingent facts remains dangerously unclear, liable to dissolve upon analysis into a multiplication of the natural, or a property of the natural self. And the self-substantiating, so-called *a priori* character of its thinking is in danger of turning out to do little more than show the way we seek for coherence and truth, by exhibiting for us those interconnections our thought can grasp, in retrospect, as internal and necessary to the world we inhabit. It cannot really be conceived as telling us in advance any 'actual' *a priori* truth. It is notable that when Rudolf Steiner aimed to untangle these and other related aspects of thought in his little book *On the Riddles of the Soul*, largely devoted to the heritage of Brentano, he spoke not of a 'shift' to a higher attitude, a break with or a bracketing of the natural attitude, but rather of a methodological *convergence*. His version of a critically validated spiritual science would actually attain its full meaning in connection with the results of natural science. Spiritual science begins with that irreducible presence of the interpreter, as the key to formative processes that cannot lie within the sense-domain.[8] But instead of building a higher, quasi-metaphysical realm of fixed essences, Steiner opened spiritual science, for instance, to ideas of development and evolution. It may be true that the world is only known as it grasped by an interpreter-knower, but the self that knows likewise only unfolds its reality in response to the world that generates and modifies its knowledge.

Thus Steiner reconstrued the kind of phenomenological purification-process conceived by Husserl rather in terms of approaches from the natural side (anthropology, in the widest conceivable sense) and from the spiritual (anthroposophy). He concedes that the two seem to begin with polar opposites, the one based on the scientific elaboration of sense-experience and the other describing the 'purely psychic' apprehension:

> *Prima facie* the two types of apprehension are divided from one another by an unbridgeable gulf. Nevertheless this turns out not to be the case. There *is* a common ground on which the two methodologies may properly encounter one another.

For the concepts which we grasp inwardly are not exhausted in being applied to the sensory domain; rather than freezing them, therefore, fixing them in that state for abstract investigation, anthroposophy notes:

> the fact that these concepts are capable (irrespective of the circumstance that they are to be related to sense-impressions) of opening a life of their own within the psyche. Further, that by the unfolding of this energy they effect a development in the psyche itself.[9]

Spiritual science, or anthroposophy, investigates this on its own terms. But this 'existentially psychic' development has to be pre-supposed by anthropology, since without it the impressions of sense remain unorganized, meaningless; conversely anthroposophy moves toward an understanding of how the inner life of the soul is actualized, individualized in the body. In place of the conventional transcendentalizing movement that yields, when we look at it, no more than an abstraction of the spirit's engagement with the world, therefore, Steiner posited a kind of convergent, or, one might better say, 'incarnational' movement, acknowledging a deeper-level continuity with the natural attitude that opens up the possibility of an encounter along the way, not with an abstraction, but with the reality of the human spirit, acting concretely to interpret and to transform. 'Rightly pursued, therefore, the two approaches, anthroposophical and anthropological, converge and meet in one point ... In this coincidence a genuinely fruitful understanding between anthropology and anthroposophy is possible. It cannot fail, if both disciplines terminate in philosophy and humanity.'[10]

The self here steps down off its artificial pedestal. Yet at the same time it is not reduced to the world it knows, but is able to reveal meaning there. The struggle over the self in the twentieth century, on the other hand, has largely swung between these two extremes of a rational Cartesian self stamping significance on a blank, indeterminate world, and that of a contingent, *ad hoc* sort of self that is merely the product of an indefinite number of experiences. In a significant way, however, the latter view has been open, especially since Freud, to a dimension which represents in some measure the 'occult,' or non-picturable component in human experience, which it has recognized in the guise of 'the unconscious.'

We have already suggested that it may be useful to imagine Steiner, as if he were present at certain points in the later philosophical debate. It is interesting to consider where he would have stood — and here again I shall try to show that in the issues that were raised by phenomenological analysis he might have been, rather consistently, on the modern side even though he strikingly declined to jump to many of the usual modern conclusions.

Criticism of phenomenology's account of the way we 'constitute' the world reached a climax with the attack from psychology led by Jacques Lacan.[11] This became, one might say, another defining moment in understanding the role of philosophy in the modern world. Psychology, he urged, could not approve a picture of a self which dominated its experience so completely and existed so autonomously. The concept of the unconscious above all, of elements in our identity not under rational scrutiny or control, had rendered such a picture unsustainable. Psychology in the twentieth century had come to recognize the self as more vulnerable — as subject both to pressures from without and even more importantly from within its own hidden depths. In particular, argued Lacan, the way we respond to and indeed depend upon other people, starting with our parents, for the roles we play and the way we see ourselves, was at variance with a 'constitutive' philosophy of the self that made even our acknowledgment of the existence of others a sort of speculation or theoretical construct! Obviously here was a crucial instance which could be used to call in question the whole basis of traditional ideas about our knowledge of the world. For it is one thing to say that all we really know about the world is the way it modifies our own sensory-cognitive organization, but quite another to suggest that other people only exist for us to the extent that we 'constitute' them from our uncertain sensory information and infer them, so to speak, in our own image. And what of the case when we see our own image in the mirror?

The latter was actually the theme of Lacan's paper. He took the case of a child seeing its own image in a mirror, and gave a brilliant philosophical and psychological analysis of this moment of self-consciousness — an analysis totally at variance with the 'constitutive' view, which gives us such power to make sense of things and even to validate other people on our own terms. For according to Lacan, the awareness of others, and most critically of ourself as one among others as when we look in a mirror, functions as a destabilizing of our unthinking, natural self-centredness. It traumatically disrupts the 'lived immediacy' of infantile experience, making us realize that others see us, as we now do ourselves in the mirror, with detachment and critical consciousness, rather than identifying with our experience of things. Instead of being able to use our own self-certainty to centre the world as the philosophers would tell us, Lacan argues, such self-consciousness actually tears us apart. It alienates us from our spontaneous ego-centrism, forcing us to identify with the view which other people have of us. We no longer really know who we are. He took the psychological understanding of self-consciousness exemplified in a child seeing itself in a mirror to work, to put it briefly, in quite the opposite way: problematizing the self, not using it as had Descartes to demonstrate the reality of the world.

Now Rudolf Steiner offers a very interesting commentary on the issues involved in what may be described as a twentieth-century showdown between rival philosophies. For we have seen that he distrusts the transcendentalizing tendency, the defence-mechanism to keep the self in control of its world. He grasped well enough that such a static self is all too open to the attacks which, since his time, have seriously eroded the very concept of the self or banished it altogether. But Steiner had actually faced the philosophical issues here in a thoroughgoing way long before. It is one of the most interesting aspects of his thought that while seeking to establish the role of the self as interpreter he was also able to confront the real vulnerability of our self-experience before the other. At the same time, however, he did not accept Lacan's basic assumption, namely that our only authentic mode of identity is a sort of pool of infantile self-ishness (unconsciousness). For what both of these approaches fail to take seriously is the ability we have to grow, to learn from the other and incorporate awareness of others in our own being. To achieve that we need our vulnerability — but also an active, constructive response to experience to extract from it what we can make our own.

Towards the end of *The Philosophy of Freedom* Steiner added a fascinating account of the way we come to know others. There were philosophers who preferred to seek a transcendental grounding, he argued,

> since they believe that otherwise they are forced to the conclusion that the whole external world, which I think is here in front of me, is nothing but the world of my consciousness, and to the further — solipsistic — absurdity that other people, too, exist only within my consciousness.[12]

His solution is however to go in quite the opposite direction: to free the discussion wholly from the metaphysical conception of the self which they are still trying to retain, and to open the matter up to what he would later call anthroposophy — 'to the point of view of the spiritually orientated observation adopted in this book'.

For it is quite untrue, he declares, that when we try to know another person we are left 'merely staring' at the other as a percept among other percepts, through which he or she comes before us, from which we must try to infer the existence of a conscious being somewhat like ourselves. The situation is actually quite different. The percept of someone does not float in this sort of philosophical limbo but also engages my interpretive thought, 'through which the percept of him becomes, as it were, transparent to the mind'. Indeed it reveals in a striking manner a disparity in our experience, not so noticeable in the usual instances of sense-perception, although there too, as we have seen, there is always the hidden element, the aspect that is not contained in the content of sense. In this case:

> In what is a direct appearance to the senses, something else is indirectly revealed. The mere sense-appearance extinguishes itself at the same time as it confronts me. But what it reveals through this extinguishing compels me, as a thinking being, to extinguish my own thinking as long as I am under its influence, and to put the other's thinking in place of my own. I then grasp its thinking in my thinking as an experience like my own. I have really perceived another person's thinking. The immediate percept, extinguishing itself as sense-appearance, is grasped by my thinking, and this is a process taking place wholly within my consciousness, and consisting in this, that the other person's thinking takes the place of mine.[13]

Albeit somewhat paradoxically, Steiner has restored the immediacy of our experience of others and has given it a meaning fundamentally freed from the lurking fear that self-awareness, as Lacan thought, must lead to a destructive crisis of identity before the other. Rather he insists upon consciousness by its very nature as interpretative, as penetrating the nature of appearances, and as fundamentally open to the other:

> Through the self-extinction of the sense-appearance, the separation between the two spheres of consciousness is actually overcome. This expresses itself in my consciousness through the fact that while experiencing the content of another person's consciousness I experience my own consciousness as little as I experience it in

dreamless sleep. Just as in dreamless sleep my waking consciousness is eliminated, so in my perceiving of the content of the content of another person's consciousness the content of my own is eliminated. The illusion that it is not so only comes about because in perceiving the other person ... the extinction of the content of one's own consciousness gives place not to unconsciousness, as it does in sleep, but to the content of the other person's consciousness.[14]

Here consciousness is not a charmed circle of solipsistic aware-ness, a transcendental construct, but a real presence, that can even therefore be threatened with extinction — loss of con-sciousness — before the other. That is the price of giving to the interpreter-consciousness real and not a protected 'transcen-dental' existence, one that is not substituted for by an abstrac-tion. It is the price above all of shared reality, enabling Steiner to give an account in which knowledge can be considered as pre-existing neither in the subject or the object, but only in a co-ordination involving a transformation of the self to include the other's perspective. The other must be allowed not only to touch us on the outside, but to enter into the very heart of the self and to change us from within.

'This whole problem is to be solved,' he continues in remarks that might be addressed to post-Freudian psychology, 'not through artificial conceptual structures with inferences from the conscious to things which can never become conscious' — he urges rather that thinkers need to 'seek the path to open-minded, spiritually orientated observation; instead of which they insert an artificial conceptual structure between themselves and the reality.'[15] Instead of insisting that the attempt to con-struct an objective world must violate the unconscious basis of identity, we might then see rather how we construct and enrich our own identity at the same time as we learn to interpret the world. The changing relationship between conscious and unconscious might also then appear in a new light.

The direction of Steiner's thought, so paradoxical in con-ventional philosophical terms, has actually been justified in the greater understanding of the developmental aspects of knowledge in the decades since he wrote.[16] A classic instance, which shows how Steiner's more radical philosophical reorientation, resolving the problem of knowledge and identity through a self that can absorb and accept the other, may be found in the increased understanding of perspective that has come from developmental thought, i.e. the knowledge we have of the relative sizes and shapes of things at various distances in space.

It is significant that perspective begins to be understood by children only at around the age of nine. But we must beware: the issue here is an epistemological one concerning the basis of understanding — and obviously this cannot be answered simply by determining when or how this happens in a developing human child. Nevertheless the evidence of developmental psychology reveals a striking anomaly that has definite consequences for the theory of knowledge. Indeed it fatally undermines any notion of knowledge that bases it either directly on perception (empiricism) or on a Cartesian self autonomously ordering its experience, as if we know the world from the standpoint of our own impression of the universe, ordered from within by principles of 'transcendental' thought.[17] For, if the ordering of things in perspective were simply a matter of sorting out how to judge elements in our perceptual field, one would actually expect children to master it much earlier. Experiments show that in fact children younger than nine, who do not yet grasp perspective, nonetheless already have very good judgment concerning the apparent sizes of things; actually better in most normal cases than in adults or older children! Yet perspective is understood only later: so that it clearly does not derive directly from perception — from direct comparison of apparent sizes. But the constitutive theory does not fit the case either: the idealist notion of matching empirical experience against an internally constructed order should equally be most easily accomplished by the child earlier on, before other developments complicate the child's perceptual achievements, which are as we have seen at their highest level at a younger age.

Psychological research thus suggests that spatial knowledge just cannot arise in either the way empiricism or constitutive phenomenology would have us believe. But why then does the grasp of perspective emerge so late? Investigation shows that it arises only when the child takes into account not only the hierarchy of apparent sizes and forms it sees itself, nor its own construction of relationships among them, but also how these appear to another viewer. 'In fact,' Piaget writes, 'the concept of projective space ... requires a co-ordination of viewpoints and consequently an operational mechanism of transformation much more complex than the perceptions corresponding to each of these viewpoints considered in isolation.'[18] We actually do not learn to judge the size and shape of a train coming approaching the station platform, for instance, in some such way as all the old theories of knowledge claimed, by co-ordinating experiences within our own closed inner world and inferring that there 'must be' a consistent reality, a fixed form, i.e. the train which remains the same size behind all the changing appearance of its size to us as it moves. The knowledge is born in us by the realization that the train already appears large to someone else further down the line, as it will to us when it is at the platform. Psychologically, as Piaget shows, this explains why it arises so late.

But the developmental data are also able to clarify the essential structure of knowledge itself, and they do so when we follow the philosophical direction opened up by Rudolf Steiner.

For what this means is that the 'high window' approach to knowledge, and its notion that we master and constitute our own experience, then extrapolate conclusions and apply them outwards to others, is flawed from the beginning. Grasping the spatial character of the world in relation to ourselves is only possible when we include in the picture, from the very start in addition to our own point of view, the awareness that it appears differently to someone else. Only then does it become knowledge, which is intrinsically something shared with others. The psychological evidence shows that spatial understanding, shared space, becomes possible only by placing the consciousness of another in the very heart of our own experience. And the knower is thereby changed, as opposed to the conventional view of consciousness locked into a world of appearances and 'constitutive' abstract ideas — the knower is made part of a cognitive structure which of its essence includes others and requires an inner modification of our own perceptual viewpoint to accommodate theirs.

Steiner often drew a religious analogy to the spirit in which his theory drew attention to the mutuality of knowledge. He called it a 'Pauline' theory, just as Paul referred his message to one who was 'not I, but Christ in me.'[19] Hence knowledge for Steiner cannot have that static, self-defining or constitutive nature that so many philosophers had sought since Descartes. Many philosophers today, it must be said, still fiercely resist admitting the far-reaching relevance of developmental researches like that utilized above. (Steiner, here above all, is still far ahead of our time.) Knowledge can be understood neither as impressed upon us from the world, nor simply as conformed to the subject, to the one who knows and constitutes meaning. Knowledge and the self in its development, as this example illustrates, are rather intimately intertwined.

Lacan in his attack on phenomenology wished simply to overturn its assumptions and substitute his own: he assumed that reality is necessarily a denial of the self and its illusion of identity. Seeing oneself as a distinct individual with a particular viewpoint can for him be only an alienation from the 'lived me'. Reflecting on the child who contemplates his image in the mirror he feels 'I am torn from myself'; and still more seriously, from his point of view, he feels threatened by the realization that he must henceforth identify with such an external image, which is all that others have of him.

If we now bring him, imaginatively, as an additional interlocutor into the dispute, Steiner can accept much of Lacan's anti-phenomenological critique. Indeed he too made scientifically precise psychological observations concerning the particular crisis in the sense of self which comes at the age of nine, even as this type of spatial awareness and its awareness of a certain alienation, sets in. But because he has addressed the underlying epistemological issue more fundamentally, his account of consciousness can actually go further. It suggests we look again at the psychologist's dogmatic assumption that all we know of others is an 'external image', to which the mirror fatally draws our attention. That same unquestioned assumption he still shares, or takes over from the traditional view of things. He no longer believes in our power to organize our experience and make it mean what we define it to mean — but he still shares the assumption that this leaves us with the outer shell of appearances, a world that is like the 'alienated image' we recognize with a shock to be ourselves in the mirror. Our lived identity with the world is shattered. Steiner's relating of the crisis to the gaining of knowledge suggests something wholly different from these assumptions, however. It is true that there can be no room here for a self looking effortlessly down, defining the world that it sees: but there is room for a self which out of the crisis will gain knowledge through admitting the other. Rather than trapping us in a world of image-appearances, the world that opens up to us in terms of spatial knowledge compels a change in the self. The threat of the other must certainly be acknowledged; but the direct connection to knowledge reminds us that the self, in spite of the threat it feels from the other, can also form a quite different relationship to it: it can allow the other into the self in a gesture of love and acceptance. It can accept thereby a shared world. The truth is that the crisis which for Lacan denies the possibility of all authentic knowledge is in reality the beginning of a relationship to the world that goes beyond the surface-impression of things, which his still unquestioned epistemological assumptions made it impossible for him to understand.

The intertwining of a psychological crisis, a changed attitude to the world which needs to overcome a feeling of alienation, and the emergence of a fuller level of knowledge as its resolution may serve as an example of how, for Steiner, the human reality of knowledge can never be abstracted from the totality, involving attitudes, feeling and actions. Indeed 'feeling is the means whereby, in the first instance, concepts gain concrete life.'[20] This does not mean that Steiner is making an appeal here to feeling (or anything else) to do what thought cannot. Other philosophers, such as Schopenhauer or Bergson, for example, have also tried to hold on to the immediacy of human involvement with the environment that thought seemed to miss.[21] But Steiner is not doing anything like this. His point is rather that thinking does not somehow demonstrate to us the world, independent of our own activity: it expresses rather our ability to grow and to overcome our self-centredness. Knowledge of the world is knowledge because there is hidden in it the fact that it is a world shared with other human beings, given equal recognition with ourselves. The notion that love is 'merely subjective' is part of the false dichotomy that has to be overcome if knowledge is to become the bearer of value, as Steiner insists it must.

> For this reason when knowledge is spoken about nowadays love is never mentioned seriously ... The essential aspect of love, the giving of oneself to the world and its phenomena is not seen to have any relevance to knowledge. Nevertheless in real life love is the greatest power of knowledge. And without this love it is certainly impossible to attain to an understanding of human nature which could form the basis of an art of education.[22]

For Steiner, all cognition must ultimately spring from love, in which alone the threat of the other at the heart of all knowledge is not only fully accepted, but affirmed.

The Self and the Other: a Social Reality

The interrelation between the self in development, knowledge, and the intrinsic recognition of the validity of the other can only be fully appreciated when we place it in this human, and specifically social framework. The rise of the social sciences is itself a symptom of the complex situation of the individual in modern society, and the struggle often needed to comprehend one's fellow human beings. It is significant, moreover, that the ways in which twentieth-century social science has attempted to explore the meaning of the individual and society have flowed, in very large measure, from the powerful methodological initiatives of Steiner's contemporaries. Nietzsche, Phenomenology (particularly once more Scheler) and the ferment of radical-revolutionary, dialectical ideas with which Steiner came into close contact during his time in Vienna, have all had a profound impact on the way social science has evolved.[23] Many of the unresolved philosophical issues were imported along with them. Arguably the contradictions and impasses rather than concrete results to which these disciplines seem so often to have conducted us might become intelligible in terms of the fundamental philo-sophical questions on which they have again and again foundered.

One might put it another way, and reverse the perspective: the full scope of these unresolved philosophical questions con-cerning knowledge, the individual and society can often be seen tragically dramatized, as it were, in the subsequent historical fate of whole societies in the great social and ideological polar-izations of our own time.

It was Durkheim who gave much of the impetus to the social sciences and especially to sociology of knowledge. Dissatisfied with the abstract stress on the subjective, the Cartesian self which bestows meaning, much of his pioneering social thought sought to redress the balance and to assert the social objectivity of the structures of thought. Therefore it radically denied the role of the self in favour of the social reality and autonomy of the structures themselves. Blossoming into the movement (or per-haps set of movements) subsequently called Structuralism, this kind of sociological thinking has directed the attention of its protagonists away from selves to the cultural and symbolic activities of societies, and revealed the inner coherence of their ideas and values. It has seemed evident to the thinkers in this line that forms of language and culture are not so much made by individuals, by a constituting 'self', as they are expressions of larger, often unconscious shaping forces. Indeed the self, they decided, can be dispensed with or denied outright.

Interestingly, Steiner rather often has more in common with this structuralist stream of later twentieth-century thought. I have discussed elsewhere, for instance, the way his understand-ing of unconscious shaping forces in myth makes use of essen-tially the approaches that have since been developed in 'structural' anthropology and sociology.[24] But of course that does not mean that he accepted the denial of the self which has so often resulted from a one-sided development of these ideas. Bold as it looks, such a denial is essentially little more a question-beg-ging gesture, rather than a real attempt to get back to the under-lying issues behind the idealist and the objectivist versions alike. Instead of shifting the emphasis decisively away from the self, and attributing the elaboration of socially objective thought to inscrutable theoretical entities, Steiner took the situation to be one in which the nature and development of the self might be observed. And it is by looking at the self in this larger context that we may really come closer to understanding how reality is 'constituted' for us. Rejecting the Nietzschean version of human self-making as a titanic-nihilistic gesture, Steiner nevertheless did not swing over to regarding the self merely as a product of society, — or an 'ideological' illusion. The social world and the role of the 'significant other' are for him actually part of the way the self evolves in a social environment. This is a uniquely human situation, and the emergence of knowledge along the way is an intrinsic part of that unique social development.[25] Social life, for Steiner, does not just exist like a natural phenomenon but actually shows such an evolution of consciousness taking place. Society exists for us to the extent that we take part in it, and our taking part in it makes us what we are. It remains the crucially important fact for Steiner that society produces actively evaluating and critically thinking individuals with self-consciousness.

He reacted therefore with unexpected vehemence when one of his own followers, the Swedish economist Rudolf Kjellén produced a treatise on *The State as Organism:*

> One can hardly imagine a more misguided or misleading analogy. If we follow such an analogy as this we shall never arrive at a clear understanding of man. Why is this? In a human organism, cells exist side by side, and this juxtaposition has a special significance. The entire structure of the human organism depends upon it ... In the totality of the State, however, the human personality is something wholly different from the cells in an organism ... To arrive at a fruitful conception, our thinking must be spiritual-scientifically grounded. This will suffice to convince us that the human individuality, or whole being of man, far transcends the state, belonging to a spiritual order of reality which the State cannot reach. If therefore you do compare the State with an organism, and the individual member with the cells, then, if you think realistically, you will arrive at the idea of an organism

wherein the individual cells everywhere extend out
beyond the skin! You would have an organism whose
cells extend out beyond the skin, developing
independently of the organism and each self-contained.
You would have to picture the organism with 'living
spines' everywhere projecting out beyond it![26]

Any attempt to make the self a mere part of the State, as if
society could exist somehow above and beyond the individuals who emerge and grow within it, must therefore fail — as
the totalitarian social experiment did fail. The self emerges as
part of unconscious, collective life. But Steiner's concept of
the evolution of consciousness enables him to describe how it
is nevertheless the self that, unconsciously, is working in society at a former stage of its development. The 'ethical individual' is the very meaning of society — not, however, as its
presupposition but as its highest evolutionary stage. We may
remember that Steiner could epitomize his moral philosophy
as the necessary response to the brilliant edifice of thought
that the scientists of evolution 'have striven to build for natural science. It is the spiritualized theory of evolution carried
over into moral life.'[27]

It is quite wrong, then, from Steiner's point of view, to
choose between an emphasis on the knowing self and a social-
objective structure. Both are opposite sides of the same coin.
Many of these philosophical problems, instead of being
addressed by the reversal of perspective that has basically con-
figured modern sociological thought, are still often left uncon-
sidered. The result has impoverished both sides of the
argument. So for example recently argued James Schmidt, in
his lucid account of the concepts which have underpinned
modern social-scientific thought. He comments gloomily on the
failure of contemporary social philosophers to break out of
these either-or assumptions, which in the end are not so far
apart even though they are sworn opposites. 'It would not be
surprising if, sneaking out of Durkheim's house in the dead of
night, they should run into a familiar figure, slipping out of
Descartes' house. Meeting in that no-man's land where, for better or worse, the human sciences seems condemned to camp

out for the foreseeable future, they might well greet one another with a smile of recognition.'[28]

He wonders whether either version as currently constituted can help clarify the way that in social reality 'structures do not simply constrain agents, they also allow agents to act in ways which frequently lead to the transformation of the structures themselves.' That would need, it is evident, a seismic shift in the underlying epistemological attitudes of the human sciences; but it precisely what they could find, if they were willing to seek it, in Steiner's thought. He had broken the mould which still constricts so many alternative versions of modern thought, by exploring precisely the way self-definition is bound up with knowledge. We become aware of objects spread out in three-dimensional space through the same act by which we become aware of our own special perspective, and at the very same time of our own perspective as only one among others — of other selves. Conscious knowledge and the self that knows do not have to be assumed as the presupposition of society, as if society came into being by a sort of agreement of fully conscious individuals and was constituted by their convergence. But nor need the knowing self be denied on principle to enable 'objective' analysis. The self comes to consciousness on a trajectory that both generates objective knowledge and acknowledges social reality. Despite his 'ethical individualism,' therefore, it is important to realize that Steiner's individualism was from the beginning seen in a social-developmental perspective, which is relevant here even before we come to consider the wider ethical implications.

In *The Philosophy of Freedom* the view that the individual exists only to realize some already constituted, objective ethical reality is likened to the ideas of an obsolete biology which saw living things as designed to realize a 'purpose.' 'Scientists, happily,' says Steiner, 'have now thrown out the concept of purpose as a dead theory.' It was once supposed that a bull has horns 'in order to butt', rather as old-fashioned morality supposes the individual to exist in order to belong to society or the state. This approach Steiner rejects; in rejecting it, however, Steiner does not let go of the evolutionary analogy. State and society are shaped by the individuals who compose them, and who are the source of their values. Yet:

> ... that state and society should in turn react upon
> individual life is no more difficult to comprehend than
> that the butting which is the result of the presence of
> horns reacts in turn upon the further development of the
> horns of the bull, which would become stunted through
> prolonged disuse. Similarly, the individual would become
> stunted if he led an isolated existence outside human
> society. Indeed, this is why the social order arises, so that
> it may in turn react favourably on the individual.

There can no more be a self-existent individual than there can be a self-existent society. The moral issues here need, first of all, the right kind of understanding of people — the right concept of knowledge.

It is the expanded context in which the self emerges and cognizes an objective, social reality that concerns us here. We cannot go into depth on Steiner's social thought. It must be enough simply to point out some of the consequences. One is that to be socialized in Steiner's approach we do not, as if we were the alien beings many theories seem to suppose, have to internalize a 'picture' of society: we are social in our very being, and society's structures are those of our developing self. On Steiner's epistemology, personal experience can be placed in the same framework as social awareness, and our individual emergence is grounded at the same time in real belonging. In fact our complex inner life is viewed by Steiner as the result of cultural history, the 'sentient soul,' 'intellectual soul' and consciousness-soul' of which he speaks are the elaboration of the soul-nature which we originally share with the animals in the course of cultural evolution.[29]

When Steiner came to expand on his social ideas in the practical context of the rebuilding of Europe after the First World War, he was able to base his project for them on a concept of knowledge in the human sciences capable of grasping the complex role of the creative individual between the conventional opposing poles. Any society needs established values, 'rights' which are attributed to all persons equally. However, the individual in the creative, 'spiritual' sphere of conscious knowledge, is a truth of equal validity, constantly offering new understandings of experience. The two are not to be played off against each other, as rival ideologies. Steiner's insight into the nature of knowledge helps us understand in particular the deeper aspects of the sphere that connects and lies between them, that of co-operation, of exchange. It forbids us from the outset to conceive of others merely as threats or rivals to the self. Self is understood as already involving others, since from its earliest phases self-understanding (awareness of one's own perspective on things) emerges alongside awareness of the perspective of others. Neither could be fixed and unchanging. The human sciences need not therefore become fixated on the unproductive task of reducing one to the other. That third sphere — of transformation, interaction, socialization, 'exchange' or economics in the broadest sense — is implied by the very social nature of knowledge as Steiner presents it, breaking out of the idealist/materialist dichotomy in which the 'self' is locked in an isolated confrontation with 'the world.' Steiner did not allow this sphere to be handed over to deterministic, externally manipulative forces (as conceived for example by Marxism); it became in his thinking instead an area of cognitive interaction and the freedom of consciousness to initiate change.[30]

In place of the subtle equilibration of spheres which Steiner envisaged, today we have dazzling intellectual feats of one-sidedness in the spheres of cultural and historical studies in particular. We may take an instance from literary studies. As the pendulum has swung away from the notion of a god-like author who makes a fictional world with effortless self-determination, we have seen the rise of a literary criticism has sought instead to conjure everything from the 'literary discourse' of the work and its time, evading reference to an author and often even denying outright that discourse can be brought under individual control. Discourse becomes a set of differences, in which by definition we can never arrive at a stable 'identity.' Or: Social history has one-sidedly stressed the economic or other unconscious social 'forces' which are seen as actually shaping events, reducing the ideas and experiences of those taking part in them to an 'ideology' or even an irrelevance, an 'epiphenomenon.' Thus a religious revival is analysed as 'in fact' social protest, etc. and the way people involved in the events understood their actions is felt to be irrelevant.

Only in the most recent phases has the wheel begun to turn full circle, and we once more have a recognition e.g. that the conscious literary aspirations of Elizabethan England, were not just an 'ideological' reflection of the changes affecting its social order, to be explained from the completely different vantage-point of modern theory. Some critics have dared to suggest that the literary representations of the period were an empowering factor, actually helping to create England's national and political ascendancy. The spiritual sphere is granted tentative histor-ical reality once again. On the whole, however, unconscious and 'objective' forces are still substituted by social scientists for what it is assumed would necessarily be a barren and solipsis-tic subjectivism.

Now, Steiner was fully cognisant of unconscious factors in history — not least in the history of philosophical thought! But he was also able to incorporate in his fundamental approach to knowledge the conscious role of the individual in bringing about creative change, and interacting with the changing society of which he was part in a way that cannot be reduced to any of the other factors. He showed the need to include, if one might think of a recent example, (and so bring Steiner yet once more in imagination into our own later domain) not only the economic failure and corruption of Communism, but also a Mikhail Gorbachev.

All this is going rather fast. But it is just because knowledge is an active component in our experience of society and the world that Steiner's concept of epistemology is important. And it is when we look at what is involved in this social and trans-formational perspective, above all, that we need the more ade-quate conception of human knowledge that Steiner championed. There are signs that others are looking in the direc-tions he has traversed. Berger and Luckmann, for instance, famously tried to break out of the methodological impasse between the foundation-statements we have named after Durkheim and Descartes.[31] One of them at least went on to explore some of the further, religious and spiritual implications, investigating in a further book what he called the 'rumour of angels' that invests human society. In reading its argument for a return to the 'human centre,' its transformational perspective that can 'relativize the relativists,' and at many other points, one feels the urge to compare his approach to Steiner's.[32] The latter would have understood his starting-point and the problems to which the social understanding of knowledge has come. He would not have been surprised, I suspect, that in the human sciences the drive for an 'objective' viewpoint, an outsider's truth, should have failed to provide us with the knowledge needed for overcoming the widespread sense of alienation and the unresolved polarization of our basic concepts. For him, the way we are required from the outset to acknowledge the reality of others is bound up from the start with the way we relate to the shared world beyond.

Reversing the widespread modern perspective, for which the emergence of self-consciousness and the awareness of others represent a dangerous hall of mirrors, and individual experience irrelevant to the real forces at work in society, Rudolf Steiner's epistemology suggests that we can reclaim society from the institutionalists as part of our self, giving a model of consciousness in which the world reveals itself to us more fully as we evolve: in the evolution of a social reality, and in ever deepening levels of truth.

Being and Nothingness

Rudolf Steiner's philosophy is once again designed, then, to avoid the unhealthy polarizations, the flying to extremes which it is easy to see has exacted a heavy price on modern thought. With their suggestion that 'objectivity' can only be won by marginalizing self-consciousness, these tendencies have resulted in a psychology which sees man as a slave to unconscious forces, or a sociology which denies the validity of the individual's own experience. Contrastingly in knowledge for Steiner, we are never outside the world we know and share by the very nature of knowledge with others; and our knowledge is not just a reflection but an active part of the society we thereby engage with, not to mention that larger society, our environment.

But though it is relatively easy, in principle, to appreciate how the validity of social knowledge — the way we can know about things around us by grasping how they appear to another — might be explained in terms of a transformation of structures or adaptation of the self to accommodate the vantage-point of others, in other areas we may feel the return of worries like those over psychologism which we mentioned at the outset of this chapter. It is time we returned to that most difficult case with which we set out to follow the emergence of Steiner's ideas. For how can the self in development be evoked to explain the truths of mathematics?

Are these not just true, independent of human relations? Even in the twentieth century, mathematicians have often adopted a virtually platonic position in regard to propositions that appear to be independent of all experience — whether they are envisaged as intellectual entities directly grasped by the mind or whether, as Whitehead, Bertrand Russell and others have influentially maintained, they are pure construction, reducible in the final analysis to logic. Mathematics also constitutes a crucial issue in the whole question of how mind is related to the world. Scientific certainty about our interpretation of that world is intimately bound up with it.

At first sight, mathematical truth appears to be independent of the contingent reality we perceive. Pure geometrical figures, for example, can never be found as such in the world we actually experience. Steiner is certainly not inclined to minimize, as he makes clear to begin with, the seeming-miraculous character of our ability to geometrize:

> If one truly reflects on this matter, that man can form the
> conception of a triangle — it will appear a marvellous
> thing: that man forms a triangle, an abstract triangle,
> nowhere to be found in concrete life, purely by
> geometrical, mathematical representation![33]

The 'timeless truth' of geometrical or mathematical propositions seems at first glance to mark them out as entities from some higher, purely intellectual world. The fascination they have exerted upon philosophers, however, has been not so much the intellectual purity that delights the mathematician, as the suggestion that they could be a unique source of certainty in an otherwise contingent world. That dream of dominating our experience, of being able to assess it from a standpoint of total mastery, has often taken a mathematical turn. Of such timelessly true propositions Steiner could agree that they 'contain something which pertains specifically to the soul — something which in its truth is quite independent of the transient process of perception.' However he was clear that the argument from psychic activity that transcends our transient perceptual experience, to the real existence of such entities, goes astray:

> The point is not that the truth thus revealed is something imperishable, in its own nature. The point is purely whether its manifestation to the soul takes place in such a way that the soul's perishable corporeal supporting-structure plays no role, or only that part of us which is independent of the perishable nature. It is the enduring aspect of the *soul* which comes before our view as soon as we become aware of experiences that are not limited to the transient.[34]

What is important for Steiner is the characteristic of the 'existentially psychic', of the activity involved. He is not inclined to look for a 'realist', or 'platonic' solution to the problem of mathematics.

Mathematics instead does turn out to have a relationship to actual experience — though one that is masked by the apparently self-sufficient, logical nature of mathematical propositions. Hence the temptation to suppose that they might be a rung we can grasp to haul ourselves up above experience altogether. But the reality, for Steiner, lies in the deeper sources of our own psychic activity. And Steiner goes on to investigate the movements that we make in the space we occupy — although we are not normally conscious of them. Indeed they need not be perceptible at all, but simply be intentional, supersensible movements which define our relationship to the world around us. These are movements that are possible because by our human bearing, our orientation in the world, we establish a plane:

> You enact unawares in space a line which actually describes a triangular movement. Such movements are actually there, only you do not perceive them. But since

your spine is in a vertical position, you are in the plane in which these movements take place. An animal is not in this plane; its spine lies otherwise, i.e. horizontally; thus these movements are not carried out. Because man's spine is in the vertical, he is in the plane where this movement is produced. He does not bring it to consciousness so as to be able to say: 'I am always dancing in a triangle!' But what he does do is draw a triangle and say: 'That is a triangle.'

In reality this is a movement, carried out unconsciously, which he accomplishes in the cosmos.[35]

Moreover our individual, willed or voluntary movements are only a part of the way that in general we are inserted into the dynamics of the space around us. Ultimately we have grown out of the world we are coming to know, so that our biological structure itself, our bones and limbs, is a part of the process. And the earth itself is in motion:

These movements to which you give specific forms in geometry when you draw geometrical figures, you perform in conjunction with the earth ... complicated movements, such as those which belong to the lines of the geometrical solids: the cube, octahedron, dodecahedron, icosatetrahedron, etc. These bodies are not invented, they are reality — but unconscious reality. In these and other geometrical solids lies a remarkable harmony with the subconscious knowledge which man possesses. This is due to the fact that your bone-structure possesses essential knowledge; but your consciousness does not reach down into the bone system. The consciousness of it dies, and it is only reflected back in the geometrical images which man carries out in figures.

Man is an intrinsic part of the universe. In evolving geometry he is copying something that he himself does in the cosmos.[36]

Thus even mathematical knowledge is interpreted by Steiner in a way that makes man 'an intrinsic part of the universe,' not in terms of ideal objects organizing experience from above. It is only that the roots of mathematics lie in an unconscious activity. Steiner remained true to the Goethean project he had originally formulated, which would take neither the object or the concept as given, but seek to trace 'the emergence of the concept from the darkness of our consciousness.'[37] And in this way we can see a way through to understanding how mathematical and geometrical figures have a relationship to the world around us, despite their apparently abstract character.

Steiner's approach to mathematics can be supported, largely from developments within mathematics itself since his time, but also by the increasingly sophisticated understanding of the relations between psychology and mathematics as empirical sciences. Within mathematics, it has come to be understood that the seeming self-sufficiency of abstract conceptual systems is illusory, at least in the sense that no such system can be self-demonstrating, a closed circle of logic. Kurt Goedel showed that a logical system such as would be needed to establish mathematics cannot be completely formalized, but must remain 'essentially incomplete.'[38] It can be established only by appeal to a higher-level system — but then to demonstrate that system, we will need to appeal to a yet higher one, and so on, and so on. This establishment of the limits of formalization, while being inimical to the formalist programme in the philosophy of mathematics, also seems fatal to the notion of self-existent mathematical objects. Similar tendencies have emerged in the developmental study of mathematical concepts as they are studied by psychology. The reference back to the activity of the individual, starting in earliest infancy and thus certainly with processes in part unconscious, has been amply documented by Piaget and others in the field.

Piaget's researches in particular convinced him, we recall, of the 'myth of the sensory origin of scientific knowledge': this has its true origins in the active intervention of the knower. Going back to earliest childhood, we develop geometrical understanding of shape and form by moving and rotating them, ultimately laying the basis of the subsequent mathematical concepts we apply to the world in science.[39] On Steiner's model of knowledge, as we have seen, it would make sense that the reality of mathematical systems would be found to be based in activity in this way. By rejecting the standpoint of consciousness, and drawing attention to the unconscious processes which underlie it, psychology helps point to a theory of knowledge that would root us once more in the world. In his lectures on 'human and cosmic thought,' one way in which Steiner attacked the philosophy which assumes we are locked in our own subjectivity, trying to interpret an alien world-out-there, was precisely by restoring concepts to movement. Thereby he sought to restore the dynamic connection involved in their essential nature between the knower and the universe in which he comes to be. The individual would thereby be liberated from the subjective, 'trapped' single standpoint to experience the circle of the sciences, or sequence of possible attitudes to objectivity — suprapersonal or cosmic thought, which puts us back into the world.[40]

The 'idealist' moment in the process of knowing, in which it seems that mind confronts the world and imposes upon it meaning, order and intelligibility, is thus reinterpreted fundamentally. It emerges as part of a dynamic of knowledge, rooted in unconscious activity of the soul. What we really witness at that moment is not the 'mind' confronting the world, but rather disentangling itself from it. We are defining for ourselves a position over against the world, so as to experience our own being. Knowledge is the bringing to consciousness of some portion of our activity as part of the universe we inhabit; but in order to bring it under conscious control, we have to suppress or 'benumb,' actually bring death into, that active involvement with the world on which, nevertheless, all knowledge is based.

Steiner's concept of knowledge sounds paradoxical, but in reality what is unfamiliar about it is simply the element of inner movement, so different from any theory of knowledge that would make of it a sort of snapshot, or for that matter a grid imposed upon the world. It can be grasped only as process. It starts with the activity of the soul, which is the knower's ability to change, to adapt and grow. But in order to become conscious of it, we have to bring this activity to a halt, to fix it in a definite form of 'objectivity.' That this is not something ever thrust upon us from without, a reality we just have to recognize, is clearest of all in the instance of mathematical knowledge, since we can never find pure geometrical or mathematical forms in nature.

The driving force behind it is rather our own urge to define ourselves over against the world we know.[41]

In thus establishing ourselves as a conscious presence in the world, we actually bring about that polarization which materialism and idealism alike have mistakenly supposed to be primary and fundamental, a fact of the world. We may recall that knowledge, in Steiner's anti-metaphysical view, is rather the relationship which *we* make with the world, dividing up reality into knower and known. '*Things* demand no explanation.' Epistemology, the science of knowledge, therefore has as its goal the reversing of what necessarily appears as the *fait accompli* by which we find ourselves consciously present in the world, observing and knowing. Knowledge sets us over against things, as interpreters; it is for epistemology to remind us of the hidden unity which connects us with the world, suppressed by our own act of becoming conscious. And just as significantly it points out to us, by analysing the situation, that it is because of our need to become separate that we suppress also the identity of our concepts (mathematical or otherwise) with our own activity, our process of self-development — in the case of mathematics, our growth and movement in the world of space, for example. Hence ideas may appear to our self, when it has achieved consciousness, to exist almost independently, in some absolute way, and their relationship to external reality can likewise come to seem mysterious and inexplicable. When I want to move my arm, the idea of doing so is translated in a way my conscious observation cannot follow into actual movement by my will; or, when I recognize something I have seen before, it may seem problematic how I can apply to a real object an idea that seems to exist only 'inside my head.'

Thus Steiner's reading of self-consciousness is deeply if subtly divergent from that of Lacan, mentioned earlier — and much more profoundly coherent. Whereas Lacan supposes that mirror-image awareness leads to a shock, jarring us out of the 'lived immediacy' of unreflective experience, for Steiner it is we who simultaneously strive to unfold our own activity in spontaneous movement and growth, and also to become aware of ourselves, arresting the flux of experience, ourselves introducing death. In Steiner too, knowledge involves a kind of violation. We achieve that 'objective' fixing of the content of awareness by handing over forces of our own life-processes to the other, which means from our standpoint, death. But we do so driven by the deep need to achieve our separateness; so that this drive is not to be set against the urge to self-development and growth but, despite its pain and terror, as the only way to its fulfilment. For knowledge, in short, is our only way of relating to the world in freedom.

To understand how this is so, we must recall just how far Steiner's thought is removed from any notion of concepts or ideas as quasi-real entities, organizing a chaos of raw experience. Rather than putting ourselves in touch with some platonic truth, by setting ourselves over against the world we have in reality reduced our involvement with it to almost or rather literally to nothing. In ideas, our engagement with things is reduced to pure virtuality, to 'picture being,' to mere representation that exerts no real pressures upon us. In fact, since there is no conceptual area, in Steiner's anti-metaphysical view, which really exists outside experience, then this separateness, our detachment from our world, places us nowhere and cannot logically be anything except — nothingness.

> A famous philosopher of modern times, Descartes, is the originator of the famous saying *cogito ergo sum*, I think therefore I am. But ... when we merely think something or experience it in thinking, it does not follow that it is, or that I am merely because I myself am thinking. For us these thoughts are at most pictures; they may be the most certain thing in us, but we do not grasp any being through our thinking.[42]

Here Steiner's account of mental images and ideas also moves decisively away from the old empiricist notion that we carry within us 'imprints' or faint reminiscences of experiences. Even if we could be shown to have such 'traces' actually marked upon us, it remains totally obscure how they could serve as ideas, i.e. how they could now refer to experiences, memories, etc. It is because we have failed to find our being in the suppressed active engagement with the world, our own coming-to-be out of our environment, that we seek desperately to reattach ourselves through such theories:

> We have ceased completely to find real being in ourselves
> ... We have no way of finding anything else in us except
> by the methods which science applies to nature — and
> then we seek our real being in that. In consequence, man
> today believes only in that part of himself which is a part
> of nature. Nature and the mode of existence associated
> with it thereby become a sort of idol which robs modern
> man of any feeling of his own being.[43]

He is aligned in his understanding of mental representations as
virtual, as nothingness, rather with the subsequent developments in Existentialism and later phenomenology. Even
philosophers more in the Anglo-American analytic line have
come to admit that, in comparison with the empiricist idea of
actual impressions as it were pressed into us, this newer analysis of the mental image is much more successful and coherent.[44]
Steiner's deconstruction of the Cogito is now complete:

> For what we have in mathematics is mental images — the
> furthest refinement of mental images that still holds on to
> a connection with external reality ... If one learns to know
> what it can reveal, one learns to know something in it that
> has as much reality as an image that we see of ourselves
> in a mirror, but which nevertheless tells us something —
> in certain circumstances tells us a good deal. But to be
> sure, one would be a fool to take the mirror-image for the
> ultimate reality ...: one is not really looking for the reality
> in the right spot.[45]

The world of mental images, of geometry or mathematical relations, is like the world 'behind' a mirror. In contrast to the tradition from Descartes which seeks completeness and certainty in
thought, it is its essential incompleteness which strikes Steiner,
and what is missing is reference to the activity which produced
it. As he had stressed in *The Philosophy of Freedom* therefore:

> My remarks concerning the self-supporting and self-
> determined nature of thinking cannot therefore simply be
> transferred to concepts.[46]

And it is reference back to this directional activity, such as our unconsciously absorbed movements or handling of objects in space, which we also need in order to explain how a 'mental image' can be at the same time an explanatory idea, which 'applies' to the real world — how the mathematical figures which arise in consciousness, for instance, are at the same time an actual engagement at a deeper level.

An analysis of being and nothingness might strike some readers as essentially belonging to the kind of hot-house culture of certain twentieth-century philosophical currents: the turgid obscurities of Heidegger or the cerebral intellectualism of the Left Bank. It is worth pointing out, therefore, that Steiner's thought here might have been helpful in a quite different, rather more robust and technical domain. It might have helped with the confusions over the extent (if any) to which the human mind works like a computer.

In the face of what appears to be the widespread if rather surprising popular wish to believe that human beings and computers closely resemble one another — or conversely that machines 'remember' and 'think,' or may soon do so — Roger Penrose has recently argued at length that 'artificial intelligence' research has achieved disappointingly little, especially in conceptual terms. It may be true that computers can do things which remind us of human mental processes; but Penrose effectively highlights also what they do not do, say, in comparison to a thinker working at a mathematical problem. It would be unwise to attempt to rival Professor Penrose's ability to explain vividly what it is that scientists do when they tackle such problems. Yet one might suggest an analogy. Agreeing with Penrose that human beings are not 'computers made of meat,' we should reflect on the more likely explanation: computers do human-like things — because they have been made by people, by human beings. They are unlikely to tell us how we ourselves operate. Bicycles are also machines designed to do human-like activities of balancing, moving, changing direction, etc. Their principle of motion is derived directly from human actions (leg movements similar to walking, uprightness, balance, etc.), though they can be motorized and move on their own. Clearly they are based on the human activity of walking, which has been turned via two wheels into a much more effective means of progression. The extension and specialization of human activity in such ways is a basic phenomenon of technology. Yet moving on wheels is not the basis of human movement; and we would be foolish to conclude that because machines move about in a fashion closely related to human movement, men are an evolutionary development of the bicycle — though that is precisely the kind of reasoning indulged in by the 'artificial intelligence' enthusiasts!

Likewise computers do not actually perform human activities, and that is not what we need them for. The theorists who would make us into computers, it seems, are leaving out of account precisely the way we use them. By concentrating on the storing and patterning of 'information,' argues Penrose, such theories fail to grasp the role in human knowledge of our striving, our activity. 'One strives for algorithms, when one does mathematics, but the striving does not seem to be an algorithmic procedure.'[47] Philosophies which ignore this can tell us relatively little about human processes of knowledge, or furnish conceptual models for our own mental life. Thoughts or ideas are simply not vast storage-jars of information. Developing a language or way of thought actually requires us to forget the information processed in the learning of it. This way in which 'information' is taken up and transformed into new faculties, in contrast, is something which Steiner saw as essential to knowledge and to the self in development.[48] It is part of his consistent recognition that knowledge is a phenomenon of human growth and social maturing, in no way comparable to a quasi-physical event like recording an image or a material mark left as a trace of an experience we have had.

Here Steiner's ideas offer more positive ways forward, one may suggest, where modern thought including the effort to understand intelligence in computer-like terms has found itself at various kinds of dead-end.[49] In contrast, it is rather disappointing that Penrose himself for example, when seeking a way out for quantum theory that avoids the subjective-idealist dead-end of making definite events in the universe dependent upon consciousness, feels he has to opt for a platonic notion of real mathematical 'entities,' and elsewhere falls back on the parallel suggestion that we 'just know' or 'just see' some important aspects of essential being. Once again thoughts are called upon to be quasi-physically 'real,' or just to present themselves inescapably to us. Penrose comes to the very verge of Steiner's 'spiritual activity,' only to fall back, it seems, at the final hurdle.

Steiner's philosophy is clear, contrastingly, in regard to these and other concepts, that their place is only in consciousness, or as one might say, in nothingness. And his point is that we do not need to attribute to them a quasi-physical actuality:

> The truth must be firmly grasped that the sphere of
> thought is in human consciousness alone. Then, it must be
> shown that the thought-world does not thereby sacrifice
> in the least its objective validity.[50]

He would have approved however of Penrose's other suggestion, about the importance of the fact that our brains are part of a living organism, rather than a sort of computer. For in a way which anticipates some aspects of modern 'anthropic' thought, he regarded the evolutionary connection between the human organism and the universe in which we have emerged as the real key to the unity between our mental operations and the world around us. The nothingness in which conscious ideas and images are projected is not, of course, any kind of metaphysical vacuum. Nor is it the empiricist conception, which also agrees in a way that in knowledge we are 'nothing,' interpreting it in its one-sided manner as absolute passivity. It is one aspect of our changing or growing — namely the aspect of our ceasing to be what we were. Knowledge changes the knower; or conversely, as we shall see in more detail below, one might think of it as a way of holding on to that adaptive ability which is a specially significant feature of human beings, extending it beyond the fulfilment of physical maturation where it biologically ends. This is another way of identifying knowledge with freedom: our inner ability to transform ourselves from within, rather than be fixed in any evolutionary niche, or determined by forces from without. Steiner here goes on to sketch out the crucial features of human development which enable this special relationship: the relative completeness of the growth of the head in early infancy, compared with the limbs, and its position of relative passivity in its relations with the world owing to man's upright position. These enable the emergence of growth-rhythms which are not immediately dependent upon the external world, but rather can be idealized into the transformation-through-nothingness which we call knowledge. The head still engages with the world around, but its actual involvement is reduced to zero, to virtuality. Freed from the pressures of actuality, it can project that completion of our limited experience which we know as thought. Epistemology has the task, however, of resisting the idealization of the process (as if we really could cut loose from actuality) and reminding us of its basis in our development. Here we touch upon that passing-over of philosophy (epistemological theory) to a phenomenological anthropology or even 'anthropic' methodology which formed part of Steiner's 'incarnational' programme for the sciences, stemming and reversing the trend to ever greater idealization which emerged in other versions of phenomenology. The lack of reality in our ideas, freeing us to envisage reality free from the limitations of our own particular vantage-point, is counterbalanced by an awareness of our deeper-level relationship to the complex interrelationships with the environment which make up the evolution of our human form. One might therefore refer to it, as he does in his later lectures, as a 'physiological conception of freedom.'[51]

But here we must stay in the domain of philosophy. And in the account which Rudolf Steiner gives of thought as nothingness, we may note among other things how the perspective has not only moved away from any materialistic notion of ideas being bits of external reality reproduced and stored within us. But notice also how the Nietzschean rebound from that view, or nihilism in regard to the world on which we vainly try to impose human significance, has in turn been thoroughly transformed. It is not the world which confronts us as nothingness, but we ourselves who introduce nothingness, i.e. the freedom to be detached and to understand, into the world.

The crisis in the world-process which we thereby create is a real one, since this is precisely our freedom decisively to alter the course of events, and to be the determining factor in things which have hitherto been determinative in (unconsciously) producing us. The world that has once been understood can never again be the same as the world of which we unreflectingly formed a part. Yet rather than bringing us to the verge of a Nietzschean abyss, reaching out into infinite alienation, or into the 'hall of mirrors' of Lacan's self-consciousness, Steiner's conception offers us a perspective in which the moment of nothingness, of nihilism, is only a prelude to re-engaging. It is the illusory side of the experience, after all, to think that we 'really have' detached ourselves somehow from the actual world and can now simply do what we like. Our ideas in so far as they are objects of consciousness may be 'nothingness,' but the reality of thought is to be found in the relations that underlie conscious ideation. In his critique of metaphysics Steiner had made clear that one could never find this reality outside experience, or beyond thinking, but only by turning attention in on the process of knowledge itself. The moment of freedom, of detachment, is nothingness — which means, nothing but a changed relationship to the world, or transformation of the self. Hence we do not leave the world behind when we seize our freedom. Steiner is important above all for his realization that the apparent otherness which marks our freedom only conceals the abiding sources of our deep implication in the world-process. Our freedom is not mere projection of ourselves into empty space, of consequence only to ourselves; we are still in the world in which we grew up, even though we grow beyond it, that is, change it in turn. To fail to understand this is truly to enter the hall of mirrors in which so much of modern thought loses itself, and to hand oneself over once more to the unconscious factors in human nature, whilst engaging in a doomed quest, perhaps distorted and no longer acknowledged, for one's own being exactly where it can never be found. The loss of the human self as agent, as the true source of 'spiritual activity,' in the mainstream of modern philosophy leads into these shadowy wastes of post-modernism, post-structuralism and the like. Steiner has the potential to lead us through the wilderness and back to the foundations of life, by showing how these same forces can be conjured into the necessary balance, unstable yet not necessarily destructive, which gives us knowledge, freedom and the harmony which is our self. Steiner does not shrink back from the affirmation of consciousness, of nothingness, fearing to become lost there:

For through it came the possibility of pure thinking.
Doubts may be professed about the very existence of this;
but in it lies the only possible basis for the impulse of
freedom. Had humanity never attained this pure thinking,
which is actually pure thinking and does not, as such,
guarantee actual reality — they would never have
reached the consciousness of freedom.[52]

By stepping into the moment of nothingness, of freedom,
instead of looking to have our knowledge determined from outside we will at last be in a position to grasp our own 'spiritual
activity.' These forces are at the same time the basis of our
knowledge, which is to say our relationship to the world-
process, our special outlook on the world at our particular point
in the evolution of consciousness — and the way we can take in
hand those that underlie our own actual growth and emergence,
making us what we are by giving us the possibility to change it.

The Contrary Powers

Steiner has moved a long way from the notion, prevalent in his
own day in scientific circles and still presupposed in many quarters today, that in order to know something objectively, we have
to form a precise replica, a 'mental picture' of it that matches the
'real world,' purging it of all else as our merely personal, 'subjective' experience. A little reflection will show we often know
what something is like perfectly well without having to have an
actual reconstruction, like a Dutch still-life, of what it looks like
in our minds. Certainly it is essential that we come to knowledge already having a model on which to base our judgment:
ultimately these 'schemata' (or *Vorstellungen*) go back, as Steiner
has pointed out, to unconscious experiences of moving in space,
relating actively to things around us, to repeated actions which
have become abilities, and so on.

But the mental picture which we can fashion from this in our
conscious dealings with the world is not usually made fully
explicit — or in general is only made so precisely where it has to
be modified to accommodate some novel experience. We
achieve objectivity rather when we balance the effect of oppos-

ing cognitive drives: one toward fitting everything into patterns we already know, the other toward breaking down existing suppositions to acknowledge the new. Keeping in touch with reality means being willing to change our assumptions, while holding on to the past in order to measure the new and make it intelligible. And it is because Steiner can conceive it in this way that he can accept the aspect of nothingness in conscious ideation without jumping to the false conclusion that human existence is, as certain existentialists have thought, absence: sheer being-elsewhere. Human existence eludes them, precisely because it is there in the process, the otherness, of change.

Neither drive alone can give us knowledge. But while we hold them in balance we are in contact with a reality that makes sense and whose meaning can be absorbed by us (and is affected by us in turn), whilst also being free to see new aspects, new relations.

Many of the features of knowledge which led Steiner to challenge conventional models fall into place when we see them in the dynamic tension between these drives, which modern developmentalists have usefully distinguished under the rubrics of 'assimilation' and 'accommodation.'[53] If we did not strive to fit our experience into patterns we have already established, assimilating it to what we already know, we would never understand anything at all. Assimilating is a process which builds up knowledge in terms of regularities, enabling us to categorize things, preserve them as instances in an increasingly well-established system. It has also become clear from our studies that if we try to close such a system completely, however, it ceases to tell us anything about the real world, collapsing into mere definition (all bachelors are single, matter is subject to conservation) or otherwise showing its incompleteness (geometrical systems cannot contain their own proofs, etc.).

Accommodation of our existing structures of ideas is also necessary, because life is never just a repetition of some one of the things we already know, to be catalogued and recorded in its proper place. Knowledge is not just fitting things into place, in a scheme determined in advance (e.g. by our nature as rational beings, as Kant supposed). Knowledge changes the knower, making us dissolve any previously fixed structure and modify

it. But if we were to become totally adaptive, totally open to
change, we could never learn anything either, or build up a systematic understanding of what we have already found out.

The one-sided empiricist approach cannot give us the human
content of experience, as Steiner had grasped early on:

> If, then, we are to comprehend what we perceive, that
> percept must have been determined within us previously
> as a definite concept. Any object of which this were not
> true we should simply pass by without its being
> intelligible to us.
>
> That such is the case is best shown by the fact that
> persons who have lived a rich mental life also penetrate
> far deeper into the world of experience than do others of
> whom this is not true. Much that passes over others
> without trace makes a deep impression upon such
> persons ... But, it may be asked, do we not meet in our
> lives innumerable things of which we have not previously
> had the faintest conception? — and do we not on the spot
> form conceptions of these? Undoubtedly. But is the sum
> of all potential concepts identical with the sum of those
> which I have already formed in the previous part of my
> life? Is not my conceptual system capable of evolving?[54]

It has been the contribution of the relatively new discipline of
developmental epistemology, its ideas somewhat reluctantly
acknowledged in wider philosophical circles, to relate these
twin process of 'assimilation' and 'adaptation' to the development of the knower as well as to the known.[55] It is in this way
that our knowledge grows: but also we ourselves develop new
perspectives, attitudes and feelings. Through the interaction of
the two drives, we are building up our own identity as a
knower. The structures of ideas we use become more complex,
rather than merely giving way one to the next, and evolve
through definite stages so that we can grasp our continuing
identity in relation to changing experience. Steiner was far in
advance of the psychology of his day in realizing that knowledge was thus intimately related to the self in development —
indeed to a whole series of distinctive developmental stages.[56]

He was aware too of the potential dangers to healthy human awareness. A predominance of one power can soon make us lose grip on objective fact, and the mind can build itself into an unreal inner world. A tip the other way can leave us helpless before a threatening, inhuman landscape.

Steiner is still uniquely far-seeing, I think, in his understanding of the relationship between freedom and knowledge here. Steiner talks about these in a way that relates them to wider issues, albeit in a somewhat 'mythological' way as 'luciferic' and 'ahrimanic' tendencies. Many philosophers from Plato onward have resorted to *mythos* to bring out the implications of an idea. But it is still worth emphasising that the dynamic of knowledge which Steiner characterizes in this manner is already described, as the essence of the cognitive process, in his early philosophical writings.[57]

Steiner was able to recognize in the imaginative pictures of the myth of the Tempter aspects of an understanding of knowledge which more formal philosophical thought had often failed to grasp. The connection of knowledge with the development of the self, and the inner incompleteness of knowledge when we pursue it one-sidedly, trying to assimilate reality to the model of what we ourselves are already — these were important features of the process which he tried to capture in his thought. But rather than follow the Church in moralizing the problem away, Steiner was willing to confront the huge expansion of knowledge in the Renaissance and early modern times, as science began to rival traditional religion in its scope for interpreting the world. This is one of the many points at which Steiner implicitly rebukes the guardians of traditional spirituality for drawing back, when they might have trusted in the resources they had been given to see the situation through. Even our modern conceptual science, for Steiner, has to be understood in the light of this 'luciferic' aspiration. Modern scientific thought is indeed the most monumental attempt ever made to reduce everything to a set of harmonious relations, a unified formula, based on what we ourselves already know. The moral immediacy of human experience evaporates:

> The impoverished humanity of modern times is presented with a wisdom that can only furnish it with a world-conception where the stars move in their courses in

accordance with purely amoral, purely mechanical forces
of necessity — traversing their orbits in a manner such
that we can in no way relate their orbiting to any moral
significance in the ordering of the world. This is a purely
luciferic world-conception.[58]

That does not mean for Steiner that it is therefore wrong, or that
it should be condemned; but we need to understand that it is a
projection, an idealization of one aspect of the cognitive process
which cannot really be disjoined from the situation of the
knower. It is the assimilative drive to make all things a reflection
of what we already are. As such it is intrinsic to knowledge, for
so long as it is grappling with the challenges of new experience;
taken as some kind of ultimate in itself, it is necessarily an
empty dream, literally nothingness, needing to be reunited with
the human reality of the 'spiritual activity' which generated it.
Likewise to the 'luciferic' aspiration belong all those attempts to
project a utopia, with which the scientific venture has often been
idealistically associated:

> All that has arisen in the course of history in the guise of
> wonderful programmes, marvellously beautiful ideas, by
> which it is always believed that somehow or other a
> return can be made to the Golden Age — all this has its
> origin in the luciferic tendencies which flow into man.
> Everything by which he tries to loosen his connection
> with reality, to soar above his actual circumstances — all
> this points to the luciferic.[59]

The luciferic drive carried to its conclusion becomes what
Steiner calls (and always in a derogatory sense) 'mysticism.'
Characteristic of it is that it allows us to remain as we are, while
in a delusive god-like way seeming to become everything —
assimilation reaching its climax in a solipsistic absorption of
everything to ourself in which necessarily all sense of self dis-
appears.

The other drive, of 'accommodation,' comprises our openness
to transformation. Once more it is an activity crucial to knowledge, namely our adaptation to the unfamiliar or new. It is clear

that the ahrimanic is necessary to knowledge, by keeping us in touch with unassimilated experience. Yet the ahrimanic too can exceed its legitimate role as one element in a balanced relationship of knower and known. The challenge of the other, as we have seen, comes to us through awareness of another's point-of-view, of another construction placed upon events or perceptions. Knowledge is interpersonal, and connected with socialization, maturity and acceptance through love. The ahrimanic pressures which can destabilize the subtle equilibrium of knowledge, however, all too easily tip us toward the sense of being exposed to the disturbing, the unassimilable. At such moments we seem to face an alien reality that presses itself upon us, indeed gets 'right inside us,' yet which cannot be understood. Psychologically, such experiences are what Freud has made familiar as 'traumatic.' Since we are unable to assimilate them, or perhaps need long therapeutic sessions to be able to come to terms with (assimilate) them, they are also a rupture with the world of social reality, leading to disturbed behaviour. The old-fashioned theories of knowledge as passive imprinting, with external 'ideas' being stamped upon the mind, are already symptomatic of a distorted, exaggeratedly 'ahrimanic' perspective. Clearly the human being described by classic empiricist theory going back to Locke, who is open to impressions like a blank screen, would really be a traumatized person, lacking the psychic defences actually employed to maintain self-equilibrium.[60] Such experiences really betoken the predominance of the ahrimanic: the overstretching of psychic equilibrium and the breakdown of socially assumed certainties, leaving the individual exposed and 'wounded.' Steiner evokes the wider resonance of human experience whilst pointing specifically to the tendency of modern knowledge, focussed on manipulative, external intervention, to push us constantly toward this area of imbalance. Our psychic resources are constantly strained in order to attain a one-sided degree of accommodation, leaving us alienated and socially disturbed.

We have already mentioned that for Steiner knowledge has indeed an aspect of violation or trauma. In evolutionary terms, our organism on the cognitive, just as on the biological level, could maintain comfortable stasis, satisfied with what it has assimilated. Such happy self-absorption is violated by the need to respond to things outside. Of course, in its (luciferic) self-absorption it is not actually self-sufficient but would in truth atrophy — or fall victim to changes in its environment of which it needed to have been aware! Knowledge is fundamentally a characteristic, we may therefore say, of equilibration in a living being, one that is not cut off from its environment but open to a degree of (ahrimanic) traumatization — not actual wounding but 'virtually,' in consciousness — from which it can recover by cognitive growth. Assimilation and accommodation, the twin aspects of knowledge, are thereby revealed as elements in a unified process of growth, the self in development. They are that same 'polarization' of experience to which we referred early on in this study of Steiner's thought, which leads to its clarification in the form of knowledge and to our ability to insert ourselves, as knowers, into the continuum of the world.

Steiner is far from wishing us therefore to avoid both luciferic or ahrimanic, which would simply be a failure to grow at all. Worst of all are those he sees:

> vacillating in-between, people who want to be neither the one nor the other, who do not rightly assess either the luciferic or the ahrimanic but want to avoid both ... But the truth is that Lucifer and Ahriman are scales of a balance, and it is *we* who must hold the beam in equipoise.
>
> And how can we train ourselves to do this? By permeating what takes an ahrimanic form within us with a luciferic element. There is nothing more ahrimanic than man's knowledge of the material world; nevertheless ... if it can fill us with fiery enthusiasm and interest — then through our interest, which is itself luciferic, we can wrest from Ahriman what is his own ...
>
> Again, what wells up in man's inmost nature today is very strongly luciferic. How can we train ourselves rightly in this direction? By diving into it with our ahrimanic nature, that is to say, by ... observing *ourselves* just as we observe the outer world.[61]

The meeting and reciprocal exchange of ideas which the philosopher of sociology we quoted earlier somewhat wistfully proposed, between the proponents of Descartes and those of Durkheim — which is to say, between those who try to constitute everything out of the self, and those for whom the self is a dead-end, a by-product of structures and social forms — is thus an urgent agenda for Steiner if we are not to be torn apart by the forces which drive modern knowledge.

The conditions for such a meeting are furnished by the framework of his thought, yet it would still be a daunting task. It would mean resisting the powerful luciferic-ahrimanic polarization, the typical flipping over between extremes, and demanding an openness on both sides. In the analysis of consciousness, for instance, it would require a recognition that the admission of the 'nothingness' of conscious ideation need not simply hand us over to compelling unconscious forces. To see it that way is not to 'discover' what human nature is really like, but to project the contrary forces (luciferic, ahrimanic) whilst leaving out of the picture the activity which spans their extremes. That is not to say that it is necessarily untrue: it may be the truth of a particular stage in our development, corresponding to widespread experience in the current world. But on Steiner's model it reveals a situation full of dynamic possibilities, not a fate hanging over the very notion of self. To unlock those possibilities would mean holding fast to that 'spiritual activity' which actually generates the polarizations, the contrary extremes, namely the human ability to grow through transformation, through assimilation and accommodation alike. Our customary modes of thinking are so orientated to grasping fixities, or products of thought, that to hold on to the crucial element of process still poses a considerable conceptual challenge. It requires us to become aware of 'the unobserved element,' our own thinking. But the result could be a way of understanding knowledge as a creative exchange between individuals and society, denying neither the need for collective values nor the freedom to find the meaning of one's life.

I have said that Steiner makes use of a 'mythological' way of speaking — and it may seem that I have myself done so in speaking of 'forces,' etc. underlying our states of knowledge.

Alternatively, they may suggest that we have reverted after all to invoking unjustifiable 'metaphysical' causes for our thoughts. The conception of a balance between luciferic and ahrimanic should really be seen, however, as motivated by the need for a deconstruction of the dialectical paraphernalia of idealist metaphysics.

By describing each as the vanishing-point of a unified activity, which terminates either when we successfully absorb something into our set of presuppositions, or when we have to change to accommodate a new perspective, Steiner takes away from them the illusory sense that we could take either as a touchstone to a higher reality, the rung on a ladder to ascend to a higher truth. The fact that we cannot account for something by means of the cognitive structures we have so far developed does not point to a 'thing-in-itself' that lies beyond our knowing; all we will find beyond our knowing is the ahrimanic denial, which is our failure (at least for the present) to adapt. The force of the reality we encountered is not something mysteriously 'beyond' our knowing, but is revealed precisely in the way that our organization has evolved in response to the need to accommodate it. Instead of crossing a 'metaphysical' boundary, we are turned back upon ourselves: there is indeed a reality beyond the 'nothingness' of our conscious imaging of the world, but the force at work in it is that which has shaped us as a part of the world we know. It is there, in an evolutionary context, that Rudolf Steiner places the reality of 'luciferic' and 'ahrimanic.'

On the other hand, a philosopher like Hegel may be seen to grasp brilliantly the paradox that complete assimilation passes over into nothingness, since essentially this forms the starting-point for his dialectic of being/not being in the *Logic*. When he takes this as an actual starting point for the world-process, what is striking is that idealism will do anything rather than acknowledge 'spiritual activity,' since it holds ideas to be a primary and irreducible reality: Hegel would prefer to attribute the instability and incompleteness of the idea-world to a kind of weird magnetic life of the ideas themselves, enacting a fantastic drama of quasi-logical deduction that ends up by deducing the thinker! The luciferic totality implied in the concept of Being for him in some way really does pass over into nothingness and begin the dialectic; Hegel can even call the dialectical Idea or Logic 'God in his eternal nature.' The conception is worked out with brilliant if perhaps slightly insane consistency. The whole 'cunning' process has as its goal 'that mind should exist': but of course what this actually means, when we step back to look at what is going on, is that at the moment where the free activity of the thinker enters the picture, the Hegelian system comes to an end.[62]

Steiner was able to integrate his account of knowledge with the wider picture of evolution, not by trying to see it metaphysically, like Hegel, as the process of knowledge writ large in nature. Quite the reverse. On the simplest level, the 'forces' involved in the cognitive process are nothing mysterious at all — they are our living, growing organism: and specifically, what happens to our growth-processes in the head, which is still developing organically up to the time of the second dentition.[63] Steiner elaborates a phenomenological account of human development.

Up to that time, the head is clearly involved in the overall maturation of the bodily form, in the early stages dominating the still puny limbs. Yet if this were simply to continue, Steiner observes, the special characteristics of human orientation and interaction with the environment would not manifest themselves. It would lead rather to animal adaptation. The head, however, does not develop into an animal 'limb':

> It has passed beyond the form which the animal world
> has developed. Man has passed through the animal
> world, as it were, in relation to this, his head system —
> gone beyond the animal organization to the real human
> organization, which indeed is most clearly expressed in
> the formation of the head.[64]

Instead of developing into animal forms, allowing the adaptive process to shape organic form to the point of full integration, occupying a distinct evolutionary niche, human beings carry the head in such a way that its special 'passive' role can emerge, scarcely in contact with the environment at all. The effect of the human carriage of the head by the upright limbs is to 'dissolve' the animal tendencies of development. Head activity is suspended as regards

further organic formation, but remains crucial to the fluid adaptability of the human beings. Thinking emerges because the
organic development basically terminates with the second teeth:
and if we want to be specific, these are the 'forces' employed in
cognitive activity, taking us beyond the animal evolution of the
jaw as a means of interacting with the environment. Instead of
adaptability we have learning, thinking:

> The thoughts of the human being are indeed a
> supersensible correlate to that which does not come to
> expression in the sense world. This continual
> metamorphosis out of the animal, streaming down from
> the head, is not expressed in the senses but works in man
> supersensibly as the process of thought.

It is not that the head is a sort of computer, exhibiting a special
activity; the facts of human development show that on the contrary its own activity uncountered is a tendency to animality,
and only in connection with the human form of the limbs and
trunk can it be 'held back in the supersensible.'[65]

Rather than adapting physically, human beings thus change
inwardly, or in other words they have knowledge. And in connection with this retention of fluid adaptability on the cognitive
level, behaviour as a whole is naturally influenced in a decisive
way.

From this perspective we can also clarify the meaning of
'luciferic' and 'ahrimanic,' since they are the moments when the
delicate suspension between involvement and detachment in
the special case of growth that we call knowledge breaks down.
Thus in both of them fluid development becomes fixed, instead
of remaining spiritual activity. Whether manifesting as illusory
completeness (luciferic) or as the intrusion of the alien to which
assimilation cannot extend (ahrimanic), we have fixity; growth
is retarded. Thereby knowledge can become an achieved complex of ideas, building up and retaining structures as well as
being open to the new. 'Luciferic' and 'ahrimanic' can be
thought of therefore in a wider sense as aspects of all evolution,
and that is how they figure in Steiner's cosmological researches
in his later anthroposophical works.

They are part of the very process of transformation, i.e. of living development and growth — more exactly they can be seen as its defining limits, points where it breaks down in the one case because of its own one-sidedness, where it becomes over-stretched, or in the other because of over-pressure from the environment. A plant which shoots up but over- extends itself and is not able to sustain its growth, and a plant which is held back by uncongenial conditions (frosts, or stony soil etc.) alike fail to establish the balanced conditions of a maturing organism. Both are essentially retardations. Growth is possible, however, between these extreme points. In the domain of knowledge, their tendencies work to suggest either that all can be assimilated to the past, or that we are helpless before uncertainty and a threatening future. Steiner's philosophy brilliantly enables us to focus on the developmental activity of which they are limiting cases, and to relate them back to the human actuality of the living present. And with that wholeness of vision, as we shall see, the moral perspective on our cognitive relationships is also restored.[66]

Thus we would pass over once more, if we were to pursue these insights, from philosophy into 'anthroposophy.' By moving away from the static models of knowledge in his philosophical account of human knowing, Steiner showed the possibility of integrating epistemology with our concepts of evolutionary development and restoring the wholeness of man's world. Knowledge for Steiner is our particular way of living with the world, and in the activity which equilibrates between the luciferic and ahrimanic we discover within ourselves not a special adaptation but adaptability itself in its spiritual form, distinguishing us from the animals which are the result of specific adaptations to the environment — so that in them spiritual activity is absorbed into, and used up in organic development. In human beings, evolution itself becomes conscious as thought.

* * *

Obviously we find ourselves here close to the heart of Steiner's philosophical programme. The kind of activity he describes at the root of cognitive relationship reaches down into the biological and evolutionary context of human existence in a way which confirms its ecological significance and setting. Human self-discovery through the freedom to resist the dehumanizing reductionism of the ahrimanic, and/or, on the other hand, the self-inflating illusions of the luciferic, gives to knowledge an essentially moral meaning by its very nature. For human beings, evolution has become the free shaping of their role in nature through thought. And yet it is here that, perhaps inevitably, that Steiner's philosophy seems to walk its narrowest tightrope. The question is ultimately whether such moral implications are really strong enough to fulfil the requirements of Steiner's demands upon them. After all, why should we not choose, if we so wished, a more comfortable existence and allow ourselves to be simply shaped by the forces acting upon us, turn back from the vertiginous brink of self-awareness and fit in where we can? Steiner has certainly shown us the possibility of the moral gesture to be made — but is there enough force there to tell us that we *should* make it? Why should we grasp our freedom and confront all the existential problems we then must face? The far-reaching process of naturalizing the ethical in which Steiner followed Nietzsche perhaps has its costs. In the *Philosophy of Freedom,* Steiner answers by saying that such acts are indeed occurring. Free spirits do arise amid the tangle of laws and restrictions and the idols which limit the outlook of others.[67] The same is said in the later, aphoristic expression of these ideas in the *Leading-Thoughts:*

> Freedom as a fact is directly given to every human
> being ... No-one can say 'Freedom does not exist' without
> denying a patent truth — even though we find a certain
> contradiction between this fact of our experience and the
> world-process.[68]

But then the more there is stress upon man's freedom as a fact, as something that simply is happening, the less it can bear the weight of moral significance needs it to bear if it is to be the motive for our inner transformation. Freedom would lose its very significance if it were merely given to us as the result of the forces at work in the world. Thus Steiner needs equally to stress its contradiction to the mere factuality of the world.

However, if we play down the actuality of freedom, his philosophy is open to the charge that the 'free spirit' is merely an ideal that nowhere actually exists, or, as he says, a chimera — and so cannot play the role of moral realism he has projected. Is there a moment where the real potential of freedom as something that is happening, as undeniable event, overlaps sufficiently with the morally demanding nature of what it asks of us to make our existential step into the unknown fulfil all the criteria at once?

From where we stand, probably not — and therefore the bold edifice of Steiner's thought linking knowledge and freedom hangs in tatters if it does not fall apart.[69] The young Steiner certainly shows signs of uneasiness at this juncture. But having come so far he does not give up. What Steiner offers us, in the end, is an answer which is more brilliant and tantalizing and hard to evaluate: namely that we will find the answer only when we have taken the plunge. It is the existential uncertainty of committing ourselves to the still unknown which ensures the moral stature of our deed, and indeed which ensures that is freely our own not an imitation of the past, because the moral self out of which we act is not a 'thing' but is found in the sense that we can go beyond what we were. That is what Steiner expresses, I suppose, somewhat vaguely, in the passage from *Philosophy of Freedom* when he goes on to characterize the free spirit as an ideal, but 'an ideal which is something real in us working its way to the surface.' So once we have taken the step, we will see how it would be a denial of our very being and of the demands of our situation in world-evolution not to have acted as we did. On the other side of the door it will be both morally clear and factually inevitable that we should cross the threshold. Later, in the *Leading-Thoughts*, Steiner returned to this crucial moment of transition:

> In ideation, humanity lives not in being but in picture-being — in the realm of non-being — with the Consciousness-soul. Thus humanity is set free from living and experiencing with the cosmos. Images do not compel, only being has the power to compel. And if humanity does direct itself according to the pictures, it is done in independence of them; it is in freedom from the cosmos.

And then as he turns to the crossing of the 'gulf of non-being' back to cosmic reality he refers, in a way that may initially seem strange, to the figure of the angel Michaël. First, let there be no crude misunderstandings. Steiner is not saying that we can get any help in our existential leap to freedom. Nor does he mean any kind of religious faith that substitutes for the inadequate nature of our thinking. Michaël is the angel of apocalypse, a visionary genre of rather definite type in which a unique individual looks into the future and addresses his community. Usually, a final resolution of current struggles is foreseen, and the apocalyptic vision may well have more of the past situation than of future events. An angel, usually Michaël, interprets the vision — but he speaks only to those lonely figures who through some special destiny of their own (such as exile on Patmos, etc.) have come to receive the vision. So Steiner can use this mythology as he has used others, giving it clear 'anthroposophical' meaning whilst connecting with the past. It does not imply that anything is fixed in advance: in fact, he speaks of consciousness 'becoming apocalyptic' and looking into the future precisely when cultural evolution has reached the point of moving beyond the recreation of past forms.[70] What it does mean is that when we of ourselves rise to the critical moment of freedom, the spiritual world comes to meet us — on the other side of the door, to continue my earlier analogy. Perhaps philosophically it is a way of saying that the moment of freedom is the completion of everything that we have been able to become in our development, but that this only has value when we are prepared to give it up for our step into the future. Only then does the value of what we are become clear. Only then can we, as Steiner puts it, 'achieve this leap across the gulf of non-being' which is discovery of our spiritual self.[71]

The Paradox of the Self

Steiner has already gone far, in principle, toward fulfilling Westphal's demand for an integrated account of knowledge — an account that does not achieve premature clarification by heaping together other aspects in a jumble of the 'subjective.' Instead of trying to freeze ideas in their 'objectivity,' Steiner stresses their developmental significance. They are the way we construct our relationship to our environment, inserting ourselves into the continuum of the world. Whereas vegetable and animal evolution is fundamentally 'locked in' to a niche in the balance of nature, knowledge is a growing beyond mere response to stimuli: instead of being an actual adaptation, it is a 'virtual' change on the level of consciousness, of nothingness; as such it leaves us free to transform the situation actively instead of being changed from without; we can unfold that special kind of constructive, directed change which builds up our unique identity, our self.

With his highly integrated account, Steiner might also enable us to solve some of the enigmas about the development of knowledge which still puzzled, for example, T.S. Kuhn when he studied the changing 'paradigms' (the basic schematizations of knowledge) in scientific thought. He understood that these were constantly transformed in order to facilitate new advances. He understood too that the drive for their transformation could not be an increasing conformation to externally given reality. It may well happen that new paradigms are initially less adequate to the description of the phenomena they are meant to explain than are the richly developed older conceptual systems they come to replace — as was the new Copernican model of the universe, in fact, in comparison with the more elaborate versions of Ptolemaic cosmology.[72] Why did it happen nevertheless that these failed to convince, and the new approach quite rapidly became the dominant one? On Steiner's model, it is clear from the beginning that the transformation which comes about in knowing is an aspect of our own living cognitive growth-process. What is happening when we come to the more radical historical shifts in the structuring of knowledge, from his perspective, is therefore never merely that we are being made to acknowledge new pressures from outside: we are witnessing rather a new stage in the organization of the self. This is how we must learn to understand natural science, for instance — getting away from the common misconception that it is defined by a special kind of subject-matter, or is a particular kind of knowledge about how things are:

> Anyone who considers the meaning of natural science, its human significance, will find that it is by no means just the assembling of so much detailed knowledge of nature. For the particulars of knowledge can never bring us to anything whatsoever except the experience of what the human soul is not. The life of the soul is not to be found in the conclusions that are reached about nature, but essentially in the process of knowledge.
>
> In working upon nature the soul experiences its own conscious life and being, and what is acquired in this living process through its activity is something far more than so much information about nature. It is an evolution of the self that is experienced in building up our scientific knowledge of nature.[73]

We know this to be the case with child-development today, when ideas of conservation of quantity, for instance, cannot be grasped by young children until they have gone through the stages of constructing the requisite pattern of relations to movement and altered size. In the process, they will also have learned to separate themselves out from the world they experience. The drive to develop knowledge is that to make conscious our own interaction with things around us and our structuring activity, thereby heightening and intensifying our awareness of ourselves as knowers. Scientific knowledge is no exception: it is driven by the urge to experience with increasing intensity the individual's power to interpret — and to manipulate. When once we understand this 'evolution of the self,' which reaches a highly advanced stage in modern knowledge, the struggle of science against earlier forms of belief can be examined without the need to demonize either party. In *The Riddles of Philosophy* especially, Steiner has shown how the essential nature of modern thought is determined by this need to construct a world-view adequate to the new sense of self-consciousness that was emerging in the seventeenth and eighteenth centuries. At the same time, failure to understand the deepening experience of self as the driving force behind scientific and philosophical advances in the 'evolution of consciousness' has led to all sorts of distortions — e.g. in falsifying the relation of knowledge to religion, false justifications of science as 'value-free,' 'objectivism,' etc.[74]

Rudolf Steiner's reference to the myths of Lucifer and Ahriman also casts particular light on the special burdens and anxieties of modern knowledge. For the myths show that in the past, human beings were not able to shoulder the burden of knowledge in full consciousness. The process of evolving scientific knowledge has meant the increasing elaboration of its luciferic and ahrimanic components, necessary to the emerging sense of self, which is built up through a complex history as we structure experience in successive transformations. In previous times, such explicit structures of knowledge were needed only in certain special domains of expertise, and broad, never consciously questioned values and ideas dominated social and collective thought. The individual never had to carry the weight of certainty/uncertainty, of finding and making the connections between different aspects of knowledge, as he does today. It need not surprise us that despite growing stronger in the course of its evolution, the self is not initially always able to balance the fears and hopes that are raised — that, for example, there should be a tendency to feel at moments the (luciferic) sense of total explanatory power, and at other times, in response to its mere ideality, the 'nothingness' of knowledge, there should be a desperate (ahrimanic) seeking of certainty in what we find outside ourselves. Conversely, knowledge often seems to scientists to be a 'reality' much greater than themselves, a burden which half-consciously leads to their investing of it with attitudes and emotions that have been borrowed from religion. The picture of humanity in the hall-of-mirrors of intensely explicit consciousness, yet at the mercy of unconscious forces, is, for Steiner, only the leading over of these polarizations into, or their recoil upon, the self which is only uneasily half-aware of its own role in creating them.

The confrontation with the contrary powers is an opportunity therefore to discover the living, growing self which underlies our knowledge. The situation just described, where we touch upon unconscious forces, is to Steiner not so much an account of how we are, but an indication of the forces that are able, if we seize upon them in the right way, to transform us, that is, to effect a raising into consciousness (and the sphere of 'freedom') of what we thus dimly start to discern:

> For at the beginning the essentially human here lies concealed behind the 'man' shown by natural scientific researches and the inner life of everyday consciousness. This essentially human reality makes its presence felt in dim feelings, in the more unconscious life of the soul. Anthroposophical investigation raises it into consciousness ... With due acknowledgment of natural science, and of a mysticism that is constrained by the ordinary limits of consciousness, anthroposophy presses forward to the perception that a new kind of consciousness must be developed — emerging from ordinary consciousness rather like an awakening from the vague awareness of a dream. The cognitive process becomes for anthroposophy a real inner occurrence extending beyond ordinary consciousness.[75]

We are close here to the very centre of Steiner's philosophical enterprise, where knowledge becomes creative power. The initial polarization of reality which we effect in order to establish our relationship of knowledge, gives way to that in which we re-engage. By becoming aware of our own active role, we cease to be just the product of these processes and grasp freely their potential for our own development. Luciferic (idealism) and ahrimanic (empiricism) both end up by denying the self its creative role. It either squanders its power in ever higher-level obstructions, or feels deprived of support from outside and falters in its strength. Steiner describes instead a poised, even serenely choreographed enactment. Our knowing sets us over against the world; our awareness of that fact in turn restores us to being part of what we know. To grasp the self in this way is already a further transformation of consciousness — not now in response to a knowledge directed outward, or adaptation to external reality, but out of our own inner dynamic of the self. In place of the paralysing opposition of inner and outer, soul and body, we begin to uncover the reality of the spirit.

Steiner believed — and clearly quite rightly — that the elucidation of the experiences stemming from this further cognitive development could in principle be just as scientific as that associated with the prior stages of knowledge, and the ordinary consciousness that is their correlative. Here, however, we cannot pursue the content he went on to derive from such a transformed relation to reality, or the spiritual character of what he believed then determines our awareness. Of the experiences he himself had along this path, and the conclusions carefully drawn from them, he himself wrote and lectured extensively. But his philosophical argument already draws attention to the issues raised by the nature of the self that is the potential agency of this higher knowledge: since, of course, in a less conscious modality, it is also the agent of our cognitive development overall. What is it that we raise into consciousness with the discovery of our essential humanity or 'self'?

In the first place, this 'it' is elusive: something that is experienced in process, in growth, in direction, and transformation, now surfacing into conscious experience. Philosophical reflection going back to David Hume had anyway long made it clear that it is quite illusory to think of the 'self' as an entity that is always there, so to speak, accompanying all our experiences and labelling them as 'ours.' Introspection fails to observe such a lurking entity, and reflection soon shows that it would anyway be redundant to any serious philosophical account. Steiner's epistemology had shown, however, that the elements in knowledge are always part of a dynamic (metamorphic) whole, always carrying more meaning than just themselves, always able to be deepened and enriched. We discover the self first of all, therefore, in the awareness of unfulfilled potential in any given experience. If we do ask what it is in itself, Steiner has described it as a sort of psychic 'hole'[76] or negative space. Whatever we may make of this initially, this is eminently a post-Humean if not also arguably a post-modern conception of identity. The self is primarily what things are not. We can find an image of our self, certainly, in the record of past experiences which have formed us into what we now are: but our real identity is not defined by these experiences; if it were, we would not be a person but a filing cabinet. Rather, we have continuing identity, selfhood, precisely because we can go on to absorb more experiences in a unified way. If we try to pin down 'what we are' at any one time, it is inherently less than the full resources of our self. But equally, if we try to cut loose from the vicissitudes of what we have done and suffered, the 'pure' self evaporates into nothingness, the 'mysticism' of the luciferic illusion. It is something of a paradox, but it is the ability to go on changing without losing touch with what we were, or the world we have known, that makes us a self, an identity. For Steiner, the self is therefore the exact opposite of something 'added' to experience, or floating additional item lurking next to it. (That would be a return to 'the subjective' as tagging on to things a redundant heap of extra significances 'only for me.') The self is our ability not to be fixed by the content of what we already know and are, but to go on working within it and transforming it:

> In his ego, man includes all that he experiences as a being
> of soul and body. Body and soul are alike the vehicles of
> the ego, and in them the ego is acting ... Feelings manifest
> themselves as effects of the outer world; the will relates
> itself to the outer world in so far as it realizes itself in
> external actions. The ego as the essential being of man
> remains quite invisible ... For the ego receives its nature
> and significance from that with which it is bound up.[77]

It is this, then, which enables us to have our unique trajectory through the world; otherwise indeed we would be finally indistinguishable from the temporarily assembled parts of it which make up our present experience. Thinking and ordinary self-consciousness are intimately bound up with the emergence of the self, but they show us nothing of the reality of it. The living, transforming reality is 'benumbed,' as we have seen it expressed by Steiner, in the process by which we become conscious of its products. We can grasp it only as an agent of transformation. Steiner's conception of the self is, as one might say, radically developmental.

It is imaged most fully in the processes connected with the head, because the head's special passive position has enabled it still to exhibit in a special form the tendency underlying all of evolution, the plasticity which in contrast reaches its limits in the adaptations of the organ- and limb-systems. Even the head and its activities are no more than a picture, as Steiner says, of the actively working spirit. But it is through them that we are able to become self-conscious, and thereby at the same time to become conscious of ourselves as an individual realization of the possibilities inherent in the world.

Such a realization is not possible for the animals, who do not orientate themselves in the distinctively human way which has enabled the evolution of thought, i.e. of an adaptation that transcends the immediate pressures of the environment. It is this, and not the possession of any special 'human' feature, which distinguishes us from the animals. Though he maintained a radical distinction between man and animal, as between spirit and soul, Steiner was therefore not at all perturbed by the body of biological investigations which had shown the close similarities between human and animal forms. Indeed to show the intimate relation of the human form to the whole evolutionary process was a starting-point for his own 'anthropic' or rather anthroposophical researches. Yet it would be a blinkered and uncritical mode of thought which limited itself to noting similarities between animals and man, as does so much modern science. 'Knowing nothing more about man than this, it has sought for the distinguishing features in the animal and says: here are the features of animal life; and here we find them again, only more highly developed, in man.' Goethe had already warned against supposing that the all-important difference could be located on any such external level. And yet the difference is profound:

> Even on the level of spatial orientation, the human being must be shown as possessing a quite different relation to the world. This, however, came to be forgotten more and more. Indeed, in virtually all the systematic scientific presentations of biological evolution, everything we actually know about human beings has been excluded.[78]

The conception of a transformative power, revealing itself in our evolution and eventually in those effects of our evolution which enable it to appear in its own nature, has recently been given renewed philosophical plausibility in the work of Richard

Swinburne.[79] Though what he calls 'soul' corresponds rather more to what in Steiner's terminology is called 'spirit,' the resemblances are certainly significant. Philosophically and conceptually coherent though it may be, however, in this domain we come up against a body of assumptions that has dominated psychology at least since Freud. And whereas Steiner could well have sided largely with Lacan and empirical psychology against the transcendentalism of the concept of self still employed in phenomenology, here he finds himself opposed by the dominant conceptions of psychology, which has been perceived as scientifically viable, one might say, fundamentally because it treated human identity as something determined. Since Freud the determining conditions have been sought first in the basic drives of human behaviour (whether the urge to pleasure or to power), and the factors which fix their manifestation in any individual have been found particularly in childhood experiences, specifically the 'traumas' we have already had occasion to mention above.

Recently, however, the whole approach to the notion of human identity as the 'product' in this way of certain drives and events has been seriously questioned — and again, on developmental grounds. The idea that what we are is the outcome of certain fixed forces in our personality in conjunction with early, determinative events has given way to a sense of ongoing adjustment and renewal:

> As research evidence accumulates ... to cast doubt on
> previously favoured theories of the continuity of
> personality development and of the great importance to
> be attached to the experience of the first three years of life,
> the issue of the effects of intervening events, particularly
> of trauma and stress, has also been open to debate. It now
> seems probable that life experiences intervening between
> early childhood and adulthood may counteract or
> reinforce earlier positive and negative experience and
> thereby influence adjustment in complex ways.[80]

Jerome Kagan is certainly sensitive to the enormity of the shift in point-of-view — and to resistance from specialists and representatives of general Western attitudes alike. But he draws his own conclusion nevertheless: 'Each developmental journey,' he writes, 'contains many points where one can move in any one of several directions. Each choice modifies, in however small a way, the probability of a particular outcome.'[81] One cannot finally separate, therefore, the influence of events from our own developmental arc. Our identity is being shaped at every stage, and not just in childhood, by our potential for self-determined inner growth through those experiences — through something, in other words, which Steiner described as the radically developmental ego or self, which 'receives its nature and significance from that with which it is bound up.'

In his anthroposophical writings, Rudolf Steiner was to draw many far-reaching further conclusions from this conception. His extension of them was indeed startling, but in no way inconsistent with the philosophically complex, modern sense of the self which he set out to explore. One was that the events and life-situations in which we find ourselves are an inseparable part of our identity, even though in a sense that is diametrically opposed to any behaviouristic reductionism. And the other, related one was the possibility of understanding human existence through reincarnation. The former extension led him to develop his own understanding of what he termed, characteristically adopting a traditional term, *karma*. The latter allowed him to conceive of a self that could genuinely grow through different life-experiences, and was in no sense the travesty often assumed of a permanent, unchanging person who puts on, as it were, a series of elaborate disguises. Steiner's post-modern self can indeed enable us to cope with the paradox of being different personalities in different lives. The case for the actuality of many lives, of course, he based on spiritual experiences which convinced him of the fact. But in the way that such a process is conceived, it is important to realize that he in no way fell back upon oriental, Buddhistic ideas. The way to understand it arose out of his understanding of the internally complex modern Western self.[82]

CHAPTER 4

Freedom and History

The Self and its Values — A Philosophy of Freedom

We may begin by pointing a contrast between Steiner's 'free spirit' and the vision of the individual in that 'gospel of modern liberal thought,' John Stuart Mill's *On Liberty*. Mill approaches the issue from the side of 'state interference.' His concern is to limit the control of the state over the individual's life, to leave a wide margin of liberty wherever one individual does not encroach on the liberty of another. Above all, liberty of ideas and of (religious) beliefs is essential. Mill is not much worried by the objection that ideas may be true or otherwise. Should this not have something to do with their value? In fact, he concludes that no one is likely to be right much of the time, and that 'liberty' is actually the best antidote to the tyranny exerted by half-truths. And yet, truth is the world we have in common. Without a sense of truth there can be no shared endeavour. Mill's all-important individual remains a sort of hole in the mesh of the state; Steiner's 'free spirit' is more challenging, more dangerously anarchistic in many ways, yet paradoxically also able to unite with others and to share in the search for truth.

Mill begins by separating his subject-matter from the question of free will and the 'misnamed doctrine of philosophical necessity': from Steiner's perspective, it may be that this is just as dangerous as the totalitarian attempt to usurp the individual's quest for truth in a cruder way by means of an imposed ideology. His philosophy of freedom is founded on the conviction that the subjects cannot be neatly separated but that all the issues must be examined together: that it is the truth which sets us free.

We have seen, moreover, that Rudolf Steiner's view of

knowledge means that he need not despair of finding truth, even though he accepts that it can be sought for only in the changing perspectives on reality that belong to particular individuals. Therefore he does not need to turn on the one hand to the merely pragmatic solutions of those like Mill who would impose upon us 'moral' actions (or limitations to our action) which cannot be inwardly felt, but are set from outside — actions which therefore by Steiner's standards lack real moral intentionality. By the same token we shall see that he need not waste his time looking for some Kantian 'formal' deduction of eternal moral principles from beyond experience altogether. Steiner admits that ethics as a normative science — a science, that is, of telling people what to do — is defunct, and for the very reasons that liberalism like Mill's takes as its starting-point: the lack of a shared basis in the values of a whole community. But his response is very different. Rather than reaching for any kind of compelling factors which would seem to rescue the situation and 'make' our actions or intentions moral, Steiner is remarkable for the thoroughgoing way in which he seeks instead to derive human values from the human perspective, from human freedom itself as he has characterized it in terms of consciousness and clarity of knowledge. Most philosophers would like to be sure first of all what our moral imperatives are, then ask if we are free to perform them. Steiner takes a different view.

He relates them in essence to the free relationship with the world which is what we have learned to call knowing, and the inner configuration of forces that make it part of our development (consciousness: including the possibility of error, of imbalance, the luciferic or ahrimanic onesidedness).

Unstable, not to say risky as many moralists would find this basis for our value-judgments, Steiner assured his listeners, in his wide-ranging course on spirituality and ethics, that with it, if properly understood, they had an adequate foundation for an ethical philosophy. Reminding them of what he meant by the luciferic and ahrimanic inner tendencies he explained:

> In this you have all that you need in order to understand the freedom of the will and the significance of reason and wisdom in human action. If it were fitting for man to

observe eternal moral principles, he would only need to get hold of these basic moral principles and then he could set off on a route-march through life, so to speak; but life is never like this. Freedom in life consists in man's being always able to err in one direction or another. But in this way evil arises. For what is evil? It is what comes about when people either lose themselves to the world, or when the world is lost to them. Goodness consists in avoiding both these extremes.[1]

Thus for Steiner, goodness, or morality, it appears, is fundamentally nothing other than the human perspective as such, which precariously balances self-assertion and mastery over the flux of experience with accommodation through inner change. It is clearly in this sense, too, and not as a metaphysical statement about 'essence,' that Steiner can say that human nature in its deepest sense is good.[2] He does not mean this in the old-fashioned way for example that Shaftesbury had meant it, that human nature is endowed with certain intrinsic qualities such as benevolence, fairness etc. We are to be guided rather by what we have already come to understand about knowledge and the knower. The presence of the knower endows a situation with moral significance, since knowledge consists in that delicate equilibrium between assimilation and accommodation, luciferic and ahrimanic drives, enabling our identity-in-change. We are then not shaped by our situation, but shape it.

Awareness of one's moral role, then, simply as a human presence within the scene, is the beginning, for Steiner, of an awareness of that dimension of spiritual activity, the active balancing of inner tendencies, in which we participate as free beings. It is thus, as we have seen, that we introduce into the situation the 'nothingness' which is the potential for different interpretation, or freedom within it. And thus it lies in our power to change the meaning of things, whether through external action or it may be simply through deeper understanding which can in itself be a healing, moral power within a situation which makes the reality of what takes place profoundly different. To act out of that 'picture-being' of consciousness, or freedom which is not determined by the past, is to go beyond what we ourselves already are — and to bring into play something going beyond what the situation is as mere matter-of-fact, as the outcome of past events. It is to cross over the existential 'nothingness' which confronts the knower of his or her own activity, and perform an act which makes things new.

What is frightening here is perhaps precisely that in Steiner's view of morals there are no set principles, even though we will (if we are wise) want to learn from the past. In fact, once we are freed from the feeling that past ideas of how to behave have the power to impose on us, we shall actually be able to learn from them in an open-ended and appreciative way. But we shall not be able to fall back on their authority, at least if we want to follow Steiner's path. Of course, we *can* do so — and Steiner threatens us with nothing if so choose, except (as we shall see) that we must live with what we become in the process. But moral awareness is always an intuition, or spiritual perception, of unique significance, in the course of which we too are challenged and changed. It goes beyond mere knowledge in that having crossed over the 'nothingness' of pure detachment, of consciousness, we actively insert ourselves once more into the interpreted world, as part of the specific reality we have envisaged, concretely, specifically, through what Steiner therefore calls 'moral imagination.'[3]

All this is going rather fast. One might choose to dwell upon many other subtleties of Steiner's treatment, such as the clear distinction between the 'driving force' behind an action and the idea or 'motive,' which forestalls so many of the profitless discussions of the moralists. But what I want to bring out here especially is the link to the human centre which we have already found in Steiner's epistemology: for moral action can be revealed as the very process by which we actualize our own unique 'higher self' across the existential divide. By relating ethics so directly to an achieved insight of our own, Steiner shifts the emphasis away from some of the traditional themes, such as the 'moral struggle.' Steiner catalogued some of those which we might still find familiar:

> We have the social struggle, the struggle for peace, the
> struggle for the emancipation of women, the struggle for
> land and territory, and so forth; everywhere we look, we
> find struggle. The spiritual-scientific approach however is

to put positive working in place of all this struggle.
Anyone who has attained to a spiritual understanding of
the world will know that this struggling has achieved no
real results in any sphere of life.[4]

We can struggle against others or against ourselves; but such
things are no substitute for the real task of bringing people
together. Steiner's conception of the moral life cannot be
achieved thus one-sidedly, but only through perceiving the
deeper potential of the world and the people around us, and at
the same time through a corresponding act of inner growth
which is how we know that higher self exists. As we take such a
step of moral discovery, it is clear in Steiner's philosophy that no
'laws of prudence' synthesising past experience, and no source
outside our own 'spiritual activity' can determine what we will
find.

Such a vision of moral significance clearly cannot point in the
direction of unalterable moral principles, but in the much more
challenging one of changing historical values, grounded only in
the experience of freedom and in human evolution — in changing human consciousness. In our own rapidly changing society,
ethical theory has seriously failed people in their need to act out
of freshly perceived moral situations. And yet do we not find so
often that past 'rules' no longer seem to fit? Ethics instead has
become analytical and in-bred.[5] Small wonder that it has so little power over events. Rudolf Steiner is one of the few to have
taken a radical lead.

One might therefore point to another basic aspect of Steiner's
ethic in its openness to history. Going beyond even what
Nietzsche foresaw, Steiner's type of moral awareness becomes
important above all because (perhaps for the first time in moral
philosophy) it sees as crucial in our moral decision-making, not
whether we can live up to a moral standard set for us whether
by society or God, but whether we can survive with our humanity intact — whether or not, in fact, we succumb to the dehumanizing pressures of the forces amidst which we have to make
our decisions. Here at once we stand again in the urgent reality
of the post-modern cultural situation. In that reality moral
awareness seems always to be determined by just the sort of

issues which Steiner placed so uncompromisingly at the forefront of ethical thought: the relationship of our consciousness, our burden of knowledge, to an immediately perceived moral need, not readily assimilable to standard types, set against the threat of dehumanization in the pressures of the world we know unless we have the strength to bring to it the kind of self-discovery, the inner achievement of equilibrium, he urged.

Perhaps two wider points can also be made here at the outset, which may further serve to signpost the significance of Steiner's approach. Steiner's ethic itself arises at a juncture in thought where the historical dimension in moral truth needed to be acknowledged and actively grasped. Nietzsche was merely the one who brought the crisis to a head. For we can easily discern in retrospect the situation of the early twentieth century, and why it was no longer enough for humanity to suppose that to be 'good' meant to measure itself against any existing criterion: the pressures of individual experience had become too great, opening the way to too many alternative perspectives, and the encounter between different cultures had exacerbated the resulting uncertainty. The 'enlightened' European cultures whose influence had spread all over the globe had now to clarify their own moral authority. Of course it was possible for some to maintain their attitude of superiority to the last — but for all who had any human involvement in the events of the end of Empire, the problems of cultural diversity and individual moral perception were becoming acute.

Steiner's historical approach offers a way through the dilemma which faced, and continues to face many people as a result. The realization that not everyone accepts one's inherited values may frequently involve a loss of trust in morality altogether, since what is highly valued in one culture, or in one section of society, is seen to be frowned on or despised in another, or because one's own society's ethic now seems to stifle and contradict the needs of one's own personal self-realization. The notion of a common ethic that was grounded in allegiance to real moral perception became ultimately hard to keep hold of — if not meaningless. Going back to Mill again, the liberal ideal of stepping on no one's toes was one way forward; but it left the problem of inner meaninglessness unresolved, gradually to become a gaping sore. Historical movement is likely to become distorted into the fanciful, luciferic notion of progress and Utopia. But Utopias unachieved take their inner toll. Instead, Steiner proposes a resolutely, even startling *realistic* emphasis. He suggests that despite the way they change in different cultures and situations, moral judgments are specifically the deeper truth of that historical setting. Moral aspiration is not given direction by escaping from our imperfect age into Utopia, but in becoming more fully what is needed by our time. What we need is to understand the internal configuration of each setting and time, which is to say, what human consciousness then brought to meet it. We cannot expect a medieval knight fighting traitors and outlaws to have our values in regard to bringing criminals to justice in modern European law-enforcement, showing respect for the rules of evidence and presumption of innocence, human rights, etc. But that does not mean the earlier standards were merely crude versions of our own, — or that the concept of 'justice' becomes meaningless since it cannot be the same thing in both cases. (If that were true, it would never even be possible to say meaningfully whether the knight in shining armour was really being 'good' or not.)

The same guidelines which enabled us to see knowledge in changing, evolving forms operate here. For Steiner, we need to comprehend each situation from inside, instead to trying to import our own standards. For Steiner, as we shall see, historical understanding of this deeper kind is inherently possible — and we shall see how he was among those who pioneered the deeper understanding of history, exploring ways of circumventing the perspective of our own time and culture, similar to those which recent historians have also begun to use in order to reach a truer perception of what things meant to the people of past times, considering them and their values not as crude anticipations of ourselves, but in their own right.[6]

Secondly, Steiner's concept of the good as existing in this extremely concrete way, as a real component in our moral perception, means that he can confront the existence of 'evil' (as he indicates already in the last quotation), in an honest but essentially unhysterical way: not, like some existential thinkers, as if it constituted a hideous bafflement and a stumbling-block cast in the way of a world that should be pure and perfect, but, after our human degree at least, as an understandable aspect of life with which we wrestle. There is nothing in Steiner of the idea with which Jung, for instance, made play, of a God who created a world and then defaced it, by an act of divine instability.[7] Steiner does indeed talk, especially in religious contexts, of a 'mystery of evil' — but precisely in order to suggest that evil is less an inscrutable, ultimate and frightening inimical force than a dimension of life which on a higher level makes sense as part of our role in the world, when we enter into it more perceptively. That is the point at which understanding becomes actively more, becomes a process of consciously transforming ourselves. It is a higher-level equivalent, perhaps, to the 'riddle'-analogy which he uses so often in relation to knowledge.[8] With the 'problem of evil' it is not in the end for Steiner that there is a problem in the world, but in our understanding. Evil is the dehumanizing pressure of unassimilable events. Painful as it is, to resolve it, we must change and become again — ourselves.

So far then: Steiner's moral thought moves right away from the idea of measuring us against any sort of fixed standard, that is supposed to be always and everywhere the same, and focusses instead upon the ability of individuals to redefine the meaning of the situation in which they find themselves: through awareness, and through transformative (historical) acts. A situation becomes moral through the potential of the specific person present, through whom its 'higher law' comes into operation.[9]

Now in all this of course Steiner was setting himself against what we may well term a dominant trend in Western philosophy, which he saw had signally failed to give scope to the kind of moral insight he valued, or even to understand it. Great philosophers who have deeply influenced our moral universe have set themselves markedly against it. For when thinkers such as Kant or Hume try to account for our knowledge of what is right, the immediate tendency is to extrapolate and generalize the situation, so as to render it susceptible of rational calculation. Kant, for example, famously argued that we can know something is morally right if we could bid everyone do the same thing in the same circumstances. The moral rightness of something thereby becomes essentially a sort of generalization we can make. But with this approach they are removing the key element of individual response, the complex striving to find one's own spiritual equilibrium, or inner balance, while at the same time stepping actively into the situation. And the result is that 'ought' and 'is,' the phenomenal world and the moral world-order, fall apart in their philosophies as they never do in actual human life.[10] There is a typical luciferic-ahrimanic bifurcation, the ideal and the real polarized and leading to a sense of the self as trapped in the contradiction between them. Steiner seeks instead to release the contradiction into movement — into history.

History and Morality

Steiner was certainly aware that his approach would be thought unconventional because it did not seek to ground morality in reasoned principles, but rather in what is clearly an extension of Nietzschean historical insights. It was Nietzsche's account of the historically explicated 'genealogy of morals' which gave him a starting-point, from which he proceeded however to apply his own characteristic approach. He was certainly aware that this moral realism would be found unusual. 'I have already remarked,' he commented, 'that what we have say on the subject of an anthroposophical ethics will be based upon facts — and for this reason will be brought forward a few facts in which the working of moral impulses is pre-eminently exhibited.'[11] For Steiner, moral philosophy needed to proceed by examining actual moral individuals such as Francis of Assisi, or the codes of values which belonged to particular civilizations. In *The Genealogy of Morals*, Nietzsche had used a similar method to devastating critical effect. He had sought to disentangle modern moral thinking from its confusions by pointing out, for instance, that the concept of 'good *vs.* bad' is quite different from what he regarded as the more modern, cowardly, fear-and-guilt-ridden notion of 'good *vs.* evil.'

The first, he says, is 'noble' — its implication of identifying with the good and of spurning low, 'bad' behaviour is rooted in generosity and bravery. A passive attitude, on the other hand, where good is haunted by the fear of what is presented as 'evil,' he suggested, has created a self-serving morality that declines to take risks, persecutes those whom it fears because it does not understand them, and congratulates itself on its own righteousness when this is in reality its timid refusal to step outside the prison it has built for itself. What such an attitude hates above all is the 'noble' morality, which is careless of self, seeks out risk and is contemptuous of everything petty that stands in its way. Nietzsche certainly exposed a rift in the conflicting attitudes which were concealed beneath the hypocrisies of the late nineteenth century society. What he offers in exchange is a kind of ruthless honesty, and in his 'wild' way he certainly cut much deeper than the moral systematizers. He managed effectively to change the whole basis of moral discourse as it had developed from the Enlightenment. In fact he went much further, since in historicizing moral values in this way rather than seeking to relate them to timeless, rationally verifiable principles, he once again revealed them to be merely a part of the 'all-too-human,' the contingency of social and historical changes which produce now one kind of society, now another. In the end, his personal preference for one or the other becomes less important than this vanishing of the metaphysical foundations, leaving morality rocking on the edge of a relativistic abyss, if not in danger of being abolished altogether. Man, for Nietzsche, is 'beyond good and evil,' and morality as a system becomes either a bugbear with which man frightens himself, or if he affirms it for himself, the expression of man's own overflowing, prodigal nature and needs no higher justification.

Steiner's historical approach takes over where the Nietzschean, with its violent reduction, leaves off. First of all Steiner is not out in the same way to take sides; and yet it would be wrong, I think, to see him as going back on Nietzsche's relativism, to interpret his kinder tone as a seeking to redress the balance, for example, over Nietzsche's account of despicable Christian morality. In choosing the examples that he does — not only a high spiritual ethic like that of St Francis or the devotionalism of India, but also the Nietzschean one of 'noble' violence in primitive Europe — Steiner indeed is clearly out to tackle the Nietzschean challenge head-on. He does not turn back from Nietzsche's historical analysis, but seeks to find out what lies at the root of it. And instead of the pendulum swing, from rational control to the opposite extreme of nihilism, he has his model of human equilibrium finding a balance from within. He tries to see what was developing, humanly, through the emergence of each ethic. Rather than rejecting Nietzsche's admired 'noble' ruthlessness for a 'Christian' spirituality, Steiner seeks to enter into the historical mode of being which brought each into being. It is actually this ancient valorous ideal, for instance, which has given us the very concept of 'virtue,' descended from the ancient 'manly energy' via the Renaissance idea of *virtù* — the creative power of the noble or superior mind.

Steiner begins on this historical note, observing that 'it is of little use in understanding the different peoples of the earth if we begin by merely applying our own moral standards':

> Modern conceptions now consider these self-same war-like deeds, which were the outcome of ancient 'virtue,' to be a relic of the past. In fact they are reckoned as vices. But the people of ancient Europe used them in a chivalrous, magnanimous manner. Generous actions were characteristic of the peoples of ancient Europe — just as actions springing from devotion were characteristic of the people of ancient India ...
>
> Now, putting to one side all the objections that might be raised from the standpoint of the 'idea of morality' — let us enquire into the actual moral effect. It does not require much reflection to realize that ... the world has gained infinitely much by that which could only be obtained through the existence of a people like the ancient Indians, among whom all feeling was directed to devotion, devotion to the highest. Infinitely much it has also gained from the valiant deeds of the European peoples of early, pre-Christian times ...
>
> So we might assert, without more ado, that something which produces this moral effect for humanity is good. Doubtless in both of these streams of civilization it must have been so. But if we were to ask, 'What then is goodness?' we stand once more before an enigma. What is 'the good' that has been active in both these cases?[12]

We seek in vain for any common rational principle that was the 'good' exemplified in both. The conventional moral idea of pre- scribing what must be valid for all humanity immediately comes up against its limits in the face of the historical facts of moral development. And a morality which is powerless in the face of facts is, for Steiner at least, no morality at all.

Once again Steiner enters a situation of threatening relativism with a coolness of nerve that is in marked contrast to the Nietzschean bravura tone. And behind this lies a deeper under- standing of the philosophical impasse. For to Steiner it is clear that, in reality, it had been the already looming fear and anxiety of historical awareness that had led in the Enlightenment ration- alizations, to a defensive counter-movement to fight off the uncertainties that were growing up. How are we to cope with the fact that other people, or even more particularly other cul- tures have a different moral evaluation of things? Unless we have strength and certainty in our own moral judgment, we shall feel weakened and attacked by the consciousness of other, 'contradictory' moral perspectives. And so begins the search for absolute principles which can effectively compel others to share our point of view.

Recent studies have indeed stressed the defensive character of the eighteenth-century Enlightenment.[13] The need to achieve agreement through reason was pressured by the growing uncer- tainties of European man, within and without. There is a certain desperation in the quest for a morality that will solve all prob- lems everywhere.[14] In Steiner's more balanced survey, the Nietzschean arguments are simply given their full scope. A true 'natural history of morality' begins to take shape.

Yet surely, the objection will still arise in many minds, there must be some things which are not just right for this or that his- torical situation, or conditionally in order to achieve this or that, but which are right and good always, everywhere? It is not that we should do such things when we want to attain a particular goal: they are things we simply ought or should do.

Much philosophical ink has certainly been shed in trying to prove that some demands upon us are absolute, like the com- mandments of a God speaking within us. And likewise, it is argued, there must be things which are not wrong in this or that situation — but which are just wrong as such — are evil? The moral absoluteness which we could attribute to the good in any such principles would give them the status of what Kant had called 'categorical imperatives,' as if uttered by some higher power.

Influential modern philosophers such as R.M. Hare have continued to maintain that all moral statements (i.e. the propositions employed in making moral evaluations) must ultimately entail imperatives. Without such implication, he thinks, morality must collapse into mere statement of preference or empty feeling.[15] Steiner however believes that moral values can survive their naturalization in the post-Nietzschean context. He is against seeing moral pressures as erupting in some way, outside of historical context, with imperative force. There is indeed a close parallel here to the process which makes us question the cognitive assumption we mentioned earlier, the idea that our own way of seeing reality is the one that is 'natural.'

Becoming conscious of these things is the key to the way moral issues actually arise — and are resolved. Support for Steiner's contention that moral significance arises from specific human awareness rather than from the dictates of an imperative might be drawn from many areas of modern experience: progress in such matters as reduction in smoking cigarettes has shown that whereas rules and regulations produce little effect or in many cases deviousness or open flouting, genuine change in behaviour has come about in proportion to the spread of awareness. Or, in matters that have to do with conserving the environment, one of the largest 'moral revolutions' to have come about in recent years has been effected almost entirely by the spread of popular knowledge and consequent awareness of the danger to our planet. The tardiness of legislators has at least served to show in a rather clear way how consciousness of a situation deepens into a moral force, able to produce changed attitudes in many people. That awareness was moralized, one might also say, precisely through the sense of the historical uniqueness of the situation, that is, the crucial difference that our presence as knowers could bring about.

In conventional ethics, the notion of general rules has vitiated the sense of moral immediacy which a crisis like that of the environment forcefully restored. It can be argued that through the influence of Kant in particular, when he denied that we can have any specific moral awareness (or ethical 'intuitions'), facing-up to historicity was thus botched in advance, and Enlightenment philosophy produced a sort of shadowy sense that failure to establish some moral absolute must mean that nothing could have any moral value at all. Its prophecy was self-fulfilled. The Enlightenment's effort to establish that we must act in ways that are rationally binding — and so binding upon everyone — in reality only led to the ever-increasing estrangement of our moral values from the actual situations in which we find ourselves. In its failure it therefore leads directly to the abandonment of inner moral certainty for the relativism of those like Mill. In the world that has resulted, moral codes have not kept their power, but come to seem abstract and unconnected with the world we know.

Steiner's alternative is to see moral judgment as a kind of 'higher knowledge.' To understand what this means we perhaps need a momentary retrospective. Many things are now starting to come together in Steiner's philosophy. The relationship between knowledge and freedom which he explored in *The Philosophy of Freedom* forms the basis for his approach to the strengthening of consciousness that we need for a moral engagement with the world, and especially to tackle the specific issues of the crisis we now face. For knowledge, more philosophically understood, confronts us with our freedom. Our increasing consciousness, being detachment, nothingness, opens up the potential for change and transformation in any situation of which we are part, which need no longer be simply determined by the past. The establishing of relationship, of inner equilibrium by which we achieve that free role already became, therefore, in Steiner's philosophy, something for which we bear moral responsibility.[16] We have seen therefore that knowledge, contrary to the escapist myth of so many scientists and others in modern times, is never value-free. Acting consciously, that is, out of knowledge, ultimately makes us become aware of our own 'spiritual activity'; freedom is the name for the many-faceted moment of 'reversal' when we acknowledge our own reinterpreting role, or participation, since coming to knowledge is also shaping our own emergent identity and life-line of our history. We determine what things will mean to us. By the very same act we are also perceiving the moral significance of our world, since as self-aware beings we are inserting ourselves into it as active agents.[17]

We are now also in a position to understand what Steiner means by certain other expressions. The 'strengthening' of consciousness of which Steiner often speaks in order to become aware of our spiritual role (which some have perhaps found a little mysterious) can now be defined more accurately: it is the inner strength needed to uphold the historical uniqueness of our moral awareness, and to take responsibility for it without trying to justify ourselves from the past, or in disguised form from a past posing as a rational-metaphysical 'imperative.' It is the existential strength, if you prefer, which we need if we are not to abdicate the moral responsibility for what we know, and so to fulfil the moral dimension of our own development. This is moral in the sense that it being ourselves always involves others. For in Steiner's view our own ego-development is intertwined throughout with that of the others whose viewpoint we acknowledge.

For the wider purposes of integrating his account of moral awareness into a view of humanity interacting among themselves and with a changing world, everything depends upon Steiner being able to derive moral significance from the actual relationships in which people find themselves, and through which they are able spiritually to grow.

We may take some examples from modern issues where many today are tempted to shelter under the umbrella of sweeping moralistic statements. Many feminists, for example, feel outraged because women in previous times were not permitted to do all the things men could do in society. Surely just wrong? It is certainly tempting to think so. But in fact everything depends on grasping perspectives. It depends on understanding the processes of development that were taking place. When we first read Milton, we come up against many assumptions from his time about the difference in 'degree' between man and woman which offend modern feeling: but as we learn more about his ideas, we discover that in his famous writings on marriage (and divorce) he has gone further than almost anyone else at his period to make human relations between the sexes full and many-sided, freely allowing that the woman may be the more intelligent, for example, and contribute in every way to the relationship. If we only assume one standard (i.e. our own), we miss the fact that in reality he is an important pioneer of modernity.[18] Though he holds many views about women which would be highly objectionable in our situation today, we can only make a sensible moral judgement when we see the spiritual direction in which he was leading. Of course, we might still hold to our absolute scale, and merely put Milton a little higher up the ladder leading to our own enlightened views: this would be the equivalent of the idea of progress in knowledge toward 'what we now know.' But Steiner, as we have seen, realized that we need to comprehend the different inner structure of consciousness in previous times. Nowhere is this more necessary than in judging moral issues.

Let us take a slightly more complex case. Aphra Behn is one of the forerunners, to many women today, of the liberation they want to achieve. In the seventeenth century she made a bold career for herself as a dramatist and writer, and without doubt prided herself among other things on advancing the cause of her sex. But when we look more deeply she did not find herself in the rather simplistic position of forging the way for women to speak for themselves, which is what Virginia Woolf, for example, later wished us to believe. Certainly she was, and very bravely, striking out a future for women writers. But by pushing the bounds of what a woman could do at that period, she found herself in a dilemma: for it seemed to her at times that by entering the masculine world, rather than winning it for women, she was in considerable danger of selling her identity as a woman. She indeed wrote powerfully and with insight about exploited women, such as her prostitute 'Angellica'; yet when she characterizes her own career, she wonders whether she is not herself hanging out her wares to please the men, under the 'sign of Angellica'?[19] In reality, then, it is not possible to give to people an abstract good (such as equality with the other sex). Not only does it need to take account of external circumstances, which Milton for instance was contending with as hard as he could —

but inwardly too it would actually rob people of their identity, failing to judge correctly how far their dynamic of identity (in the way we have come to understand it above) can be stretched. It would only be of moral value for Aphra Behn to find a writer's voice as a woman, in other words, if she could do it as herself. For then she would experience being morally free. When Steiner summed up his view on the 'women's question' by saying that it could not be answered, but had to be given over to women themselves, he was not indulging in an intellectual sleight of hand, but going to the very heart of the question itself.[20]

Moral Perception

Such experiences, where abstract moral perspectives turn out to fail the real need for change, are by no means unknown today. It remains open to question how far the pressure exerted by groups such as feminists have brought a real sense of liberation to women. There has been some notable successes and genuine social change, which liberates everybody to develop in new ways. In other respects, however, women have appropriated many traditionally masculine roles and domains but failed to bring about new attitudes and values. People feel trapped as they did before. Rudolf Steiner's is one of the few moral philosophies to have grappled seriously with that relationship between the moral value of our actions and the way we thereby achieve the deeper integrity that we can describe as our spiritual, or 'higher self.' To do so we need to draw upon those deeper resources that for Steiner belong as such to the self in its development, profoundly unrecognized though they are by contemporary thought that denies the self. Conventional moral thought paved the way for such denial when it substituted, for actual moral achievement, the abstract motivation and duty which alone were supposed to have an ethical charge.

To act out of the self is of course an enormous challenge. It is, as we have seen, to act freely, i.e. out of conscious insight. Ultimately it is a deeper form of that ability which is already present in all true knowledge, and in the paradoxical character of real selfhood: the strength to allow the other into the heart of our own existence. 'A good man is one who is able to enter with his own soul,' as Steiner explains,

> into the soul of another. In the strictest sense, all genuine morality depends upon this ability to enter with one's own soul into the soul of another ... without which no true social order amongst people on earth can be maintained.[21]

We can be courageous enough to do that, however, only if we know that, across nothingness, leaving behind all that has made up our existence in the past, we have the inner resources and trust to give ourselves to the other and not be lost, but inwardly renew ourselves:

> The experience of goodness really unites us with the world of which I have said that it is always there if only we would reach out our hand — we would be reaching into it! But while he is on earth, man is separated from this world which he will enter again when he passes through the gate of death. On earth, the experience of goodness points towards this world and is a true link to it for humanity. When someone lives in a true spirit of goodness, his deeds on earth engender forces which endure beyond the gate of death.[22]

The experience of the moral order is therefore one of spiritual, i.e. eternal reality; and of this Steiner similarly remarks elsewhere that 'it is characteristic of the world of spirit that it is there for us only when we take the trouble, even if only to a small extent, to become different from what we were before.' It is in this way, in fact, that we act morally rather than selfishly, and in so doing 'when we act in the physical world, we bring down the spiritual into that world.'[23] In this incarnational process we are making our identity.

Paradoxically the essence of our link with the eternal is that it gives us the inner strength to go through change. If we suppose that we only consist of what has happened to us, our physical make-up and the sum of our past, we must shrink from the existential nothingness or face it with Sartre's sense of condemnation to freedom. But we can risk leaving it behind with the confidence that we can find ourselves once more if we can rise to the awareness of 'the good' as Steiner presents it — as a real power in events. And it enables us even more importantly to take responsibility for what happens as a consequence spreading out beyond our own acts, continuing on beyond our own situation and perhaps even our life. Thus we are already working while on earth to create the spiritual future, not in some abstract sense — but through finding the moral strength to assert our existence in history.

One of the most striking consequences of Steiner's thought along these lines is that actual, historical deeds and events are given moral reality. In his account of the specific moral intuitions which are actualized through the self and its 'higher knowledge' he is close again in some ways to Max Scheler, and the latter's controversial 'concreteness' in regard to moral values. 'There is a mode of perception,' writes Scheler, 'whose objects are totally beyond the grasp of the intellect ... a mode of perception nonetheless which presents to us real objects and an eternal order among them – namely values and their hierarchy.'[24] We do not work out the value-aspect of something we do or experience by means of an act of calculation after the event. We perceive it directly by virtue of our existence as a self, able to see more in things than the mere externally given. Steiner calls this kind of higher perception an intuition, which for him replaces that supposed rational deduction of what is right which many previous theories of ethics asked us to believe was the basis of value-judgments. For Steiner it is rather a direct observation we make about the nature of the world. (This also means incidentally, despite Steiner's use of the term 'intuition' to describe the way a specific content of moral awareness arises, that he is at the very opposite extreme from the celebrated 'intuitionism' of the Cambridge moralist G.E. Moore. The latter regarded such things as goodness, fairness, etc. as 'non-natural' qualities utterly underivable from the specifics of things as they are: perhaps the ultimate case of *ought* sundered from *is*.[25]) Scheler, the Phenomenologist who so often has much in common with Steiner, is interesting here in that for him as for

Steiner, morality was a matter of a kind of specific moral perception rather than the application of an abstract rule. In this both are being true to the fundamental characteristics of moral experience: the unfairness of an act or the brutality of something that has been said are clearly just as immediate a part of it as the force of the hand that performed the cheat or the loudness of the voice that spoke the words. It is quite artificial to suggest that we only invest such actions with moral value in a roundabout way through deductions about their universal application (such as reflecting, 'they are bad because if everyone made untrue accusations, for example ...'). Moral theory has been just as culpable in this regard as the far-fetched theories of perception which tried to make us believe that the chair we sit on is known to us only as an uncertain matter of inference, while abstruse and concocted entities such as sense-data were held to be the only certain truth. Moreover, Steiner could rightly claim that in particularizing moral perceptions rather than generalizing them he was specifically in line with the real origins of Western ethics — that is to say, in the Bible, specifically in the raising of moral awareness evinced on many crucial occasions in history by the prophets of Israel.[26]

Now it is true that more recently philosophers have made gestures toward breaking free from the notion that in order to convey moral significance something has to be generalizable. Philippa Foot for example, looking back over the philosophical arguments which occupied her, where the issues took the special form of problem of the relationship between 'descriptive' and 'evaluative' elements in the meaning of good, observes, 'It had not occurred to me to question the often repeated dictum that moral judgments give reasons for acting to each and every man. This now seems to me to be a mistake ...'[27] It is interesting nonetheless to see her reservations about one of the most serious attempts to bridge the divide between 'ought' and 'is,' undertaken by the modern philosopher John R. Searle. Essentially, like Steiner seeking the 'bridge between the ideal and the real,'[28] he is objecting to the whole idea that an 'ought' is a sort of extra ('imperative') entailment which is tacked on to the meaning of a statement, making it obligatory to all. He chooses as an example to consider a specific account of promising, or being under obli-

gation, and seeks to show how it could lead on 'internal' premises to an understanding of the moral forces involved, so that an
account of 'is' would be at the same time an account of 'ought,'
without having to bring in anything further — like a transcendental or non-natural imperative.[29]

Whilst admitting the force of Searle's challenge in principle,
Professor Foot nevertheless objects to this *internal* analysis. But
it is precisely this kind of approach, it seems to me, which
Steiner wants to take, and which points toward the inner moral
reality, which he argues cannot be and does not need to be, validated by any sort of 'extra' ethical component, tacked on to the
situation as such, and telling us what to do about it. And then,
in a fascinating extension of Searle's presentation, Foot argues
against herself, seeking in all fairness to open out the crucial
arguments involved to their fullest extent. She suggests that
Searle might appeal for support to the insights of post-
Wittgensteinian linguistic philosophy. Philosophers in that line,
notably the Oxford academic J.L. Austin, have made use of the
technical term 'illocutionary' to characterize the way that language acquires under certain circumstances further nuances
from the situation in which it is uttered. Thus for example to say
'The writing is on the wall' can have in certain situations the
meaning of a warning, or admonition, even though it is logically
and linguistically just a statement. Foot advances the idea that
instead of seeking for a concealed moral imperative in descriptions of language, it might be possible to appeal to an 'illocutionary' model, showing how a statement becomes a moral
directive without the intervention of an indirect or otherwise
mysterious 'hidden' component, short-circuiting the need for a
'special' moral kind of meaning or concealed imperative.

Despite the very different terminology, this is ultimately very
similar (unless I am much mistaken) to Steiner's account of how
we insert ourselves, freely, into the world. We do not come bearing an abstract imperative; but the meaning of the situation is
changed by the complex new meaning a proposition acquires
through our wider awareness, which gives it its moral resonance.
In Steiner's thought this is part of the way that the luciferic, ide-
alizing drive has to be redirected by conscious human activity,
i.e. becoming moral-spiritual activity. The drive toward nothing-

ness, toward an idealization that is finally divorced from engagement with the world around us altogether in search of complete
self-fulfilment, becomes in moral life the basis of the division
between ought and is. It is the luciferic drive which projects an
absolute, timeless good — but one which, as moralists have
always discovered to their cost, fails to produce any acts which
live up to it. But in the linguistic philosophers' account of 'illocutionary force' one may see a parallel to Steiner's insistence
that, instead of giving in to the luciferic projection as if it could
lead us to something metaphysically real, the abstract consciousness we have attained must be inserted into the world once
more. As a matter of fact, Steiner speaks of a 'deeper life' of
words when thus inserted into their context (see p. 221 below). It
is in that reinsertion into the complex, manifold present actuality, rather losing ourselves than the endless pursuing of an ideal,
that knowledge becomes moral, and we find ourselves again as
morally responsible agents. Knowledge always becomes moral
knowledge when we remind ourselves of our own involvement,
and that it is therefore knowledge in specific circumstances. The
complex, expanded awareness which has been referred to as illocutionary (where we know that a proposition means more than
its superficial content) reflects such a sense of the setting, whilst
the specific, objective meaning remains. (The parallel also suggests that Steiner's thought need have nothing to fear from the
valid use of linguistic-philosophical approaches. Its relevance
may simply become more clear.) Of course, the moral force of
such subtle moral perceptions can never be as clear-cut as a good
old-fashioned imperative: but then, that is surely what Steiner
means about the strengthening of consciousness, and why he
characterizes his ethics as first and foremost 'a philosophy of
moral tact.'

Yet Philippa Foot is uncertain. Once again, however, I think
the kind of problem she senses is one where Steiner's historical
grounding of moral ideas, however, might actually be a help.
Her objection in respect of cases such as the old code of
duelling[30] shows up the need for precisely Steiner's historical
dimension to the discussion, which alone would enable us to
disentangle why such obligations may have had an 'ought' to
them in the past, but may not be morally incumbent upon us

now. One of the most important aspects of Steiner's moral philosophy, in fact, is its potential for helping us in just such an increasingly unstable world, like the one we now inhabit, where moral certainties cannot be assumed for all time any more than they can be imposed upon other moral individuals. What is happening in such cases certainly does not betoken a failure of his type of philosophical account to provide a morally convincing analysis, but the emerging of the clear need for recognition of the historical character of morality as such, where new significance emerges, not in the form of added imperatives, but in an expanding and deepening awareness.

Natural Symbols and Modern Taboos

Behind the strength of feeling connected with these issues, we may sense that something deeper is at stake than philosophical reasoning. For the whole attempt to rationalize morality is of course deeply connected with specific (that is to say, historical) attitudes and social developments that have transformed modern European society. Broadly speaking, they are the 'liberal' attitudes which emerged out of the Enlightenment and out of the attitudes of those like Mill. By exposing the unconscious driving forces which nevertheless impel the attempt to bring moral response under control of the comparing/assimilating power of reason, Steiner enables us not so much to reject these but to understand and transcend them. His perspective of the 'evolution of consciousness' is needed more than ever if we are to face down the forces confronting us here.

Nothing is felt to be less 'enlightened,' one might almost say, than the very idea of an intrinsic moral charge to certain concrete actions: evoking archaic associations of taboo, quasi-ritual pollution or purity — primitive confusions of moral and physical, as they are taken to be: to the return of whose Gothic world we must not open the door even by the smallest chink! The real importance of Steiner's challenge to moral thinking is perhaps therefore to be appreciated more when we see it in relation to areas of social psychology and even social anthropology, since it involves the complicated factors and symbols that shape our lives — factors about which moral philosophy has all too often failed to enable us to think clearly.

Unusual perhaps in directing her professional skills so extensively upon her own culture, the anthropologist Mary Douglas has contributed many penetrating observations on the nature of modern Western life. Not only is her work thereby brought close to Steiner's project of cultural-historical self-awareness, but she has been especially concerned with the impoverishment of the 'symbolic' values which in many traditional societies communicate shared experience. Traditional societies have been able to invest acts and exchanges with immediate spiritual and moral significance: but Western enlightenment has all too often produced erosion and moral alienation. Is Steiner therefore necessarily dragging us back into the irrational, into a world invested with the aura of the primitive? Or can he give an account of direct moral perception that also shows the way to fulfil the step we have taken into intellectual self-definition? If we wish to bring Steiner in on a contemporary moral argument as we did into recent debates over knowledge and on the self, it might best be here. For whereas academic philosophers have tussled over the analytic plausibility of moral principles, it is only when we measure these against the catastrophic spiritual decline and loss of moral direction experienced by so many today that we can estimate their true importance. An anthropologist has opened the door to questions about what gives symbolic-ethical reality to societies and their relations with nature, and tried to sketch out an answer based around the metaphorical possibilities in particular of the human form.

Mary Douglas bravely takes as an issue a highly charged situation from modern social-religious life. It is all very well for the liberal philosopher to assert that moral value does not reside, for instance, in observing a Friday fast or dietary observance. From the liberal point of view, Mary Douglas admits, to suppose that there is anything intrinsically valuable in such practices is to risk being associated with the 'bog Irish.'[31] Liberal philosophy, in the wake of the ever-increasing division between 'ought' and 'is' which has infected Western thought, is insistent above all else that morality cannot be grasped in these terms, but gauged only in respect of the well-meaning intentions, the personal benevolence or contrition, etc. in which the act is done. It takes it for granted that goodness cannot be measured by concrete observances, or ritual, but only in terms of the attitude in which it is done, the individual's feelings. And the philosopher can argue, in theory, that the moral principle involved can suffer no conceivable loss through being abstracted from the primitive observances which were supposed to have been necessary in former, less enlightened ages and beliefs. It can make no difference, rationally considered, to the principle and indeed can only be an advance if instead of fixed observances people are encouraged to make their own gestures of goodwill, or perform their chosen moral 'good deeds' instead.

But there is a problem. Despite the theory, people are prepared to defy danger, social pressures, even the threat of death to preserve their allegiance to 'primitive' observances, which evoke a degree of commitment that frequently amazes and baffles the liberal onlooker. On the other hand, it is equally clear from recent history that the attempt to substitute well-meaning alternatives quite rapidly loses allegiance, becomes banal, and fails to hold people's commitment in times of difficulty. Despite its 'proven' validity in principle, rationalized liberal morality does not survive in fact. Despite all the efforts to prove that it can be sustained, from Kant to the present day,[32] in historical reality it does not work. It increasingly becomes emptied of content, meaningless. Where the 'bog Irish' mentality can inspire individuals to acts of commitment and self-denial for the sake of its practices, detachment from the specifics of their way of life finds no living substitute in abstract-personal moralism such as is demanded of most of us today by official society. 'As soon as symbolic action is denied value in its own right, the flood-gates of confusion are opened.'[33]

The 'anthropological' approach to the question, with its relation to facts, would have been congenial to Steiner: as in his moral thinking generally, the abstract issue needs to be put back into the world of history to find out what actually happens — only there does its moral significance emerge. Perhaps it is not surprising that in dealing directly with questions of value anthropology here comes close to 'anthroposophy' in Steiner's particular cognitive sense, for which his philosophy of course provides conceptual support. Indeed, Mary Douglas uses social and anthropological theory to uncover the human dynamic behind the conflicting value-systems in a manner which in certain respects approaches Steiner's anthroposophical approach. In her analysis, she follows research on language and social upbringing that points to the progressive 'elaboration' of speech which takes place in the children of some homes. (Whilst one may question some of the detail, the research has been fruitful and its ideas influential.) She distinguishes especially developments that take place in more affluent and 'entrepreneurial' families, though making it clear that what she means is not just connected with greater social ambition. She is talking about features that belong to the kind of thinking that emerges.

These children's increasingly complex language contrasts with that of other families, which tend to use 'restricted,' even formulaic phrases and expressions, and in attitude tend toward settled roles ('little boys don't play with dolls,' 'that's not how to do it' etc.). In the 'elaborated'-speech children, the increase in the possibilities of linguistic expression leads on the other hand to greater experimentalism and a concern with inner distinctions ('let me try to explain exactly what I mean, or how I see it'). In the unelaborated or 'positional' family children, the constant reaffirmation of socially accepted ways of describing things leads to a sense of underlying ritualism, an attitude only rarely inclined to examine personal motivation or the role of the self.

Mary Douglas notices that the quality of intense expression seems to open up new worlds of self-development, even as it undermines the older ritualistic-social attitudes by seeming to offer a more heartfelt personal meaning to life. Yet the sense of infinite personal potential turns out in many ways to be illusory — luciferic, in Steiner's terms. The forms of expression appropriated for personal use in this way seem at first to offer boundless possibilities, but are in practice soon afflicted by uncertainties and inner contradictions. For communication and social, i.e. moral activity depend on *shared* interpretation, on 'symbols,' which 'are necessary even for the private organizing of experience.' By substituting for ritualized certainties personal elaboration of ideas and feelings, she notes, 'the child is freed from a system of rigid positions, but made a prisoner of a system of feelings and abstract principles ... Instead of internalizing any particular social structure, his inside is constantly stirred into a ferment of ethical sensibilities.'[34] In this confusing situation, intentions become personally meant but have less moral force: promises may be sincerely made but are less likely to be kept. In prizing individual consciousness and personal ethical commitment, Western culture has given free rein to these developments in its philosophy and many associated cultural forms, right up to Existentialism and beyond. By reinserting philosophical abstractions into history and society, using the methods of 'structural' anthropological analysis, Mary Douglas approaches an 'anthroposophical' clarification, focussing on the spiritual activity, the inner forces at work behind the thoughts. And in her extended investigation of the 'luciferic' consequences, she is at one with Steiner in many of her assessments. The search for ultimate personal fulfilment and inner satisfaction, she concludes, is self-defeating since shared significances cannot be incorporated into it by definition, and yet the individual can only exist in society. Hence:

> we are moved all our lives by longings for an ideal,
> impossible harmony ... Alas for the child from the
> personal home who longs for non-verbal forms of
> relationship but has only been equipped with words and
> a contempt for ritual forms. By rejecting ritualized speech
> he rejects his own faculty for pushing back the boundary
> between inside and outside so as to incorporate in himself
> a patterned social world. At the same time he thwarts his
> faculty for receiving immediate, condensed messages
> given obliquely along non-verbal channels.[35]

At the moment it seems to offer most, the luciferic drive collapses in self-defeat, in inner nothingness. And the implication is that the cultural and philosophical direction empowered by it is based on 'ignorance' of the meaning and power of ritual, and of unconscious symbols. Evidently we need to reaffirm something beyond the individual if moral value is to have real force once again in society.

With much of this Steiner may concur. Indeed the analysis

strikingly overlaps with his ideas and methodology. But he has a further dimension to add, and he most profoundly and illuminatingly disagrees with the conclusion.

The further dimension is an awareness of the other pole, or 'ahrimanic' aspect in addition to the luciferic. For if the liberal and personal ethic shows profound ignorance of the power of symbolic ritual, Steiner will counter that it is also quite illusory to suppose that those 'floodgates' of personal development can ever be closed once they have opened. Any attempt to 'go back' to a settled symbolic world, in other worlds, is just as unrealistic as to suppose that charity will flow inevitably into the categories of well-meaning personal-ethical talk. That is why all efforts to reassert and to exalt communal values over the individual, as happened notably in the totalitarian regimes of communism, become ahrimanic: they lose moral integrity, enforcing outer obedience in an endlessly deferred promise of renewal. The attempt in the last century to shape societies without the renewing spirit of individuals, based solely on the collective, showed simply once more that it does not work. Now, the point is not that the Catholicism, for example, of the supposed 'bog Irish' cannot teach liberal Western intellectualism something valid about the real moral powers ruling in society as Mary Douglas says. Certainly it is not ahrimanic in its original form; quite the reverse, it has strong and largely unconscious life. But it is a mistake to imagine that the spiritual vitality found there could be recaptured by any sort of turn-around, or retreat from the personal awakening that has taken place. The forms which work unconsciously and effectively cannot be validly imposed on self-conscious cultural life without themselves becoming hollow. In the place of inner unconscious power comes social pressure, external constraint, and the spiritually real moral force is lost. There is nothing for it but to take the individual awakening a stage further, rather a stage back. And that is what Steiner's 'ethical individualism' actually does, giving to the individual to perceive moral significances concretely once again.

It is typical of Steiner's originality and philosophical insight that by making us face up to the reality of 'no way back,' he does not leave us simply imprisoned by our situation as might first appear. It is precisely this recognition, rather, which makes us realize that we cannot stay where Mary Douglas' analysis would leave us, longing 'for an ideal, impossible harmony.' Steiner gives full recognition to the horror of taboo at the thought of reversion to atavistic forms: it is the horror of our own denial of the spirit that is still working within us, changed in form though we be. At the same time, however, we cannot but realize that the abstract personal consciousness traps us. All-important is that knowledge of our own involvement in how we got here. In Steiner's ethics, understanding the balance of the two inner forces of luciferic and ahrimanic when we become aware of them, actually frees us to move on, and thereby out of our historical own development we are able to envisage a transformed society into which we will be able to reintegrate on new terms:

> It must go further still; that soul must become its own betrayer, its own deliverer, the one activity, the mirror turn lamp.

But neither the model of Western liberalism where the individual is cut loose to think and feel, but community disintegrates or becomes abstract, nor communistic subordination of the individual spirit can furnish an adequate framework for full understanding of the individual as a power of renewal and social change. We need to identify with our history. Steiner's evolutionary and inwardly dynamic approach to ethics and the individual as part of an evolutionary process, combining 'anthropological' scope with spiritual insight, is still one of the boldest visions we have of the way in which 'the good' can be a real force once more in human relations, both among ourselves and with the world around us.

Ultimate Questions

Why should we be good? In the end only because our own human existence consists in going forward to new insights, resolving situations in which we stand in inner relationship in a way that involves more than the outer necessities that would otherwise determine events. Steiner took over an Eastern term,

which signifies the connection between a person and his or her ongoing spiritual existence — their transformation through more than one life of earth. It is will be evident that quite alien to Steiner's concept, however, is any hint of *karma* as punishment for deeds in a past life.[36] To think in terms of one's *karma* is just the opposite of feeling that one's present sufferings are 'inflicted' because of guilty actions in previous lives which have to be expiated now. To think in terms of *karma*, from Steiner's point of view, at least, is to affirm the present life as a free creation stemming from one's own deepest self. Certainly that means acknowledging what the past presents — for past lives, he tells us, are included in the survey open to our spiritual self. But we take our sufferings upon ourselves as a part of our transformation, they are not imposed: they are part of the very process whereby we can then free ourselves from the past and realize what we are striving to become. *Karma* no longer works as an unconscious, compelling power as in Eastern thought, but is given the character of conscious freedom when we reach the stage of deeper insight into the self, into what we are. Until we reach that point, of course, we are inevitably working somewhat in the dark.

But this certainly does not mean that, after all, we are subject to external moral judgments from some all-powerful cosmic authority. Rather, *karma* may be understood most profoundly as the concept which spans the gulf between our moral awareness, which the moralizers make so important, and what we actually are and do, which for Steiner is what carries real moral weight. *Karma* is the full meaning of our identifying with history.

I have repeatedly mentioned the fact that Steiner says very little about good intentions. In a system of ethics which appeals to 'rational,' formalistic standards, it counts for much if not everything that an action is directed by an intent to fulfil some good principle — even when the results are in fact less than wholly successful, or even downright disastrous! At least it was not our responsibility; and we tried. Steiner's moral realism, however, attaches moral value to what we actually know, and do, not to the intentions, neutral, benevolent or otherwise which express our limited view of the situation. Freedom demands the achievement of real insight. Hence we risk ourselves in every moral action, since we have not the artificial certainty of fixed and unchanging standards; we carry in a much more direct way the responsibility for what we try to bring about as 'free spirits,' with little room to excuse ourselves. Another way of putting this is that morality is loving action: and we give up some part of ourselves for another. *Karma* in Steiner's Western formulation is essentially a matter of 'karmic relationships' — not, I think, a formulation found in the East.

Now after death, according to Steiner's anthroposophical account, we see again the events of our life on earth. This vision is the basis of our future destiny, our *karma*. Owing to the nature of spiritual experience, we see it from an un-earthly perspective, however, for we no longer see it from our own point of view. We do not experience what we wanted or intended to do, but the effect of our actions on those around us. Our spiritual part, after all, is what we give up of ourselves for others. Such is the spiritual reality, as he describes it, behind the popular reward-and-punishment theology which says that after death we are tormented by the consequences of our deeds and the wrongs we did to others. Steiner's account does not go into that ethical *cul-de-sac*. For the 'punishment' we receive is seen to amount to nothing more than this: we see the reality from the vantage-point of the spiritual world of what we have done. Then, in shaping a future life, we close that gap, which we could not always close on earth, between the deed we meant to do and what actually happened; that disparity works on us, on the spiritual plane, as our *karma*. 'This state of suffering,' explains Steiner, 'is the school for the destruction of the illusion in which a man is enveloped during physical life.'[37]

Steiner's spiritual descriptions can in no way be predicted from his philosophical writings, and the latter cannot for a moment 'prove' them one way or the other. Nor, conversely, can the knowledge of spiritual realities form the foundation of his philosophical doctrines or prop them up in any way. All we can say is that his philosophy enabled Steiner to comprehend the spiritual process of man's self-creation in the working out of his destiny in a genuinely moral way. What he describes is not a judgment passed upon us: it is the full understanding which was temporarily denied to us by the limitations of our self as it was at a particular stage on earth. It is the knowledge we are always striving for, however, because to act out of knowledge is to be free. The problem that Steiner's moral realism requires us to act beyond the sphere of the controllable (which ultimately is only our intentions and motives) is solved, not in argument, but in the real force of that disparity to lead us forward in striving for the future. It is the vision, painful yet liberating, which frees us to resume our self-creation and to affirm a future life. The process of the 'incarnation' of the ideal can go forward. Freedom becomes destiny.

CHAPTER 5

The Critique of Modernity

The truly apocalyptic view of the world is that things do not repeat themselves.

Wittgenstein

Myths and Modernity

I hope that we have seen in this book how much Steiner has to contribute, if we will allow him to do so, within many of the developments that have revolutionized our approach to knowledge itself in the century since his time. His insights seem obviously relevant to a morally responsible science that can no longer close its eyes to the fact that we are part of the world we know; his inwardly dynamic concept of freedom gives new meaning to the modern experience of self, one that is open to change but not crippled by uncertainty; his new form of ethical realism, combined with a radical individualism, gives us ways of facing up to a society where the power of the old value-symbols, which ordered life in a more collective way in times gone by, needs to be renewed in a changing and multiform culture such as ours. In formulating his ideas we have seen too how Steiner was already elaborating many of the concepts that have had such an important history in twentieth-century physical and social science, or in educational psychology: central 'phenomenological' ideas, 'structural' approaches to a range of new problems from biology to art, and a developmental understanding of human growth — in all these areas Steiner seems to have grasped the essential new perspective, and indeed already to have come upon many of the twentieth century's supposed discoveries from his own point of view. As a thinker who proposed a spiritual view of the world that is compatible with the scientific, critical consciousness of modern times, Rudolf Steiner may be important in the end, in fact, because he thereby challenges one of the most potent myths perpetuated by post-Enlightenment culture.

Readers of Steiner are sometimes tempted to believe that Steiner is the 'hidden genius' behind many modern ideas; but even if it were true, that is not at all Steiner's real significance.[1] The point is his difference, not his similarity; for Steiner arrived at all these eminently modern ways of thinking out of his own spiritual *Weltanschauung*, or 'attitude to the world.' And it is there that he challenges most profoundly the treasured modern myth, which argues to the effect that the great shift to modern attitudes and modes of thought could only have been achieved by an iconoclastic act, a bitter break with the past and with its 'spiritual' orientation, in order to give us power in the sphere of the practical and material resources all around us.

The eighteenth-century Enlightenment thinkers —by their own account — had to dethrone medieval Theology from her place as queen of the sciences, had first had to debunk 'priest-craft' before freethinking became possible, to replace superstition and credulousness with 'critical' thought, the old unreal metaphysics with empiricism. Without John Locke, it is clear, there could not have been the American Constitution, or (more or less, therefore) modern democracy; and later, Darwinism had to liberate biology from the old teleological and 'providential' vision of a God-designed world which still dominated Newtonian science, so as to allow 'survival of the fittest' the full grandeur of its scope as an explanation of the living world including ourselves. Modernity, so the myth goes, only emerges after a drastic watershed, a critical reversal that replaces acceptance with scrutiny.

The myth, or plexus of myths, is important because it gives to contemporary attitudes their characteristic conviction of incomparability. Our culture is considered to be simply not measurable in terms of the past. We stand utterly distinctive, alone.[2]

Musing on the question of why Steiner's thought is so widely rejected, Owen Barfield doubted whether the use of particular terms (such as the dread 'occult') could really have undermined its credibility among apparently intelligent people.[3] Such matters are especially vulnerable to the influence of myths, and we may suspect that Steiner's thought has really suffered precisely because it refuses to go along with this prevailing mythology of the uniquely modern, based on the reductive and materialistic. It urges instead that modernity, critical thinking and self-consciousness are most fully realized in terms of a spiritual philosophy — whereas the myth presupposes that spiritual thinking must in some way conceal an allegiance to those old, unreconstructed attitudes of the past. When Rudolf Steiner arrives at modern ways of thinking about child-development, or form and structure, out of a spiritual perspective, therefore, he is actually attacking one of the cornerstones of contemporary culture. In insisting on the validity of those spiritual approaches which he makes so fruitful in so many domains, Rudolf Steiner mounts what is in effect a new critique: a critique of 'modernity' itself.[4]

When he develops Goethe's ideas in biology, on plant 'metamorphosis,' for instance, into a far-reaching spiritual-developmental approach to living things, he slips through the net of the prevailing categories of thought. Look at the way that in his discussion of 'Romantic religion' Stephen Prickett rather casually pigeon-holes Rudolf Steiner as a 'great nineteenth-century vitalist' — whereas that is exactly what he was not.[5] Vitalism is the idea that 'life' is a special kind of force, conceived as analogous in some way to physical forces. Living things are supposed to be distinguished by the presence of a 'life-force,' and therefore have to be explained in terms quite distinct from those used for inorganic things. But Steiner repeatedly stresses that his conception is quite different from that of the nineteenth-century vitalists. Indeed, he expressly rules out any kind of quasi-physical status for a 'life-principle,' pointing out that the condition of the body immediately after death cannot be distinguished in this way from its previous state by the absence of any such quasi-material factor.[6] And on a deeper level, his persistent criticism of Bergson and the neo-vitalists shows that he realized the philosophical problem behind all vitalist thinking. If one once adopts the approach that completely different principles of explanation operate in different domains, there is fundamentally no rational explanation of anything at all. One might then basically mark out any area of study and insist that things there have to be explained in a special way that does not apply elsewhere. Alice can have as many wonderlands as she pleases. That is why Steiner preferred and threw himself so consistently instead behind the 'monism,' the unified explanation of the world, that was being demanded by the materialistic scientists such as Ernst Haeckel, alien and rather narrow-minded though their approach now appears to us to be.[7]

Steiner 'jumps' unfailingly in the modern direction. Spirit cannot be conceived in a mixed-up way as a special sort of agent that intervenes in material processes and makes things work completely differently. And therefore it looks as though he must go down the 'modern' road: life must finally be reducible to material processes, since it has to be explained in the same terms as the rest of the universe. There is the inescapable watershed. But not at all. Steiner jumps in the modern direction, but he takes the opposite view to the materialists about the relevance of spiritual thinking. For one can just as coherently draw the conclusion that a unified explanation of the world must include the spiritual dimension of living things — and therefore include it as part of its approach to explaining so-called material phenomena too. Certainly spirit cannot be brought in as an adventitious special agent, operating arbitrarily in one area of understanding, but few thinkers have had the courage to follow Steiner's route, which argues that therefore we must rethink our unified science, of material things too, so as to be able to include a convincing science of life. Unless we do so, our science actually fails the 'monistic' test. It must be replaced by an approach which includes a spiritual science, not to supplement the successes of natural science but to restore its coherence. It is actually implied by the successes of natural science that they must be part of an explanation for all the universe. Yet in the twenty-first century, we know all too well the inheritance of a science which has produced many wonders, but at the expense of fragmenting and making incoherent our existence. Indeed ultimately, science must be open to include ourselves as knowers, and can therefore never be compartmentalized. Steiner insists as an element in all real knowledge upon the spiritual dimension or anthroposophy, starting methodologically with the knower, which he conceives on a convergent course with the development of natural science. Its point is to put the universe together again, instead of rending it apart from our human experience of life as tacitly happens whenever we try to live, — as opposed to abstractly conceive — the typically modern, reductive version of science.[8]

One of Steiner's earliest books was his *Mysticism at the Dawn of the Modern Age*. Surprisingly, perhaps, we find that it contains a good deal of material about the history of science, and the kind of consciousness that developed to make it possible. Though concerned with the inner life, it covers pioneer scientific figures such as Paracelsus and Giordano Bruno. Steiner shows how the deepening of spiritual self-exploration, usually called mysticism, was really part-and-parcel of the intellectual evolution that gave Renaissance humanity the beginnings of its mastery over the empirical world.[9] His contemporaries, on the other hand, he regarded as failing to learn the lesson of the history of ideas — or better, perhaps, the evolution of consciousness.

They were falling for the influential myth of modernity, the myth of the watershed, according to which 'mysticism' belongs to the old, pre-modern world; 'science' to the modern world. In reality spiritual development and natural-scientific development had been closely intertwined. Steiner's kind of science, arguing for the inclusion of the spiritual evolution of humanity that brought science about, was simply one which claimed to be true to the history of science itself. Materialism was a danger and a limitation, in his subtle but far-reaching idea, not because it denied the spirit in order to give man material power, but because it actually denied the basis on which science, even material science, really grew up and the spirituality which was essential to knowledge as a living activity.[10] Characteristically, Steiner wanted to put knowledge back into history. He denied the mythology of watershed, of the unprecedentedly modern, on the grounds that it took away so much that really belongs to modernity by right and is inextricably bound up with its emergence. We have become unfree in our science partly, at least, because of the influential but extraneous myth which it has helped to foster, and which until very recently has robbed science of a proper understanding of its own history.

Names like that of Frances Yates, who have reillumined pioneers such as Giordano Bruno out of Hermetic and magical sources, have since become well-known for their rediscovery of the 'hidden' side of emergent science, and similar dimensions have been found to the work of giants of the scientific establishment such as Newton and Boyle.[11] In the history of ideas one must certainly recognize Steiner for an earlier but not less uncompromising advocate of their line. Not only does he ask us to re-evaluate the past role of science, but also to restore to it its meaning for our own inner growth. They have shown how the Enlightenment followed on the heels of a more 'radical Enlightenment' with a potent spiritual agenda and a detailed history.

And yet, even nowadays, the influence of the modernist myth remains a potent one among those who write our cultural history: one need only think of the urbane and learned intellectual historian Peter Gay. No one can fail to admire his scholarly acumen and poise as he learnedly traces the background of the rationalistic eighteenth-century Enlightenment, the world of the French materialists, the *philosophes*. Perhaps it goes without saying that he is too knowledgeable to swallow the crude form of the myth, to the effect that modern science was a completely fresh start only possible when superstition and priestcraft had been swept away. Commenting instead on the spuriousness of that very claim, he says wryly: 'If there were a debtors' prison for intellectuals who failed to acknowledge their obligations, it would be filled with the natural philosophers of the scientific revolution.'[12]

His example (which he admits is but one of many) is Descartes' demand for what we would call psychology, or as he put it a theory of the passions. According to Descartes' own statement, all previous thought on the subject is so unsatisfactory 'that a total revolution is necessary' — and yet, Descartes' work on the subject is full of materials borrowed from ancient philosophy! The claim is admitted to be nothing but empty 'talk ... but it was obviously essential to the morale of the innovators of the age.'

What is still more remarkable yet, however, is that such a clear-headed chronicler of intellectual history can expose a similar situation time after time whilst oddly failing ever quite to disown the 'shabby talk.' He chooses instead to speak of a 'curious duality in the Enlightenment's historical verdicts' — their myth about themselves, in other words. Historically, it is a pack of lies. But the fact that he does not come out and say so roundly means that in the last analysis he too is not willing to abandon their morale-boosting self-delusion, preferring to have us believe that though 'the *philosophes* were ungenerous and prejudiced' they were still (amazingly) 'right in substance'![13]

History Again — *and* Logos

A perspective on the past which justifies and highlights the supposed special nature of the present is naturally found easy to accept. What is at stake here is not only our assessment of the symptoms of a dubious attitude to history which Rudolf Steiner was one of the first to challenge in a thoroughgoing way, but perhaps even the seriousness with which we take historical insight.

If we accept the myth and then look back, what we have is a view which selects out of the past what is important from the standpoint of the present-day. It is a view which finds continuous 'progress' in history, because it chooses those features of past thought which, as we now know, were taken further and are still with us in later guise. In these features of their thinking, it maintains, past thinkers were right and progressive. As for the other aspects of their thought, we need take no further interest but concentrate on those things of which they 'already' had correct knowledge. The other part thereby becomes a great blank *terra incognita* or, when it has to be acknowledged, is characterized as still riddled with confusion or as childish superstition. It is worth reflecting on the process, because it enables us to see how easily history can be distorted into a *fable convenue* (a phrase of Voltaire's which Steiner often quoted). It is all too easily made to tell us that history is meaningful where it points toward ourselves.

This distorted perspective itself has a history. For it was long used to support the 'Whig' party viewpoint, which was the forerunner of modern liberalism. Its pernicious role is nowadays increasingly recognized. Against this 'Whig' view of history,[14] Steiner posed one which required us to enter into the different consciousness of previous times, to appreciate the sometimes radically different way things were experienced then. We must learn to take the past on its own terms. And instead of supposing that history was aiming all the time toward our own attitudes and ideas, we have to see that our own consciousness is a transformation emerging from previous stances toward and the resulting relations with the world in the past.

Strangely enough, it was actually in reply to the up-to-date ideas of science, I think, that Steiner formulated his point most clearly. The great scientist needed to apply his principles to his own thought. 'Devout enthusiast for Haeckel's work as I am,' he wrote, 'it reflects badly upon a representative of "scientific" thinking ... when he will not give to prior forms of thought, which are the stages of development leading to his own truth, proper recognition for their evolutionary role, choosing rather to represent them as worn out, childish systems of belief.'[15] It was especially unfortunate, Steiner noted elsewhere, that Christian thinking was so vehemently rejected by the modern scientists. For on an unprejudiced examination, it was Christianity which had prepared the way for much of what we find in our scientific world-picture, as well as in religion. The idea of evolution itself has clear roots in Christianity (yet another irony to 'Genesis v. Geology').

For ancient thought, individualization had meant nothing but the fissure of primordial oneness, the world falling apart. Individual existence had no significance apart from the cosmic whole, but was merely fragmentation, just as in ancient society individuals had no real meaning apart from the structures of kinship and social role. And when the classical city-states lost their power under the great Empires of Greece and Rome, individuals did not automatically find the power to make their own coherent world: many felt existentially abandoned and lost, wandering through life or glad to shelter under the massive strength of imperial rule.[16] In late antique thought, the engendering of the individual is a disintegration, a catastrophic threat to the whole. Only in Christianity was the individual conceived as more than a fragment, more than a lost traveller. On the decision of many individuals through faith and commitment depended humanity's salvation, depended the gradual coming-into-existence of the community of salvation or Church, a transformed society based on the order of divine grace and love. We now know that applying this as a model, thinkers such as Augustine (or in other ways Origen) forged concepts of evolution, because with their Christian attitude to individuality they were capable of formulating a concept such as the emergence of significant differences out of an original state a principle for understanding the world.[17]

Quite apart from the misunderstanding which relegates Christianity to a pre-evolution, pre-enlightened stage of thought — quite wrongly — Steiner's point was that history told in the 'progress toward ourselves' sort of way makes us feel justified and artificially highlights those aspects of the past most congenial to our own society, but in the end seriously impoverishes our culture and estranges us from the real forces of the past which have shaped our own world. Looking back, we discover only what fits our predisposed set of assumptions. In reality, people of the past did not share our sense that certain features of their experience stuck out from the rest, that the 'rest' constituted a mass of superstitious and uncritical notions, or that they were enveloped by massive blind-spots of 'the unknown.' Steiner has been followed most productively by Owen Barfield in this sphere, who has helped to remedy the perspective by examining the way familiar words in historical situations previous to our own bore connotations, as we experience them, that cut across our presuppositions and usual boundaries of thought. They have to be understood in terms of the different consciousness, the different cognitive relationship which gives them their significance.

To take only one striking example, which shows how Barfield has been able to use linguistic techniques to carry forward Steiner's insights, it seems to most of us that people in the past were mixing up quite different things in their notion of 'spirit,' which in most languages has a root sense which includes wind or moving air, and also the notion of an invisible source of inner or volitional movement.[18] Modern analysts may adopt one of several attitudes, but they tend to share the idea that the overlap between the inner and outer meanings must be a confusion — animism, or crude self-projection. If the context is a religious one that is sympathetic toward the notion of spirit as an inner, volitional force, then the quasi-physical model of wind or gas will be dismissed as the vestige of a crude and primitive stage of thought. If the context is one that is more hostile toward an inner principle, on the other hand, it will be easy to debunk 'spirit' as no more than the illegitimate extension of a physical experience, a fantasy reducible to the workings of a confused mind.

But Barfield has shown precisely, through an historical investigation of its semantics, that neither inner nor outer meanings of the archaic usage can be assumed to have been originally separate in this way. Whichever one we choose to approve of now, the fact is that before a certain stage in the development of consciousness, the distinction itself could not be made. We have to realize that what are to us mental or physical attributes were previously experienced as part of a larger and different meaning, from which ours is descended but which was not yet carved out.[19] Steiner's anti-metaphysical idea of meaning, as a polarization which we effect within an original whole, thus shows its full potential specifically as an *historical* explanation of meaning of the kind Barfield traces.

At the opposite extreme, so-called historicist interpreters tend to stress the absence of inner connection to the past, which perplexingly survives only in its 'material traces.' In contrast to many versions of the 'new historicism' which has emerged in recent decades, however, the Steiner-Barfield model of historical difference does not leave us merely stupefied before the otherness of the past. In the eyes of many modern thinkers, awareness of history shows us only the left-over material traces or texts which for many theorists can never yield up their inwardness, but are externalized as ideologies of past ages, laid out for examination *ab extra*. 'Ideology' in this sense means primarily that the ideas are regarded in such a way that they no longer have any power to engage us in their own right, and challenge us in turn, but seem mere products to be accounted for — and indeed the presupposition that people and perspectives are no more than products of the circumstances of a given time is the underlying assumption of the theory. The argument thus really chases its own tail: it is the theorist's preconception which has selected the materials and the view of them as products is reflected in the result.[20] Steiner's approach to the matter is simply more interesting and, importantly, more developmental. The modern historicist's treatment is actually designed to neutralize history in a subtle way by making it merely external, alien, and so giving it no power over our own standpoint. It seems the essence of many of these accounts that we do not need to learn from the past, or open ourselves to it, but feel that we need only look back upon it with the power of superior judgment. Steiner's concern is to reimmerse our own perspective into the flux of history, and to experience it as a part of the changing relationship of consciousness, of which Barfield has traced the living record in language. History becomes a real power of change, which we must allow to infiltrate our own thinking. We have to acknowledge the disturbing otherness of the past; but we learn also that the different world we find there is the basis on which our own has developed, and is in a sense still there in the underlying web of presuppositions and meanings on which our particular stage of consciousness depends.[21] It is something of a paradox, perhaps, that by seeking to find our present anticipated when searching the past, the 'Whig' view alienates us from the reality of former ways of seeing. Acknowledging our own view as a successor to different ones in the past means that we can find an inner link to the past, and with proper sensitivity we can rediscover the 'self' of those times precisely because it is a part of the developmental history of our own.

Steiner thus as always demands a precarious and subtle kind of self-assertion: we certainly must not run away from the past by building defensive walls and intellectual ramparts to prove that we of the present are alone right; but we must have the confidence in our own unique position that is needed if we are to establish our extension of the past into the present moment, moving forward in 'freedom' in a way that is not determined for us by past relations but actively determines their meaning for us. History, in short, is our ability to learn from the past.

Seeing what the past means as the basis for our own step forward, therefore, is dependent on seeing that the past was genuinely different. If we mix up the two, we will find that, because

one cannot really assimilate the past to our present, we tie ourselves to the past, we are unfree. Perhaps one might say that historical knowledge requires us to go beyond interpreting the
world we experience: it becomes a drama in which we must also
speak and play a part:

> But follow thou, and from spectator turn
> Actor or victim

For to Steiner, that existential moment of stepping free from the
past is also, as we have seen, the essence of moral perception
(intuition). Having rejected the spurious version of modern
'uniqueness' mentioned earlier, we rediscover it in its true significance here. By entering into history we must indeed gain the
strength to act uniquely, creating a new pattern of relationships,
determined out of our spiritual being. All the existing patterns
we have grasped or understood are changed by our ability to
add new elements, and so change their meaning, at least in part.
This is where something enters in that can only be understood
spiritually, not materially.

Spiritual life is thus above all shown as historical existence.
And if we must acknowledge the burden and anxiety of facing
life as a unique possibility, as an ego, as history, for Steiner it is
always outweighed by the recognition of our identity as spiritual beings, which is precisely such openness to advance, to the
bringing about of creative change. But such recognition apparently involves a challenge to the notion of structured and self-
coherent knowledge.[22] How can the assertion of historical
uniqueness accord with the basic need to make patterns, which
are inevitably based on the recurring and the similar? We seem
to have come to the verge of a 'showdown' between fundamental opposites, between cosmos and history.

Once again Steiner has some highly original suggestions as to
how we might heal the tensions that in our official culture are all
too often left to smoulder unresolved.

'History is bunk' — at least, this well-known expression is the
form in which Henry Ford's words are generally quoted.
Lacking in subtler nuances though the comment may be, it is
oddly penetrating and encapsulates, effectively enough, the sci-

entist's mistrust and almost instinctive hostility toward the concept of historical significance.[23] How can it be of any real importance whether something occurs a little earlier or a little later? Surely the only true meaning we can find in things resides in patterns that reveal the intrinsic, timeless 'laws' of nature?

The social sciences (as the claim implicit in the very term already indicates) similarly try to demonstrate the working of essentially a-historical rational principles. T.E. Hulme, one of the most influential pioneers of modern cultural history, expressed his distaste for the whole notion of applying evolution, for example, to society and the arts. That is no doubt why he was particularly dedicated to opposing Romantic literature and art in favour of the classical, with its 'timeless' aspiration: Romanticism is centrally concerned with change and transformation.[24] No doubt too that is why Romanticism has been surfacing insistently in our argument, and Owen Barfield is certainly right to link Steiner's philosophy profoundly with the essence of the Romantic movement in European thought and history. According to Barfield, Romanticism itself failed — or failed at least in the achievement of its high goals — primarily because it did not have a sufficiently profound grasp of history, and he calls Rudolf Steiner's work in this respect a 'Romanticism come of age.'[25] That is because Steiner is still one of the few thinkers to take seriously the historical dimension of knowledge, and its deeper implications for the kind of world we know.

If all knowledge has moral value, that can only be because it too is essentially historical. We cannot give knowledge moral value without accepting our own historicity, and in that cognitive sense carrying the existential burden of our uniqueness.

The seminal expression of this is already to be found in Steiner's early *Outlines of a Goethean Theory of Knowledge*, in a short and stimulating chapter on 'history' as one important mode of the cultural or spiritual sciences, — in effect, as the science of freedom. It is a brilliant piece that is still, I think, somewhat overlooked.[26] It is significant that it takes its point of departure from the underlying moral issue — from Lessing's famous brilliant flash of insight into the nature of moral action, *'Niemand muss müssen'*: literally 'no one must "must".' Steiner's discussion however takes off from the less-quoted further comment of Lessing, that 'He who has insight also wills.' Steiner concludes: 'There is no impulse, therefore, for our action,' speaking from the perspective that is also the starting-point for history, 'except our own insight':

> A free human being acts according to insight, without the intervention of any sort of compulsion, in accordance with self-given commands ... The departure-point for human action is only to be found in man himself.
>
> For this reason, in history too, the subject of which is human beings, we must not speak of influences from outside upon man's conduct — of ideas belonging to a particular time, etc. And least of all must we speak of a 'plan' constituting the basis of history. History is nothing except the unfolding of human action ... In the same way it seems fallacious from our point of view when the effort is made (as Herder does in his *Ideas for a Philosophy of the History of Humanity*) to set historical events in due order like facts of nature, according to the succession of cause and effect. The 'laws' of history are of a far higher kind. In physics, one fact is determined by another in such a way that a law stands over the phenomenon. A historical fact, however, as something ideal, is determined by the ideal. One can speak of cause and effect only when one depends completely on the external. Who would believe that it is in accordance with the facts to speak of Luther as the cause of the Reformation? History is the science of ideas ... Every step beyond that is unhistorical.[27]

Several things about the passage may seem surprising. In the first place many people may be aware of Steiner's emphasis on the rhythms of cultural evolution through the unfolding of certain aspects of human development, which necessarily take a period of some centuries to reach their full expression. He quite rightly saw that philosophy was in no way exempt, and that a thinker could only take up and develop ideas in the form they were presented in his time.[28]

It is impossible to consider a philosopher simply as exerting an influence on his time. He is much rather an expression, or revealing figure of his age. What constitutes the unconscious soul-content of the great mass of mankind ... is advanced by the philosopher in his ideas.[29]

But that is not history — any more than the nappies of baby-hood, the trials of learning to speak and write, adolescent emo-tions or even typical events that everyone is likely to experience make up a personal history — such that we would expect them to figure in a biography, for instance. Moreover we can take this further. Just as we can look at any baby and make a plausible estimation that he or she will go through these infantile upheavals, so even such things as that by twenty-five he/she will be married and have two children (in a Western society), that by forty-five he/she will have peaked in career-achieve-ment, that he/she will be slowing down and overweight by fifty-five (given some statistics to work from we might even be very specific here), etc. etc. And all these things may well be true. Further: even the way that we think about things also has its developmental basis, so that this too may be predictable, as when educational psychologists point out that we start to use a particular sort of concept at a definite developmental age.

But the history or biography of the person will only emerge when we know also what they meant specifically to that indi-vidual, who by confronting and assessing them in a free way will also have been able to redirect life away from the standard pattern, to a greater or lesser extent. The same is true on the large scale. Much may unfold in a culture in a predictable man-ner. A large-scale configuration like this is comparable, Rudolf Steiner suggests, to a developmental stage in the evolution of humanity. For Steiner, however, scientists are misguided in try-ing to reduce everything in human development to patterns that can be predicted. Methodologically they are thereby missing the possibility of the specific dimension that for him is truly history. This occurs, not when 'cultural impulses' work themselves out, but when an individual person is able to reinterpret the past configuration of events and so envisage a different future.[30] For we have seen that by really understanding the past, and not try-ing to make it like our own time, we are actually enabled to move freely forward and shape something new.

That is what he means in the present context, I take it, by 'ideal': the way a configuration of events is perceived by the individual agent is intrinsic to historical reality. Taking in his stride the point made by Collingwood's much-discussed dictum that 'All history is the history of ideas,' Steiner goes on to sug-gest a vision of history that grows out of the pattern of cultural evolution and is always fundamentally reinterpreting it. Individuals are rooted in their society, but his concept of history is a way of recognizing how individuals also outgrow it and become a factor in its transformation.[31] This is that 'becoming free' which Steiner as always wishes to treat, not as a meta-physical conundrum, but as an event that is actually happening in human evolution. Its concrete manifestation is the emergence of those 'free spirits,' or individuals, in history. In Steiner's approach, instead of trying to reduce them to a generalizable pattern of causes and effects, individuals are acknowledged as irreducible and unique. That is the very essence of history: that a situation is treated as having aspects simply not assimilable to any other.

The human pattern-finding or pattern-making urge, which in its most far-reaching forms underlies the scientific enterprise, is therefore for Steiner not ultimately capable of fulfilment. As Henry Ford feared, history is indeed a radical challenge to cos-mos. For it tells us that the world we experience can never be wholly assimilated, much as we would like to think so for our own sense of security, to the patterns that have emerged so far. Our world, if we are true to our experience of it, therefore, can-not ever be reduced to a thing, to something we can define and control. If there is any truth in history at all, it indicates that real-ity is ultimately personal. The ultimate conclusion to emerge from the human sciences, for Steiner in his philosophical expli-cation as it was more intuitively for Goethe, is therefore that the 'the rational world-order is to be conceived as a great immortal Individuality' which is the prototype of our way of giving meaning to the experiences which come to meet us, and which 'thereby makes itself master over the fortuitous.'[32]

Rudolf Steiner returned to this point in much later, in the lectures on what he called 'historical symptomatology.' We may readily understand this in terms of the foregoing account, to the extent that it means events have a different signification, are 'symptomatic' of the consciousness in different periods, as in the example he takes from the modern period of growing self-awareness which he terms the present 'Consciousness Soul' age. Particularly valuable philosophically, perhaps, are the passages where he tries to clarify the pathos and the potential of historical change.[33] What is involved here is pre-eminently a philosophy of history: that is to say, the way we need to think in order for the meaning of what we are studying to become clear. He puts it in a graphic manner. Especially in modern times, with the emergence of free spiritual individuals and so of ultimately different meanings to a situation, we become aware that historical problems, as he says in effect, are ones which have no solutions:

> You must feel how things have come to a head and end as insoluble problems ... And that too is a symptom! The naïve imagine that there is a solution to everything. Now an insoluble problem of this nature (insoluble not to the abstract intellect, but insoluble in reality), was created in 1870–71 between western, central and eastern Europe — the problem of Alsace. Of course, the pundits know how to solve it ... But those who are realists, who see more than one standpoint, who are aware that time is a real factor and that one cannot just bring about what lies in the bosom of the future — in short who stand with their feet on the ground — are aware that this is an insoluble problem ... This situation is an obvious symptom, like that of the Thirty Years' War which I mentioned yesterday in order to show you that in history it cannot be demonstrated that subsequent effects are the consequence of antecedent causes.[34] The consequences of the War were unrelated to the antecedent causes; there can be no question of cause and effect here. But what we have is a characteristic symptom ... Problems are raised which do not lead to a solution but to ever new conflicts and end in a blind alley. It is important to grasp this: these problems

> lead to total deadlock, so that people cannot agree
> amongst themselves; opinions must differ, e.g. because
> men inhabit different geographical regions of Europe ...
> And in the midst of all this we see the continual advance
> of the Consciousness Soul.[35]

It is because there are such problems that life cannot always be resolved into a pattern to be elucidated as 'cause and effect.' Rather there is lack of resolution: suffering, conflict and ultimately death.[36] These things are involved in the very existence of the emerging free spirit which could not, in any other way than in history, find expression for its uniqueness, its self or 'ego' in Steiner's anthroposophical terminology. We actually and actively take death into ourselves, so as to realize our freedom. If in order to find spiritual activity as *thinking* we must cross over nothingness, in order to find it as moral activity we must further enter into and contend with suffering and death.

In summary, then. For Rudolf Steiner, history is a model for the 'spiritual sciences,' in that it cannot be conceived from outside — as if we could trace its meaning in external relations of cause followed by effect. It has meaning only from inside, in accordance with the changing possibilities that depend upon people's stage of awareness. If we want to have inside knowledge of the world, therefore, of the kind demanded by the situation today in its political conflicts, its ecological demands and our own need to find knowledge answerable to our sense of 'becoming free' through self-awareness — it must be historical knowledge, with all the pain and conflict of change, of coming up against the insoluble in terms of our present situation, of things which cannot be understood by assimilation to the past. Any other way of conceiving our relation to the world will result in the loss of our spiritual activity as a morally perceptive agent in the process. The attempt to deny our historical destiny of freedom, e.g. to return to 'nature' as often popularly envisaged by those looking for a short-cut solution to our ecological plight, is in essence to deny our own future. However it is disguised, it is therefore fundamentally to retreat from the necessary burden of our uniqueness and the unique responsibilities which attend it. History is the model, indeed the foundation-approach for all the human or spiritual sciences, and increasingly so, one may observe, in Steiner's later anthroposophical work where he puts notably less emphasis on the analogies with natural-scientific procedures.[37]

Steiner's direction of thought is not unrelated, I should say, to the considerations which have led a number of challenging thinkers in recent years to question the 'scientific' attitude to psychological and cultural phenomena, and to propose more historical perspectives. To these approaches nevertheless Steiner would give his own characteristic, liberating twist. Obvious examples have recently included the 'histories' of gender, and even of madness.[38] Instead of trying to reduce these to their supposed causes (biological, pathological, etc.) and so define their meaning externally as if they were natural phenomena, it has become possible to see them as ways of trying to say something. As such they are historically variable, and the changes in what they have to say, their spiritual direction or intentionality are the essential: efforts to define gender by biological causes, or insanity against a supposed psychological norm only lead us away from their essence. The spiritual and historical approach on the other hand can liberate us to see the point of their specific behaviour. Instead of needing to protest against being 'trapped' in a gender role, we can explore with inner freedom why people needed to play particular roles, and how new versions of those roles can be fulfilling to us now. Instead of condemning the actual person as supposedly damaged or insane, we may be able to recognize the human spirit, that is yet speaking to us through 'disturbed' behaviour. The basis on which we are able to do so derives its force from history: in the phenomenon before our gaze there is nothing to suggest the deeper truth unless we are prepared to think in terms of a 'history' belonging to the spirit that is speaking to us through the phenomena. Only the acknowledgment of such an extension beyond what we actually observe, of a further history past or future belonging to the person, can open the door to such recognition. Steiner no doubt startled some of his lecture-audiences when he chose to add to these examples of things which reveal their secrets only in historical perspective such matters as sleep, and even death.[39]

It is actually one of the basic distinctive features of our modern society that it discounts more or less entirely the side of life that belongs to sleep. In previous cultures, which did not do so, sleep of course meant something entirely different. Sociologists may think they are stating the obvious when they assert that its character as shared reality 'sharply differentiates everyday life from other realities of which I am conscious. I am alone in the world of my dreams ...'[40] But many cultures have experienced in sleep the presence of the ancestors, spirits or the gods. Hence they did not draw the 'sharp' differentiation line we think is there. Can we meaningfully say that the line of differentiation was always there, and it was only that ancient and other cultures failed to notice it? Is sleep biologically defined and so always the same — or has sleep really been different to different times?

Or to take the latter instance: if we think of the moment of death of an individual, we find that this can, as the recurring legal problems and debaters of medical ethics show, actually be fixed in physical or biological terms only by somewhat arbitrary proceedings. Physically, as Steiner noted, there is no specific change of state that distinguishes the body immediately before or after death. Here too it seems much better to explore the suggestion that death is not so much a 'phenomenon' that requires recognition, but takes on its rich range of meaning (conceived historically in so many diverse ways by different cultures) from the changing conditions of consciousness. For Steiner, death actually was something different for different cultural epochs. It may indeed have been from Steiner that one of Yeats' poems took its fine thought that 'We have created death.' That is not to say that anyone can pretend death does not exist. But it arises as we have seen from the very conditions of a free consciousness that it must take into itself death-forces, the ahrimanic — and overcome them, by spiritual activity, from within. In all of these cases it becomes a matter of being able to recognize the spiritual, and the potential for spiritual activity, which is inherent within what appears to the culture-bound and time-bound as externally 'given.'[41]

Yet it may appear on reflection as though Steiner is walking on a razor's edge once more — not so much because he is extending the ideas so much further (though he certainly does so) as because he is rather in danger of proving too much here.

The kind of thinking which initially seems to be wholly inside the reality it describes, and so in touch directly with its spiritual dimension, has to many modern thinkers seemed to fall out of touch with reality altogether. If there is no definable 'phenomenon,' the historically changing perspectives seem merely to become baseless constructs — the endlessly shifting tapestries spun by human activity with no foundation. History becomes for most moderns therefore a desolating relativism. Its meanings are merely imposed upon the world, and in themselves are historically diverse and unrelated. If we lose hold of any last trace of the unchanging, 'objective' bedrock underlying changing human relationships, it seems that we are left only with subjective, diverse efforts to gain a grip on the ungraspable. The way to a discovery of deeper sources of spiritual activity that are integrated into the world we experience just runs into the sand. But it is here that Steiner takes his greatest and boldest leap, and precipitates the biggest of his reversals of conventional philosophical assumptions. For it is here that he appeals instead to his concept of Logos.[42]

History in the radical sense we have characterized must bring such a collapse — if we are using any model of knowledge that assumes meaning to be something imposed on the world by ourselves, *ab extra*. Steiner's view of knowledge, contrariwise, by insisting that the knower is all along part of the world that is known, suggests that meaningfulness is inherent in the known. Rather than being a construct imposed upon the given, it is brought to consciousness by that polarization of an initial wholeness which enables us to find ourselves as knowers. History, as the way we shape and define our own conscious self over against the world — becoming a unique though changing vantage-point of awareness, becoming moral — for Steiner must therefore still be an unfolding of what is inherent in the meaningful world, that cosmic wholeness of meaning: the Logos. As a matter of fact, no other approach can ultimately satisfy the criteria of radical history as he characterized it, in the sense of something based on the unique meaning of persons and events. For by any of the other current models such an historically specific construing of the meaning of things can only be a relativistic skein of subjective wishful thinking spun over cosmically meaningless events. Now in one way, now in another, it would then appear that people throughout history had tried to make the world meaningful. But the very need which we have emphasised, to recognize the essential differences between the consciousness of one historical period and another, dooms all these efforts to contradict each other as an account of the way the world is (unless of course we were to contemplate such dead-end solutions as to be willing to backslide into idealist nonsense and say that the world only exists subjectively, and therefore actually was different for different minds, and so on and so on). Otherwise, by any of these standards history must indeed be bunk or, if it is humanly valid, undermine any real truth in human understandings of the world: the hall of mirrors once more. Steiner's solution is brilliant and radical. In his view, the different understandings reached by different minds in the course of history are not alien attempts to find meaning that is imposed upon things, but partial siftings from the infinitely rich meaning which is the fabric of the world. Indeed, through us it rises to new levels of conscious realization.

Steiner's view of history is thus the polar opposite of, say, Dilthey's, where the build-up of historical knowledge is conceived as gradually freeing us from the limitations of any one particular culture. God-like as this sounds, it is ultimately a picture of an alienated intelligentsia, able to find out a great deal but with little moral leverage in its own society. Knowledge abstracted from engagement with particular experiences and attitudes becomes luciferic, luring us away from the reality of our freedom. Steiner's reversal, renouncing unreal universality and urging us to affirm the kind of knowledge appropriate to our particular stage of consciousness, is a source of freedom, because it enables us to see our particular form of knowledge as nonetheless rooted in the intrinsic meaningfulness of life as a whole.

We saw earlier how even mathematical truths were viewed by Steiner in an anti-Platonic way, as emerging from our activity, our initially unconscious engagement with the environment. Reaching even deeper, to examine the origins of language and reason itself, Steiner turns to the Logos-concept in the context of cosmic evolution.

It appears outwardly, he remarks, that man as a thinking being, not only able to experience the world but — still more significantly — able to communicate the experience back to the surrounding world by means of words, comes as an end-product of evolution, or pinnacle of the natural order. As a result man may be represented as one who stands e.g. higher than the animals. But in the thought-world of the Gospel of John, with its Logos-doctrine, on the other hand, he finds it was taught that:

> what appears outwardly last, in the human being, existed in the world from primordial times. We may suppose that man in his present form did not exist in the earlier conditions of the earth; but in an imperfect, mute form he was there and gradually evolved into a being endowed with the Logos (or Word). This was possible through the fact that what appears within him as a creative principle was there from the very beginning in a higher reality. What struggled forth out of the soul was 'in the beginning' the divine creative principle.
>
> The Word which sounds forth from the soul (the Logos) was there in the beginning and so guided man's development that at last a being came into existence in whom it could reveal itself. What appears as the last in time and space was already there spiritually from the beginning.[43]

The implication is that meaning is not something we add to the world as-it-is, by virtue of our own more advanced faculties. It is the basis on which we ourselves have developed, which then comes to expression through us in our particular, partial way. Our nature as thinking beings presupposes a meaningful world. In terms of modern evolutionary thought, Steiner contends that the Logos-idea makes powerful sense. In pre-evolutionary thinking it had to be supposed that beings such as animals or men existed, and the fact that their environment suited them was due to some deliberate, purposive arrangement to provide them with what they need. Grass-eating creatures existed, and so their creator thoughtfully furnished a world for them in which there was grass. But this notion has given way to evolutionary understanding, whereby the fit between creature and environment is no longer grasped teleologically, but as an indication of their intertwined development. Likewise, Steiner proposes, the idea that the meaning we find in things emerges in us as thinking beings, and that this fits the world, as if there had been a special arrangement made for it to do so, can no longer be upheld. Instead, he argues, the world we know and the cognitive make-up which enables us to know it are alike the outcome of a shared prehistory. Steiner had tried to develop these ideas in an evolutionary, 'anthropic,' way already in his early *Anthroposophy. A Fragment.* The cognitive structures which we supposedly impose on our experience, he argues, are in reality our clues to understanding the forces of the world which actually shaped our evolution into knowing, thinking beings. He does not infer metaphysical realities that are beyond our actual knowing, but turns our attention back on indications of the ways we were actively transformed and made to adapt by the nature of what we know.[44] It was in this way, we recall, that he came to his active conception of the spirit, or supersensible forces which have shaped us.

Such an approach came together with some of his earliest epistemological conclusions, too, about the problematic nature of the 'given,' or raw experience at the root of our knowledge.[45] In his account of the 'polarizing' into knower and known he really points to the starting-point of a plenum of meaning, to which we ourselves belong, as the one half of the subsequent equation. His liberating reversal of conventional theories of knowledge now becomes complete. We define our standpoint, our identity as the knower, not by stamping ourselves on the world but by limiting its too-rich potential of meaning so as to find our own identity, our own finite existence in the world. We could never do so if we lived always in 'vital continuity' with that world:

> The manner in which the mind suffers its cognitive
> process to peter out into the abstractness of concepts is ...
> determined by the laws of development of man's own
> existence, which laws demand that, in the process of
> perception, he subdue his vital continuity with the outer
> world down to those abstract concepts that are the

foundation whereon his self-consciousness grows and increases.[46]

In place of the universal Logos we retain only those 'benumbed' abstractions' which have the characteristic of non-being, so that we can insert our own being into the world through morally significant deeds. Our thoughts are emptied of reality, not because of the spiritual nothingness of the world, as Nietzsche would have us believe, or because we are mere products of historical changing circumstances, but because only in that nothingness can we define our own identity.

It is in this way that Steiner arrives at his conviction of a spiritual fullness, the primal Logos which is charged with vital creative power. For what is contained in the content of ideation could not possibly create the world, as Idealism vainly sought to show. Rather it is by turning the question of the actual validity of thought back upon the knower that Steiner finds the deeper level of spiritual-creative power, based on an 'anthroposophical' understanding. In the philosophical search for the link between mere 'thoughts' and actuality, he says,

> anthroposophy demonstrates that, beside the relation to man ... which is there in the sensory field, there is another relation as well. This latter does not, in its immediate specificity, reach into the ordinary-level consciousness. But it does subsist in a *living* continuity between the human mind and the sensuously observed object. The vitality that subsists in the mind by virtue of this continuity is by the systematic understanding subdued, or benumbed, to a 'concept.' ... Reality furnishes man with a living concept. Of this living content he puts to death that part which invades his ordinary consciousness. He does so because he could not achieve self-consciousness as against the outer world if he were compelled to experience, in all its vital flux, his continuity *with* that world.[47]

Knowledge is our affair. Therefore it is through self-knowledge, and through responsibility for our act of achieving the conscious otherness of modern detachment, that we may also look to heal the spiritual wound. It is by finding the Logos again that we finally understand our own history and the identity we have gained. In other words, the rediscovery of meaning, of Logos, as Steiner indeed reiterates after the passage just quoted, is to be made not by the return to the forgotten paradise, but by following the road of self-consciousness through to its end. For its meaning is history itself, the inexhaustible particular realizations of the Logos..

The Rediscovery of Meaning

It is all starting to sound rather grand. The conception of meaning as the divine fullness we are scarcely able to bear, and which we need to fragment and benumb into abstractness if we are to find ourselves, consciously, in the partial realizations of history. But does this have more to be said for it than that it is a grand speculation? Certainly it offers a new vision of the relationship between history and cosmos, in which we find genuine certainty and truth, though partial, in knowledge that is part of the historical process. But is it anything real in that precise, historical way that Steiner himself demands? Can it connect in any significant way with the questions that are pressing upon us so urgently as we enter the third millennium?

In fact it does. We can possibly best appreciate this by means of another of our imaginary encounters where Steiner might contribute to crucial issues that have been raised in the development of our thought. A last one might be engineered, a trifle confusingly, perhaps, between Rudolf Steiner and George Steiner (no relation, at least in so far as I know). The latter, a highly regarded professor and cultural historian, has tried to deal with the current crisis of meaning in a profound and challenging manner in many of his books. He has come to some of the same insights which have led Barfield to the possibility of 'the rediscovery of meaning.'[48] I find it hard not to think he would be helped to take forward the consequences of his ideas, as may become clear through an imaginary encounter such as this, by Rudolf Steiner.

The situation from which Professor George Steiner starts, as he himself explains, must be understood by tracing to its roots the recent revolt against traditional philosophies of meaning. He looks at the way the revolt has come to a head in modern-day linguistic theories, post-structuralism, deconstruction, etc., and he does not underestimate the seismic nature of the upheaval that the underlying shift in the apprehension of meaning itself has brought to modern cultural life, or the threat to the humane, as he puts it, that it contains. And just as importantly, nor is he altogether convinced by the reasoning of its protagonists.

Looking at those linguistic foundations, we come in the end to the concept of 'difference.' For the idea of meaning which we derive from linguistic theories starts from exactly the other end to Rudolf Steiner's — from the benumbed, dead products of the process he describes. It is based on the observation that meaningful utterance is apparently based on a system of differences. Languages or systems of signs can be many and various, but within them we must be able to differentiate: at the word-level, sound patterns or written signs must indicate that this word is being said rather than that word; then, on a syntactic level, we must be able to mark that one possible mode of expression within the system is being actualized rather than another. The language as a whole is the range of differences that are available to the speaker. The meaning of any particular speech-act depends upon them.

Now once we look at the meaning of an utterance in terms of differences in this way, we are liable to be driven rapidly to a number of conclusions. One is the modern linguist's principle of the arbitrariness of the sign. It does not matter whether we make the difference that between *bow* and *wow* or *ding* and *dong*. It is the systematizing of them as different, as opposing signs, which we require for making language. Then they can figure as different words, indicators or determinatives. Secondly, we may conclude that the notion of a meaning residing in what we say is an illusory one. There can really be no such thing, since the meaningfulness of language consists solely in the fact of this possibility *rather than the other*, or strictly, in the difference between them. The more we try to isolate the meaning of our particular utterance or speech-act, the more the meaning will therefore evaporate. We will finally be left with the sense of confusion, meaninglessness, or in the technical terminology, aporia — being utterly at a loss. The theorists may go so far, on this basis, as to tell us that there really can be no meaning at all, and that all we thereby seek to describe are 'meaning-effects' which arise from the interactions of the system. Along with such a process of 'deconstruction' of apparent meaning, the subject, the speaker, is also inevitably called in question. The sense of someone speaking is part of the illusion. Language is essentially collective, and we cannot make it the bearer of personal meanings in the way the idea of a subject or an author tempts us to suppose; these ideas are themselves only created by the system, by the gaps between the components of the assembly. Meaning is dissipated into the spreading context of language, of signs (semiotics) generally, of communication, of society, of human and animal behaviour, and so on to infinity. And the fact that the limits of the system cannot be specified is further reason to think that definite individual meanings within it can only be illusory, in that the set-up of the language has apparently been arbitrarily fixed somewhere and regarded as complete.

But here George Steiner is right to object. 'The fact that there cannot be, in Coleridge's macaronic phrase, any *omnium gatherum* of the context that is the world, does not mean that intelligibility is either wholly arbitrary or self-erasing. Such deduction is nihilistic sophistry.'[49] In fact, the very powerful, sophisticated nature of the linguistic model enables us to put it to the test here. For if it fails, it seems hard to see how any similar model could succeed. And by requiring that meaning, if it is to be other than arbitrary of delusive, would require the spelling-out of the whole systematic context of the world, its sophistry is indeed revealed. For it depends upon a methodological sleight-of-hand: while setting out to explain meaning, it concludes by telling us that meanings are really only meaning-effects. But this is nothing other than the failure of the theory to explain what it claims to! And we should therefore conclude that the fundamentals of the theory are wrong. Meaning cannot depend on the kind of specifying it requires, which is obviously unachievable. Yet the theory has gone so far in elaborating the attempt to explain meaning in this fashion that it is hard to see how it could do more; therefore, suggests Professor Steiner, we should choose to look elsewhere for the answers, rather than try to hold on to it further, sophisticate it further and assume that sooner or later it will get things right. If meanings are not meaning-effects, neither are they the result of meaning-causes. We should either have been successful in explaining meaning, or we should shift our efforts radically in other directions.

Professor Steiner thus brings out the challenge which deconstruction poses to the culture which has produced it. It has brought us to a point of decision, where we can see clearly whether these machinations of modernity work — or not. If they do not, he concludes, there is nothing for it but

> a readiness to envisage, literally to look upon the face of,
> foundations beyond the empirical. We must ask of
> ourselves and of our culture whether a secular, in essence
> positivist, model of understanding and of the experience
> of meaningful form (the aesthetic) is tenable in the light
> or, if you will, in the dark of the nihilistic alternative.[50]

And he asks whether any of our accounts of meaning 'can be made answerable,' as he puts it, 'to the existential facts, if they do not imply, if they do not contain, a postulate of transcendence.' Meaning must contain, in other words, more than the means we use to express it. Rudolf Steiner was as ever acute here. The whole notion that if meaning is to exist it must be derived from the interaction of fixed-value units is roundly rejected:

> It is among the hardest things of all for the external
> approach of our modern culture to comprehend that the
> same words mean different things in different contexts.
> People's attitude in contemporary culture takes it for
> granted that particular words, in so far as they are
> physically definable entities, must always give rise to the
> same result. Here is a point at which modern minds are
> especially liable to be ensnared in Ahriman's net,
> preventing them from seeing that it is only when they
> are viewed in the particular context in which they stand
> that the deeper nature of words actually awakens to
> life.[51]

It is as though Steiner had already foreseen the illusions under-lying the deconstructionist misadventure. But we must, if we cannot accept the deconstructionist account, give one which begins from a greater meaning than can be literally specified, or than can be defined so as to function as a 'cause' of what we say. There is no longer anything left between nothingness or real meaning, real presence. Either language has no basis, and is inherently destructive of meaning, or we have to do with what another recent philosopher has called 'the Logos-structure of the world.' He too would emphasise that by understanding the nature of the processes involved in meaning we have the oppor-tunity, even as we gaze into the ahrimanic darkness, of making the greatest of the inner acts of freedom such as we have repeat-edly described.[52] The alternative is dark indeed. But the begin-nings of awareness are themselves a sign of hope. The cultural situation in which we find ourselves, according to George Steiner, has brought us to the verge of that very step, the bold reversal of perspective that leads back to Logos, which Rudolf Steiner was willing to make.

Appendix I

Legends of the Fall

In Steiner's philosophical account of ethics, we are guided by no external criteria but only by the deepest insight of which we are capable into the situation and its meaning in relation to our self. It naturally requires us therefore to be sure that we live out of our deepest self perception, which will further our inner growth and process of self-transformation — out of the selflessness, in short, which is paradoxically what distinguishes the self from any *thing*, or material continuity, for instance, in our existence. Any thing less than such selflessness, indeed, will be being untrue to the unique possibilities which are brought to the situation by our presence, and will stifle our own spiritual life as well as failing those others who are involved.

But in life as in thought it is possible to mistake idols for the true self — comfort, vanity, security, fame, power and so forth. In a certain way Steiner's ethics thus returns us to a hallowed moral theme, though one which is more familiar in religious tradition than in philosophy: the theme of temptation. The real threat to our ability to live out of our highest self is precisely the temptation to be side-tracked by the superficially attractive veneer of things which mirrors back our vanity, or by the wilful blindness to our true potential which covers over our fear and uncertainty before the challenge of making good. Steiner was as usual highly perceptive about the farther reach, as it were, of the traditional, 'mythical' accounts which spoke of humanity being tempted and undergoing a Fall. The attempt to justify our actions rationally, which had obsessed ethics especially since Kant, was actually less revealing of the forces which pressure us in the moral life than the legends of the Fall.

Nevertheless, he used them in his characteristic 'anthroposophical' way, not accepting them on their own terms but using them to explore in a free manner the inner dynamics of moral action. In accordance with his historical and evolutionary perspective on such matters, he requires us first of all to see within the traditional themes two quite different emphases — so that we must all along recognize changing circumstances and perpectives. One or other of the legends may have fulfilled a dominant role in the past, but now we need to be aware of multiple possibilities, and dangers. If we recognize the Lucifer-figure of pride and inner inflation from the biblical story as a morally real tempter, it cannot be in the attempt to escape from his challenges as did ancient humanity in submitting themselves in humble obedience to a fatherly God. Steiner sees the truth of the tale, that in acquiring an identity of our own we become subject to temptation. But he wants us to explore this as an inherent dimension of the human moral dilemma. We must not run away from the insight, but learn to comprehend the forces that are at work within ourselves. At the other pole, the myth of the ancient Zoroastrian demon of fixity and outer darkness called Ahriman seemed to him to contain the essence of the threat from without. The fact that we have engaged so strongly with the outer world in modern times actually makes this figure from ancient imagination all the more strikingly relevant. But we are not being asked to retreat from that engagement when Steiner talks of the threat of the Ahrimanic: we are affirming the dangers on the path of development which we need consciously to recognize so that we can go on. Both encounters arise inevitably from our meeting with the world. Absorbing the world we know in terms of our own self, and stepping out into the world at some risk to what we have made of ourself are features of all cognition. The moral dimension is at once obvious when we notice our own activity being involved, since either can become one-sided, a threat to the human. But without them no engagement with the world would be possible at all.

'Luciferic' is the more familiar term, recalling as it does the ancient legendary account of Lucifer, the 'Light-bringer' who was also the primal Tempter, that has remained definitive for much of western culture. Theological tradition for long con-

nected the so-called 'fall of man' with the story in the Bible
(Genesis, 3), according to which the first man and woman were
duped into accepting the Tempter's promise of knowledge:

You will be as gods, knowing good and evil!

But although 'their eyes were opened,' in gaining it they had
transgressed against the conditions set for them by their Maker,
and they lost the effortless, harmonious relationship to the
world which had characterized their existence in Paradise. Prior
to its moralizing interpretation by the Church, the myth has its
origins before Christianity, in the 'apocalyptic' and esoteric literature of Judaism such as the *Book of Enoch*. There the Tempter
is represented as one of the cosmic powers, a great angel,
though one who had already rebelled against God, and he
together with his powers betray to humanity secrets of knowledge which include much of what we would nowadays call scientific knowledge (mysteries of the workings of nature,
techniques for metal-working, dyeing, and so on). Elements of
this wider meaning of the myth persisted in the later legends of
Dr Faustus, in Rosicrucian and other esoteric teachings.

According to the implications of this myth, knowledge takes
place in a dialectic between aspiration and self-delusion. The
myth grasps brilliantly the way that knowledge is an assimilation to the self: all its protagonists from the original Lucifer
down to Dr Faustus are inflated by the sense of inner expansion
and power which their greater knowledge brings. Their fate,
though it may be moralized as divine punishment, is presented
as fundamentally the result of the ultimate emptiness of their
aspirations — the failure, in other words, of their knowledge to
give them the fulfilment they seek. The myth contains an imagination of paradisal fulfilment, but seems to imply that it is ultimately inherent in human nature that 'Paradise' is lost. Yet
especially in the older and in the more esoteric versions of the
myth, there is a real ambiguity in the aspiration itself despite the
dangers involved: it is by no means clear that Faustus was
intrinsically 'wrong' in his longing to know; or in the older literature that, for those who developed the spiritual strength to
receive them in the right way, the 'divine secrets' might not be

legitimately divulged to the few who were worthy. As a matter of fact the final hardening of the Church's moral interpretation only came in the sixteenth and seventeenth centuries as it was starting to be challenged by scientific 'natural knowledge.' All through the previous centuries, it had generally been felt that Christ had made it a 'fortunate fall' by coming to redeem humanity afterwards, and human knowledge too could be redeemed and brought into accord with religious truth. The luciferic drive was a dangerous but nevertheless an intrinsic aspect of the journey towards knowledge.

If the luciferic drive ultimately becomes a will to nothingness, or mystical inflation in which we lose the sense of self, the 'ahrimanic' in its ultimate extension threatens the self in its precarious balance too. For as well as empowering us in the recognizing the other, it evokes the terror of losing oneself in the unknown, of alienation. Steiner found a mythical and profoundly imagined exploration of this aspect of knowledge in the Mephistopheles of Goethe's all-embracing poem of modern life, *Faust*. Goethe's devil is only in a rather incidental way the traditional Tempter-figure (an aspect largely internalized in Faust himself), but dramatizes much more fully the ahrimanic features of Faust's cognitive search. Steiner sees an evolution here from the conventional standpoint of the Church. The moralizing restraints laid upon earlier human thought, taken together with the reassuring reference of all things back to God as Creator, not only limited man's luciferic drive to self-expansion: it also protected him from the full intensity of the sense of the other. In contrast, this must be faced by the relatively unprotected, solitary seeker after ultimate answers today.

Though it could gather many relevant insights from the traditional 'luciferic' myths, therefore, a spiritual philosophy for Steiner needed to recognize the much greater threat of the ahrimanic which arises out of the modern emphasis of knowledge, which is conceived less as shared belief and more as restless exploration, discovery, a challenge to each individual mind, bequeathing to us also many shadowy fears. Goethe was once again a pioneer — and Rudolf Steiner would clearly have liked to take his terminology from the great writer's work. But Goethe had actually not been clear enough about what he was doing,[1] and in the end Steiner reached back to the archaic original myth about the alien power, the darkness coeval with the divine light: the myth of Ahriman.

The myth is the foundation of the Zoroastrian religion, whose founder Zarathustra had lived in prehistoric times. Worship of the divine Lords or powers of Light was older still, but it is in Zarathustra's revelation that we find them for the first time placed in eternal combat with a co-eternal essence of Darkness. Ahriman is agonized or negative thought, associated with doubt (especially self-doubt) and denial — in general, the Lie. Wherever human hopes are met with crushing defeat by outer circumstance, or life is undermined by sickness and death, or wholeness is disintegrated in a family or a society, there the hand of Ahriman was felt. But human beings could choose to align themselves with the Wise Lord, the power of Light and life. Then they too became fighters in the universal struggle against death and denial. The religion of Zarathustra thus involved choice and commitment, dramatized in an exemplary way by the two spirits themselves who 'in the beginning' had chosen their respective paths. Adhering to the religion fostered a kind of self-awareness, therefore, and at the same time depended directly upon knowledge: knowledge of the tendencies which shaped the direction of the universe. It was as a myth about knowledge that it interested Rudolf Steiner.[2]

What the ahrimanic myth has to tell us about knowledge, he noticed, is interestingly different in its implications from the more familiar luciferic versions of the West. The Lucifer-story comes from a stage in the development of thought and society where human beings are tempted to rival the gods, i.e. by wanting to know for themselves, to make their own decisions, to have their own absolute identity. The myth of Ahriman comes from a much more archaic stage, when the self is much less developed, and feels corresponding more threatened by the external world. The myth does not deny the self — indeed encourages it to grow by decision-making. But the frightening 'otherness' of things when we set out on the path of knowing can be faced, it implies, only through solidarity and collective values/beliefs. The luciferic aspect was not at that stage isolated for analysis, but remains an undifferentiated part of the Light-side of the equation since we are encouraged to feel that knowledge is part of a god-like mission shared with the Wise Lord. In this way above all the myth suggests that even in the weak state of self-development we can grasp the forces at work in the world and, quite specifically, control it. Agriculture in particular emerges as the focus, suggesting a way that knowledge furthers the work of the Light and life, creates a stable society mastering and transforming its environment, fostering skill and commitment to consistent purpose in human life. It provides the basis for a far-reaching attitude to the material world and the potency of knowledge that was vastly influential on later thought. The luciferic myth of knowledge, in contrast, centred fundamentally on issues of authority and independence, of inner autonomy, and very little on the possibility of action.

It might seem odd that Steiner should reach back to so stark and primordial a myth, coming down from almost the beginnings of human society, to explain the threat as we leave traditional restraints behind. Yet he makes a case for its relevance precisely in the modern age when the authority-issues of a culture long dominated by the luciferic myth, originating in more complex and introverted societies, have to some extent been transcended. Certainly we should be worried about the dangers of self-assertion, now that the authority of common religious faith no longer regulates the social meaning of knowledge; we ourselves now need to control and balance the luciferic drive. On the other hand, we have repeatedly mentioned that Steiner does not recommend an attempted return to older moral restrictions which the dynamically conceived self has outgrown. In a way, therefore, we face once more, but now as separate individuals, the challenges of stepping out unsupported into the alien world, of knowing it and deciding its value, and acting upon it with meaningful intent. (It is eminently characteristic of evolutionary progression that earlier forms are not left behind, but reappear, modified and in altered contexts, at a higher stage.) But beyond everything else, Steiner does not intend us to return either to this or its alternative mythology uncritically — he is rather employing the old myths for their wider insights beyond the modern compartments of ideas, then combining them creatively on the basis of his independent philosophical-developmental approach. Or to put it another way: both his luciferic and ahrimanic myths must really be grasped in relation to an understanding of knowledge that balances assimilative and accommodative aspects; the role of the self which has emerged in modern philosophical thinking obviously cannot be found in any archaic myth.

The challenge of Ahriman in the modern world, in these terms, however, is vividly conveyed.

Kant and the Post-Kantians: Steiner's Relationship to German Idealism

Now the enthusiasm for abstract truth is an exceedingly fine thing, as long as the truth which is the object of the enthusiasm is so completely abstract as to be altogether out of the reach of the human faculties ... And therefore I have called my son Immanuel Kant Flosky.

Mr Flosky, in Thomas Love Peacock's
satirical novel Nightmare Abbey

One of the undoubted drawbacks to *The Philosophy of Freedom*, for a modern reader, is the excessive amount of attention it devotes to disentangling the ideas of the neo-Kantians. Steiner returns almost obsessively to their insidious implication that because we are trapped in the limitations of our own consciousness, there are many essential things about our world which we are intrinsically unable to know.

This circumstance has an obvious explanation in the historical ascendancy of Kantian thought at the turn of the nineteenth century — especially among scientists. It is perhaps rather surprising to us that scientists should be attracted to a philosophy which denies that we can ever know what things are 'in themselves'; but neo-Kantian ideas actually served very well to limit any challenge to empirical knowledge. By accepting the impossibility of positive metaphysical knowledge, they were thus able to claim that sensory knowledge was the only real knowledge possible (so long as we do not challenge the assumption that any 'higher knowledge' would be speculative and abstract in the traditional metaphysical manner).

From the Kantian point of view, it is not just that we do not, as a matter of fact, know what lies beyond the range of our sense-perception, and those postulated ideas (such as cause and effect, and so on) which we must employ to make sense of it in our minds: Kant had argued that in the nature of things we never can know.

Kant had attempted to break out of the dichotomy posed by empiricism and scepticism in the late eighteenth century. The appeal to what we can all see and touch by Locke had unleashed a sort of dialectical process working itself out in the thought of that time. Perception can only show us how things appear, how they are felt. But this meant that the question of what they actually were could not, by definition, be solved in those terms: hence it seemed that after all we must remain uncertain about the very matters the Enlightenment had hoped to have such concrete assurance. So that unless we were prepared to follow Berkeley and assert that there were only appearances (maintained in their consistency by direct act of God), the scepticism promulgated with such subtlety and inescapable logic by Hume must be our only recourse. Our ideas about things, beyond the way they appeared to us, were for him only habits of mind — postulates that we cannot ever ground in the nature of things 'out there'. Kant, however, saw a loophole in the logic of the situation, which he brilliantly exploited to turn the tables once more. He accepted that we make postulates about the way appearances are related, but that we can never know how these are grounded in the nature of 'things in themselves'. But, he contended, the postulates of our reason are such as we must make if we are to arrive at any coherent understanding of experience at all. We order our world in cause and effect, for example, because we need to think in that way; the result is perfectly valid, for us and for our experience. Only we cannot ever know whether there is a corresponding truth in the nature of things themselves. The certainty that attaches to our knowledge is founded upon the necessity of our own mental constitution, our ways of thought. And the price of attaining that certainty is the realization that we can never know anything beyond the range of the empirical experience to which those modes of thought apply. To project them as if they told us a truth beyond our own minds was inherently contradictory, because it was to forget the manner in which they apply to experience.

Strange as it may seem to us, Kant's views proved highly congenial to many, not only scientists. Kantianism set limits to human knowledge, but also invested the human situation with an aura of logical inevitability, as though the scientific attempt to organize our experience were the only kind of knowledge possible, on the one hand, and the kind that therefore had to be accepted by all rational beings, on the other. We trawl our world, according to Kant, with a sort of mental fishing-net of our reason, and we should not be surprised that we catch only those fish which are of a size to lodge in its meshes, on the one hand, or that those which are not slip through without any possibility of our catching them, on the other. As for smaller and larger fish — we shall never know.

Kant's whole theory depended on the logic, the internal necessity attaching to the ways of thought he called 'rational'. In the philosophy of the twentieth century the actual contingency of these 'rational' assumptions has, however, been repeatedly exposed. The idea that we cannot intelligently think in other ways than those endorsed by Newtonian scientists was challenged, not least by the overthrow of classical physics in the wake of Einstein's theory of relativity. And on a more philosophical level, it was a part of the later Wittgenstein's importance to show that Kantian demonstration of the limits to the application of a concept, leaving an area which we know really exists but about which we can only say that we know nothing, cannot have the sort of significance which Kant supposes. Such boundaries can only be established internally, and do not permit us to measure their success against a supposed unknown 'reality' that we can at the same time never know.[1]

Looking back, therefore, few will now disagree that the intellectual culture of Steiner's day was aptly diagnosed by him, in one of his earliest philosophical works, as 'suffering from an overdose of Kant.' Steiner constantly had to fight against the claims of Kantianism to have established a universal rationality that must determine all subsequent critical thought. The ever reiterated claims of the Kantians to have shown in principle whatever can be known even prodded him into moments of

uncharacteristic irritability — though maybe there is still something worth pursuing in his suggestion that we should look critically at the logical propositions in the *Critique of Pure Reason:*

> Reverse each and every one of these propositions and you
> will arrive at the truth. The same applies even more to his
> theory of space and time ...

Nevertheless, Steiner's strategy was not fundamentally one of
refuting Kant in order to arrive at an opposing philosophical
truth. He did something much more interesting and important.
For what he rather did was to apply to Kant his usual approach,
designed to free us within the framework of thought that we are
using, liberating us from the false supposition that it represents
an inescapable way of thinking imposed on us by the nature of
things, making us see it for what it is: one way in which we
engage with the world around us, cognitively useful it may well
be but for which we also carry responsibility.

It is obvious that in Kant's case the struggle must be particularly hard-fought. The whole thrust of Kant's brilliant thought is
directed to proving just what Steiner must show to be a mirage
— the inherent necessity, the finality of the Kantian solution. But
Steiner's technique is, as always, to get to the bottom of the
philosophical enterprise, and to uncover the assumptions, the
particular perspective, on which it is based. In this sense he is
not hostile to Kant or out to catch him in a failure of logical
deduction, but sets out to reveal the particular limited way in
which Kant is true — so as also to expose the way in which we
are liable to become fixated, stuck in a way of thinking instead
of responding creatively to different cognitive situations when
they arise. In reality, the illegitimate extension of ways of
thought to become a straightjacket on the thinker, beyond which
is only the intrinsically unknowable, rather serves to displace
the problems of knowledge instead of solving them. And
because he stakes everything on the claim to know the only
valid ways of thinking, the Kantian thinker is particularly prone
to such illusions.

Nowhere was this more apparent than in that section of the
'Transcendental Aesthetic' where he attempted to show the

nature and limitations of our sense-experience. Kant began by assessing critically the claim that we know the real world because it impinges on us through our senses, and that our ideas about the world are merely reflections of what we have thus experienced. He was quite right in his conclusion that this theory could not be true. The outcome of such a sensory bombardment could never be a clear and coherent knowledge of the world, but only what a subsequent thinker termed a 'buzzin', bloomin' confusion.' If we do nonetheless find a meaningful world-order in our experience, it must therefore be that an element of thought is introduced, necessarily, into our sensory perception. Any world that we know, he rightly concludes, is an interpreted world. The empiricist theory is therefore plainly wrong. But instead of abandoning the simplistic theory, Kant locks into the way of thinking and projects it into an extraordinary metaphysic: he does not reject the theory, but supposes that we actually *do* experience a sprawling confusion, a 'sensuous manifold' upon which our mind 'imposes' meaning in accordance with its necessary assumptions. Kant sees that we can know only an interpreted world, but he treats this insight in an oddly dualistic, metaphysical way. He takes this rich and various world to be only our 'mental picture,' our interpretation, which interposes between ourselves and the 'thing-in-itself.' Having seen that the theory cannot give an account of how we know the real world, he continues to accept the theory and then supposes that there must actually be a world of real things-in-themselves that we can never know.

The insight from which Kant began should have been a stimulus to change his way of thinking. Instead, Kant has carried over a way of thinking that can only trap us and delude us with the spectre of a logical 'necessity' in which we seem caught, unable to break out of the assumptions imposed by our own minds. But in fact, Rudolf Steiner points out, the account solves nothing at all. It shows that with his talk of 'things-in-themselves,' Kant has only apparently

> abandoned the naïve point of view while unconsciously retaining the type of thought which it necessitates ...

> Whoever thinks in this way is merely adding another
> world in his thoughts to the world already spread out
> before him. But with regard to this additional world, he
> ought strictly to begin his whole process of thought over
> again. For the unknown 'thing-in-itself' is conceived in
> exactly the same way ...[2]

What was urged upon us as metaphysical truth turns out to be
really an infinite regress.

Extending his argument to Kant's problems — and those of
his followers — about mental pictures, Steiner diagnoses the
underlying perspective to be that of detachment. Kant has
taken over from the 'naïve' model the notion that the observer
is ultimately other than the world he observes. That is why the
problem reappears again after being displaced into the imaginary realm of things-in-themselves. Yet the problem is that the
gap between onlooker and world must simultaneously be
bridged:

> In explaining mental pictures, philosophers have found
> the chief difficulty in the fact that we ourselves are not the
> things out there — and yet our mental pictures must have
> a form corresponding to the things.[3]

Instead of indulging in the Kantian metaphysics, Steiner insists
that we must reject the whole terms of the argument in order to
resolve the issue directly:

> On closer inspection it turns out that this problem does
> not really exist. Certainly we are not the things out there;
> but we do belong together with them in one and the
> same world ... For a relation to subsist between my
> organism and an object external to me, it is by no means
> necessary that something of the object should slip into
> me, or make an impression on my mind like a signet ring
> on wax. The question: 'How do I get information about
> that tree ten feet away from me?' is utterly misleading. It
> presupposes that the boundaries of my body are absolute
> barriers ...

Behind the barriers is a Kantian consciousness, and somehow, it seems, information filters into it. Steiner shows that the interpreter is part of the world he interprets, and the same 'world process produces equally the percept of the tree out there and the percept of my self in here' — so that the impossible questions which metaphysics tries to answer are really misguided. What we need is a relationship to things, not to reproduce them 'inside' us which only poses the question of relationship again and leads to the infinite regress. Detachment — separateness — is part of what defines any relationship. But whereas Kant sees only detachment, and so projects the separateness of the mind into an abyss of the 'unknowable,' Steiner sees detachment as the knower freeing himself, separating himself in order to enter freely once more into connection.

Kant's moral and ethical doctrines are also determined by his inability to resolve the problem of detachment. His concept of duty betrays the standpoint of the person with no particular involvement, who must therefore be told the requirements for interaction in a wholly abstract and impersonal form. The imperatives of moral duty therefore seem to exist in a rational void, and Kant is oddly blind to their obvious communal and social origins. To protect the helpless or the innocent becomes a 'duty' when we consider it in isolation from concern or sympathy with a particular person. Kant's moral stance, which insists upon remaining at this level, is thus that of a perpetual alien, inwardly separated from the world in which he acts, refusing to identify.

Instead of appreciating his own starting-point, however, the sage of Königsberg interprets all this in a resolutely metaphysical way: the vacuity around his moral imperatives he takes to signify their 'higher' origin as if from the mouth of God; their impersonal form, identical for all (outsiders, that is) suggests to him that the 'practical,' that is, ethical, reason acts out of realms inaccessible to the speculative mind. His basic conclusion is therefore that we should stand outside our own situation, and act as we deduce everyone must act in similar circumstances. Our question should always be: What if everyone were to ...? Ethics thereby becomes a subject of universal rationality, exactly analogous to the epistemological project which we have already examined, and just as crucially involved with the same far-fetched metaphysics. For Kant's theory of freedom to make any sense, we have to believe in his world of 'noumenal' reality since we can attribute freedom only to Man as a *noumenon*, not as a phenomenon — or in ordinary parlance, as he actually is. It is hard not to agree therefore with Lorenzo Ravagli, when he argues against the proposed criticism of Steiner that he has not given Kant his full value as a defender of freedom.[4] The great danger in Kantianism was once more precisely that Kant claimed to have solved an issue which in reality remained urgent and festering in modern culture.

Steiner was clear that once more Kant was carrying over into spiritual domains a way of thinking that was inappropriate and materialistic. 'People nowadays approach nature,' he comments, 'in the light of their educational training. Nature proceeds in accordance with natural laws ... Everything is seen from the standpoint of natural laws. So in addition to laws of nature there is "moral law". Kantians in particular feel that we are subject to the categorical imperative, making us an integral part of a moral world order.'[5] And yet, he adds, the actual result is rather anaemic. After all, if moral significance attaches to the generalized principle, to the 'What if everyone ...' element in the formula, the specific case, the moral act, is stripped of its ethical reality — which inheres rather in reflection, conscience, the awareness of good intentions or guilt. The attempt to give the moral order a necessity like that of natural law fails. 'If we are really honest, moral ideas are unrelated to the natural order, to what natural science regards as the fundamental realities. Moral ideas have become emasculated. They are strong enough to determine men's actions and the dictates of conscience — not strong enough, however, to give the impression that what one envisages as a moral idea today is a concrete, vital force in the world.'[6]

And so he reverses the main propositions of the *Critique of Practical Reason* too. Thus Steiner:

> Kant's principle of morality — Act so that the basis of your action may be valid for all men — is the exact opposite of mine. His principle means death to all

individual impulses of action. For me, the standard can
never be the way all men would act, but rather what, for
me, is to be done in each individual case.

But it is superficial to read Steiner as saying simply that Kant
was wrong. His point is always to comprehend what really lies
behind a philosopher's insights, and free us to make full use of
it. The Kantian ethical outsider is not wrong in suggesting that
there is a moral reality as well as a natural one: he has not found
the way, however, to actualize it by fully living it, as an individual, belonging to and identifying with a community. Steiner values the moral detachment which comes from questioning the
values of our particular society just as much; and he wants to
employ the analytic resources of the intellect just as stringently
in order to evaluate it critically. Here indeed is the source of the
individual's freedom. But Kant draws back from his own
insight. Rather than re-entering the community as a free agent,
Kant's ethical individual chooses rather to commune with a
hypothetical society of purely rational beings, like Swift's
Gulliver among the Houyhnhnms. As soon as we look away
from the metaphysical blind alley into which Kant has thus
turned, it is obvious that what we really have here is the abstraction of the compulsive power of society, which Kant has
detached from its historical and concrete reality. Since he must
remain in principle an outsider, Kant's individual necessarily
meets community only in the form of demands. Any recognition
of belonging would give him the opportunity, in addition, to
discover society as a domain in which to fulfil his own individuality: but it would 'unfreeze' the relationship, robbing it of the
features of inbuilt structure (the outsider as such, society as
demand) which Kant grandly elevates into logical features of
the moral world. It would cast morality loose into the flux of
history, and moral values would be perilously dependent upon
concrete and ungeneralizable acts. Steiner, following Nietzsche,
was willing to historicize morality; Kant held back. He refuses
at the last hurdle, and instead of recognizing an order in which
moral 'law' is as real, in its full independence, as the natural
order, tries actually to assimilate it to the generalizing scientific
cast of mind.

History, however, was unimpressed — or to put it another way, the Kantian individual who became free only on condition that he would act only in accord with pure rationality, i.e. the sum of previous experience, and do nothing to change things, did not conceal his true potential from the many thinkers who followed Kant. They experienced the master not as the austere setter of limits he aspired to be, but as intoxicating philosophical liberator. Kant's dialectic initially opened the way, not for a final definition of what we would never know, but for an awareness of intellectual process (Hegel), inner freedom and struggle (Fichte), and generally all those adventures of ideas which constitute the dazzling, impressive and sometimes bizarre domain of 'German Idealism.' In this we have historically the shift from the Enlightenment individual who reaches out to others only in so far as they are rational, not real, to the Romantic individualism which seeks to unite real individuals into a movement for social and spiritual change in its 'passion for reforming the world.'

Owen Barfield has repeatedly stressed Steiner's place in the deeper transformation of modern attitudes and values which flows from that Romantic upheaval. And Steiner himself was at pains to bring out the underlying impulse behind the thinkers who so unfaithfully followed Kant where he had told them not to go. Yet it is most remarkable of all that Steiner followed the spirit, and not the metaphysical form in which, liberated by Kant's transcendental dialectic, the German Idealists pursued their new philosophical mission. They still tried to give to freedom itself a quasi-logical and deductive form. Rather than discovering the thinker whose spiritual activity relates him to the world freely in thought, Hegel attributed the dynamic to an extraordinary mystical life-of-their-own in concepts as such.

It is Steiner's independence of that all-infecting metaphysics which is the sign of his modernity and his truly liberating philosophical power.[7] And it is that independence which enables him to adopt a sophisticated attitude to Kant. He at once condemns the late nineteenth-century attempt to reimpose the caveat of the 'limits of knowledge' which is the most metaphysical part of Kant's system, whilst recognizing that Kant had indeed done the 'groundwork' for the liberation of the thinking individual, giving the philosophical issues related to it their distinctive modern form. That is why the *Philosophy of Freedom* retains so much that is Kantian. Steiner's science of knowledge, we remember, is one 'without presuppositions': its task is not to put new presuppositions in place of the Kantian ones, but to achieve a clarification of knowledge. That involves the dissolution of the metaphysical illusion, the sense namely that this special (e.g. Kantian) formulation of knowledge has a direct relation to some kind of ultimate or absolute feature of mind or the world. Steiner seeks to show knowledge as a relationship based on freedom, and constituted by changing perspectives. He therefore attempts, not to refute the neo-Kantians but to make them aware of the real potential of human thinking, including their post-Kantian — indeed perhaps especially their post-Kantian — way of thinking, once its illusory metaphysical side is unlocked.

When Steiner described his conception of these changing perspectives (his version of the circle of the sciences) so liberating us from the fixed standpoint, he used the analogy of the solar system and the apparent movement of the sun against the stars, the 'mental signs of the zodiac' which are possible approaches to thought.[8] In the detail of its working-out, his circle of sciences is very un-Kantian. But clearly he sees his own liberated thinking, with its awareness of changing cognitive relationships, as the real fulfilment of that 'Copernican revolution in philosophy' which Kant optimistically claimed he had brought about. He put Man at the centre of philosophy, albeit in a flawed, 'metaphysical' way. Steiner's anthroposophy is a more thoroughgoing enactment of the 'anthropocentric' shift that is central to all distinctively modern thought.

A good understanding of what Steiner was doing was evinced by his pupil Carl Unger, in a number of philosophical essays but perhaps especially in 'Some Thoughts concerning the Philosophy of Contradiction.'[9]

Kant had argued that some illusions do not go away, even when we realize they are illusions. Because our reason makes certain assumptions so as to render experience intelligible, but does not give us access to things-in-themselves, it is possible for us to reason faultlessly and yet arrive at contradictory results. The apparent 'truths' of our reason are to be explained as 'transcendental,' according to Kant, i.e. we transcend experience in our reasoning, but are then unable to prove any truth; yet we need this reasoning which goes beyond what we experience in order to shape that experience, to interpret it into any sense at all. We may see through ordinary illusions and they dissolve. 'Transcendental illusion, on the contrary, does not cease to exist, even after it has been exposed, and its nothingness clearly perceived by means of transcendental criticism. Take, for example, the illusion in the proposition: The world must have a beginning in time ...' Under the heading of 'The Antinomies of Pure Reason', Kant demonstrates that this proposition is just as logically consistent as its exact opposite.

Kant remains committed to his usual metaphysical reading of this situation. There is nothing wrong with our reasoning in either case. And he remains convinced that there is a reality beyond our knowing and reasoning. The sign that it is inaccessible to us is precisely the way that when we try to go beyond things as they appear to us, our reason becomes intrinsically contradictory, mocks us with an illusion.

At this point Unger enters in. He takes it for granted that thought and especially art are permeated by this kind of view of life as contradictory (a slightly startling assumption, perhaps, to our own less dialectical age). And he takes up the philosophical cudgels in the cause of a spiritual science, or anthroposophy, not by rejecting that view but by entering into it with overt enthusiasm. It soon emerges, however, that his procedure is, though on the face of it highly Kantian, subtly disruptive of the Kantian metaphysic. All his main concepts reflect the Kantian assumptions; for example, the opposition of ego and non-ego as a primary distinction, corresponding to the notion that we start with an underived consciousness somehow having to get to know an alien world. The Kantian consciousness, Unger amply confirms, will experience life as contradictory. Nevertheless Kant is wrong, quite wrong to blame the nature of things: it is Kant who wants to hold on to a way of thinking and continues to identify with it, even when he has gone beyond its sphere of application. But what really happens then is not that we touch upon some mysterious chasm, transcendentally reflected in illusions that will not go away. It is rather that here our knowledge has to change into knowledge of a different sort. For systems of rationality are not (as Kant had supposed) closed in themselves and complete. Unger shows that in constructing geometries, for instances, we do not have a system that is complete in spatial terms. We construct our understanding of space by defining out of our experience of movement the element of time. In geometries, time is eliminated to a point approaching zero, for 'the factor of time, which is contained in the concept movement, plays no part in them. In order, however, to develop that content, time is made use of at the beginning and then eliminated. That one must, as it were, touch upon time in order to lay the foundations of spatial science can also be felt elsewhere in geometry, — for instance in all questions of continuity ...'[10]

When we have to understand movement, it will necessarily contradict our purely spatial, geometrical ideas (which are nevertheless completely right in themselves). Unger's response is the very un-Kantian but very Steinerian one of pointing out our own role in changing the way we think. Instead of feeling the metaphysical paralysis, the sense of limits of knowledge, we are invited to recognize the different ways in which we engage with reality. Instead of desperately trying to hold on to a system of understanding that is supposedly static and complete, when we find it contradicted we should become aware of shifting our perspective. Kant, on the other hand, allowed man to occupy the Copernican position at the centre of philosophy only under circumstances which he considered to establish him in a perspective that was unique and necessary, not dependent upon his changing way of looking at things.

Unger therefore worms his way ever deeper into the conceptual framework of his philosophical contemporaries, but with the ostentatious aim of moving there freely. If our way of thinking subjects us to manifold contradictions, and seems to imprison us in the needs and limitations of our own nature, it is not reality which is at fault but our wrong-headed attempt to measure our thought by some external standard, such as the posited unknowables which Kant wants to infer beyond the contradictions. Unger urges us to affirm our own nature as a way of experiencing reality. We will then no longer feel it as a crisis when we come up against something which makes us change (contradicts us): 'On the contrary, we feel only satisfaction if a result is born of it. We obey it gladly because we recognize in it the reality of our own nature. Thus rightly viewed, our own nature only becomes a compulsion for us if we sin against its reality. To be in accord with one's own nature is more accurately styled freedom.'[11] Instead of feeling limited when we come up against contradictions, we feel fulfilment. As Shakespeare's Celia and Rosalind express it:

> Then go we in content
> To liberty and not to banishment.

We can freely accept Kant's way of thinking, and involve ourselves, layer upon layer, in the contradictions that result, which are actually the way that the world changes us to accommodate its ever revealed and inexhaustible deeper levels of meaning.

Steiner explicitly approved of Unger's work, which as I have intimated may not be so different in its approach from the strategy behind the *Philosophy of Freedom*. Freedom from the Kantian limits is attained in a kind of meta-Kantianism, demonstrating to the metaphysical theorist the way to disentangle himself from the fixities of his own theory. This was precisely, I think, what Steiner felt was needed. With Unger, however, there remains more of the sense that we actually should think as Kantians and can therefore only know ourselves through six layers of contradiction; and somewhat less of Steiner's own brilliancy of making us aware of all ways of thinking as expressions of changing (and by no means exhausted) relationships between the thinker and his world. Unger is emphatically not wrong, and Steiner wanted us to be free within the thought- and value-structures of our own age and culture, not as aliens to it. Indeed in that way it fulfils Steiner's intentions better than Steiner himself.

A somewhat similar case is that of Kreyenbühl in ethics, whose work Steiner enthusiastically hails as one of 'the most important contributions to present-day philosophy.'[12] Kreyenbühl too had wormed his way into the Kantian mode of thinking in order to show that it had to be turned inside-out, arriving at the notion of the 'ethical *a priori*' — a concept which from a normal Kantian point of view ought to be a contradiction in terms (it was fundamental to Kant's moral programme to show that there could be no moral intuitions of the implied type). In Steiner's own case it is much clearer that his thought does not actually arise in dependence or from dissatisfaction with Kant, but can be applied to it and to all historical realizations of human thought. Kreyenbühl's meta-Kantian free individual is like a fish-out-of-water (or so it thought), glad to realize that it is really still in the pond and free to swim about. Steiner's free spirit, possessed of that 'power which lays hold our moral conceptions and creates out of them a new world,' might take an evolutionary step forward, and finally leave the pond behind altogether.

* * *

After Kant, a word about Fichte may perhaps be in order: not least because his *Wissenschaftslehre* was the subject of Steiner's doctoral thesis, and because Steiner's own first mature philosophical reflections grew out of his response to Fichte's thought. It is the more necessary, even, because of the now uncongenial mode in which Fichte's thought is couched. In fact he is now remembered by most philosophy students (if at all) as a typically nineteenth-century speculative Idealist, hardly to be taken very seriously in his talk about Absolute Spirit and his laboriously opaque propositions such as 'The Ego opposits in the Ego a divisible Non-Ego to a divisible Ego.'[13] Yet Steiner's 'Prologue to a Philosophy of Freedom' (the subtitle of *Truth and Science*) began life as a thesis concerned with the technicalities as well as the general thrust of Fichte's theory of knowledge, for which Steiner received his doctorate in 1891. And the reasons behind Steiner's grappling with Fichtean ideas are not far to seek when we discover that Fichte is the first thinker who attempts to provide a comprehensive analysis of the concept of freedom — indeed, Fichte claimed that his entire system was nothing less than such an analysis.

Fichte's response to Kant certainly anticipated and perhaps influenced Steiner's in its general approach. Fichte saw his own work as the intellectual equivalent of the French Revolution, designed to shake 'humanity loose from the fetters of the "thing-in-itself", from any external influence, and establish him in his first principle as an autonomous being.'[14] The link between knowledge and freedom, crucial to Steiner's thought, came to prominence for the first time in Fichte when he kicked away the last metaphysical constraints, the unknowable, mysterious things-in-themselves. Zealous for the cause of freedom, the philosopher formulated a view of the dynamics of knowledge, according to which our understanding of the world, far from reflecting the way things are, actually determines it. We come up against reality, he argues, not in contemplation but in active struggle. Merely spinning thoughts, we do not encounter anything real; the world is real for us to the extent that we master it, subdue and dominate it and thereby establish our freedom. The world is what we make of it, and any notion that we can say what it is like 'in itself' is worse than nonsensical.

One can see here in a strangely distorted light a version of that way out of the Kantian impasse which Steiner took. It seems to the contemplating mind that Kant must be right: the universe is knowable only in so far as it accords with my own faculties of perception and thought. The contemplating mind forgets that it has not always been contemplating, and that its organization was shaped and formed by the forces of the environment in which it struggled into existence. Instead of restoring the balance, however, Fichte chooses to turn the struggle toward consciousness into a weird metaphysic of the will, eventually coming to believe in a grand cosmic will playing itself out through individual selves or Egos, pushing toward an all-embracing or Absolute Self-Assertion which is also self-defeating. For if it no longer has an adversary to fight and strive to dominate, the Ego would lose its *raison d'être*. The Ego must therefore create its own adversary ever and anew, as the 'other,' as 'Nature,' in order to rule over and annihilate it. A shocked Coleridge rejected this system, and denounced it in horror as 'a crude egoismus, a boastful and hyperstoic hostility to NATURE, as lifeless, godless, and altogether unholy.'

Steiner too would have nothing to do with the German metaphysics of the will — for reasons he spelled out in *The Philosophy of Freedom*. For him, Fichte's restless, destructive Ego is anything but free. But the influence of Fichte's language was not limited to those who entered into his late speculations. Its assumptions echoed a much more widespread attitude to nature which became the staple of technological dreams: 'To subjugate all non-rational nature to himself, to rule over it freely and according to his own law, is the ultimate goal of man ...' When he rejects Fichte's will-driven dream, therefore, Steiner is at once correcting a misinterpretation of the very materials from which his own philosophy is formed — and challenging an attitude, based on that misunderstanding, which has gone far toward creating the world we know today. The 'mastery of nature' by such means, he contends, will cheat us of real freedom. By failing to understand the forces that drive us, we give in to those very 'shapings of the unregenerate mind' *(The Eolian Harp)*, perhaps, which Coleridge in a poem about the new Pantheism feared would replace the old God-given directives.

Coleridge — momentarily in his poem — and Fichte, it seems, more permanently, were swept somewhat off their feet by the intoxication of freedom. It was for Steiner to show that a sober estimate of philosophical freedom may counteract both their anxiety and their wilder dreams. His answer was not (to continue the bathing analogy) that we have to keep our feet firmly on the bottom, which would be the metaphysical 'foundations' theory, guaranteeing values from without. We must, since the advent of modern knowledge, learn properly how to swim.

Notes

PREFACE

1. See T.H. Meyer, *D.N. Dunlop. A Man of our Time* (London 1992) pp.201–246.
2. See J. Tautz, *W.J. Stein. A Biography* (London 1990) pp.187–207 (esp. p.190).

INTRODUCTION

1. A good documentary life available in English is: Johannes Hemleben, *Rudolf Steiner* (Sussex 1975); or, in German, there is the very readable Christoph Lindenberg, *Rudolf Steiner* (Hamburg 1992). Selections from Steiner's wider spiritual or 'anthroposophical' (as opposed to his more strictly philosophical) writings, with extremely useful bibliography, are available in R.A. McDermott (ed.), *The Essential Steiner* (New York and San Francisco 1984); articles on many aspects of Steiner's work as it fanned out into different areas are to be found in A.C. Harwood (ed.), *The Faithful Thinker* (London 1961); and J. Davy (ed.), *Work Arising from the Life of Rudolf Steiner* (London 1975).
2. Steiner, trans. M. Wilson, *The Philosophy of Freedom. The Basis for a Modern World-Conception* (London 1964; 1999); also trans. R. Stebbing *The Philosophy of Spiritual Activity* (New York 1963). Related materials assembled in O. Palmer (ed.), *Rudolf Steiner on his book* The Philosophy of Freedom (New York 1975). Surprisingly, there is no available collection of philosophical materials from Steiner's work.
3. E. Lehrs, *Man or Matter* (London 1961) p.26.
4. O. Barfield, *Romanticism Comes of Age* (Connecticut 1967). Preface to the new edition.
5. The 'concept' of freedom is livingly embodied in the Goetheanum building at Dornach in Switzerland, which Steiner designed as the headquarters of the Anthroposophical Society. Rex Raab writes of the forms used in the structure of Steiner's masterpiece in 'eloquent concrete,' the circle and its modifications. The point of Steiner's building is not at all one-sided artistic self-expression by the architect, dominating the form as in so many of the towering glass or concrete structures built today, but emerges only in encounter and freely active dialogue with those visiting and using it. 'Were the plan dominated by the concentric principle alone, it would be rigid and above all under the spell of a self-centred, "egoistic" principle. It is of decisive importance, therefore, that two sections of the building in the west — the protruding sculpturally treated staircase above, the projecting main entrance below — break through the charmed circle, grow out of it, one might even say actively push their way through ... In the face of the plain circle a person sensitive to form will feel that he is placed

on his own resources, resting within himself. To begin with, this unarticulated line allows of two characteristic tendencies. In the first of these, rounded protrusions appear in the form of a wavy line, proclaiming the "victory from within." In the other, a zigzag line indicates that external forces have won the victory': Raab, with A. Klingborg and A. Fant, *Eloquent Concrete* (London 1979) p.104. The result, he adds, is an architectural language that does not demand acceptance but free engagement, a language 'communicating immediately with the spirit of man ... whose forms call for further partners in conversation' (p.162).

6. Steiner, *The Course of my Life* (New York New York 1977) pp.296ff.

7. Steiner, *The Philosophy of Freedom* p.40.

8. Steiner, *Outline of Esoteric Science* (New York 1997) p.15.

9. Steiner, *Philosophy of Freedom* p.26.

10. A sizeable section of *The Riddles of Philosophy* (New York 1973) is of course devoted to 'Darwinism and the Conception of the World' (pp.284–313); see also Steiner, *Goethean Theory of Knowledge* pp.1ff for the relevance of Goethe to Steiner's evolutionary ideas. Also, O. Barfield, *Romanticism Comes of Age*, which contains several essays on Steiner's thought: especially relevant here is that on 'The Time Philosophy of Rudolf Steiner' (pp.184ff).

11. The fittest are defined as those who survive; the organisms which survive are said to do so because they are fittest. Cf. the observations in D. Holbrook,

Evolution and the Humanities (Aldershot 1987) pp.9ff.

12. Peter Gay, *The Enlightenment. The Rise of Modern Paganism* (New York and London 1966) p.326: the comment paraphrases a remark made concerning the high-profile rationalistic defender of Christianity Samuel Clarke, that 'no one had doubted the existence of God until Dr. Clarke tried to prove it'. It was the religious selling-out to rationalism, in other words, which upset the balance, not the overwhelming of religious ideas by a rampant scientism or victorious Enlightenment. On God in eighteenth-century science, cf. further M.C. Jacob, *The Radical Enlightenment* (London, Boston and Sydney 1981) pp.93–6: the usually implied progression from religion, *via* religious (Newtonian) science to naturalistic science, she demonstrates, is historically false, and the attempt to link religion and rationalistic science is actually a secondary, basically defensive mechanism. Historically, it seems increasingly clear that it was fundamentally religion which trapped itself in an attitude of destructive insecurity which has led to its recent unravelment.

13. A useful account of the incident involving the *Giordano Bruno Bund* may be found in A. Oldenburg (ed.), *Zeitgenossen Rudolf Steiners im Berlin der Jahrhundertwende* (Dornach 1988) pp.17ff. Rudolf Steiner's response to Aquinas is most fully developed in his lectures translated as *The Redemption of Thinking* (ed. A.P. Shepherd) (London 1956).

14. Steiner, *Occult Science* pp.7–8.

15. See Charles Nicholl, *The Chemical Theatre* (London 1980) p.60 on Paracelsus' theory of a 'specific arcanum' to cure each disease.
16. J. Kagan, *The Nature of the Child* (New York 1984) p.70.
17. Recently translated as Steiner, *Towards Social Renewal* (London 1999).

CHAPTER 1

1. W. Stark, 'Introduction' to Scheler, *The Concept of Sympathy* (London and Henley 1954) pp.ix–x.
2. A vivid account of the 'Panopticon' may be found in William Hazlitt's sketch of 'Jeremy Bentham' in *The Spirit of the Age or, Contemporary Portraits.*
3. Steiner, *Friedrich Nietzsche. Fighter for Freedom* (New York 1960) p.39.
4. A rather full account of Steiner's involvement is now available in David Marc Hoffmann, *Zur Geschichte des Nietzsche-Archivs* in the series *Supplementa Nietzscheana* (Berlin and New York 1991).
5. *Philosophy of Freedom* p.94.
6. G. Ryle, *The Concept of Mind* (Harmondsworth 1973) p.198.
7. Steiner, *Nature's Open Secret* (New York 2000) p.114.
8. 'The endeavour of human thought in the course of its development does not produce clear-cut and well-defined solutions to the riddles of philosophy. Rather they are ambiguous and apparently contradictory ....' Steiner, *Riddles of Philosophy* p.xx. This emphasis on the riddling nature of philosophical concepts is reflected in the insistent use of the term in Steiner's titles (*Riddles of Philosophy, Riddle of the Soul, Riddle of Man,* etc.), even

more striking in proportion to his published output when we remember that his lecture-cycles were at first only circulated privately. It must have seemed almost a trademark. The term has its background, no doubt, in the *Welträtsel* of Nietzsche, but more immediately perhaps in the writings of Haeckel whom the young Steiner so admired (*Riddle of the Universe,* etc.)

9. See Steiner, *Human and Cosmic Thought* (London n.d.) pp.17–18.
10. Steiner, *Philosophy of Freedom* p.78.
11. *Philosophy of Freedom* p.92.
12. Steiner, *A Theory of Knowledge Based on Goethe's World-Conception* (New York 1968). Steiner's pioneering studies have recently been presented in Steiner, ed. Barnes *et al.*, *Nature's Open Secret. Introductions to Goethe's Scientific Writings* (New York 2000). See further F. Amrine *et al.* (eds.), *Goethe and the Sciences: A Reappraisal* (Dordrecht 1987); H. Bortoft, *The Wholeness of Nature: Goethe's Way toward a Science of Conscious Participation in Nature* (New York 1996).
13 Cf. discussion in R. Steiner– O. Barfield, *The Case for Anthroposophy* (London 1970) pp.10–11.
14. N. Davidson, *Astronomy and the Imagination* (London, Boston and Melbourne 1985) pp.3–4. See further discussion below, pp.86ff.
15. See below, p. 129–30, for more from Steiner on Descartes' programme.
16. Cf. the relationship to Husserl's ideas discussed e.g. in W.J. Stein, *Die moderne naturwissenschaftliche Vorstellungsart und die Weltanschauung Goethes, wie sie Rudolf Steiner vertritt* (Stuttgart 1921). The centrality

of Brentano to understanding the origins of Steiner's thought is highlighted in W. Klingler, *Rudolf Steiners Menschenbild* (phil. Diss. Basel 1986) For more on Brentano, cf. below pp.60–63; and for Scheler, pp.179–80.

17. J.D. Barrow and F.J. Tipler, *The Anthropic Cosmological Principle* (Oxford and New York 1988): a brilliant exposition, including an awareness of the essential historical dimension. It is a shame that even in its later 'corrected' editions it still contains some extraordinary historical 'howlers,' such as the reference to the 'Mediterranean island of Ionia' (p.31) or, more seriously to Roger Bacon's views, 'typical' for the thirteenth century, expressed in the 'Wisdom of the Ancients' (*De sapientia veterum*), which was unfortunately penned by Francis Bacon, in the seventeenth (p.111)!

18. Steiner, *Anthroposophie. Ein Fragment* (Dornach 1980) p.41ff.

19. Barrow and Tipler, op. cit. pp.4ff.

20. Writing on 'The Dangerous Defiance of Science' in *The Sunday Times* 24.03.96. The article is interesting too for its distinct suggestion of paranoia about the hatred scientists are supposed to evoke. An other hint about the half-awareness many intelligent people of the double-standards concealed in the 'objectivity' ascribed to knowledge —an anxiety fended off, as I take it, by being presented as hostile criticism coming from others.

21. Cf. *Anthroposophie. Ein Fragment* pp.24–5: spiritual science 'advances the conception that our inner being is not something completed and fixed, but that it is something capable of being developed, evolved.'

22. Steiner, *Wahrheit und Wissenschaft* (Dornach 1980) pp.11–12.

23. Consider only the pressure to believe that the mapping of the human genetic make-up means we 'now know' what makes people as they are. Surely if genetics is true, there can be no place for a unique 'spiritual' aspect to people which gives them their individual value? Not only is this to forget that it is we in our thought-processes who have decided in the first place that the essentials of 'what people are' is equivalent to those factors which can be determined genetically — but one should also read Steiner's description of the spiritual at work in heredity, to see just how much we are trapped by either-or assumptions. The reason for *accepting* his account must be found in our relationship to the experiences he describes, but the way in which he shows it is possible to understand it reveals just how impoverished our ways of thinking can easily become! See Steiner, *Evolution of Consciousness* (London 1966) pp.160ff.

CHAPTER 2

1. Still the best introduction, perhaps, is Edo Pivčević, *Husserl and Phenomenology* (London 1970). Also see the same writer (ed.), *Phenomenology and Philosophical Understanding* (Cambridge, London and New York 1975).

2. Westphal, *Colour. Some Problems from Wittgenstein* (Oxford 1987) p.88: 'What is needed here is not a reduction describing what

happens at the surface of perceived objects ... and the physics
of this, but a wider understanding of the whole relationship
between the organism, the eyes
and the visible scene, the physiology of colour-vision, and ultimately the evolution of the
colour sense' – in short, 'clearer
and more imaginative theory'.
Westphal is influenced by
Steiner, as well as by Goethe's
colour-science. He is appreciative but not uncritical of Steiner,
cf. his article in *Journal for
Anthroposophy*. In his treatment
of experience, Steiner strongly
protested against the partition of
the 'objective,' leaving what was
presumed 'subjective' in opposition to it as a heap of the worthless and illusory. He pointed to
sensory-deceptions, such as the
way the moon appears larger
when it is low in the sky: this is
a phenomenon governed by
strict conditions and in no way
an 'illusion': see further B.
Kallert, *Rudolf Steiners
Erkenntnistheorie* (Stuttgart 1971)
p.14 and n2.

3. W. Stark, Introduction to Scheler,
The Nature of Sympathy (London
1979): moral perception,
pp.xiv–xv; changing the past,
p.xxiii; evolution, pp.xxiv–xxv;
psyche and spirit, pp.xxvi–xxvii.

4. See Steiner-Barfield, *The Case for
Anthroposophy* pp.69ff. Also
Steiner, *The Inner Nature of Man*
(Bristol 1994) pp.60ff.

5. See in particular *Case for
Anthroposophy* pp.82–3:
Brentano's description of psychical experience as representation, judgment and love-hate is
confused as regards ordinary
consciousness, Steiner argues,
but is reaching for the account
of spiritual levels of conscious-

ness which are taken into
account in anthroposophy. 'It is
not only the private content of
the soul that is being experienced, but also a somewhat that
demands judgmental acknowledgment or repudiation,' indicating that 'there is added to the
representation a soul experience
deriving from spirit.' It was only
Brentano's attachment to traditional (Aristotelian, Thomist)
ideas which prevented him, in
Steiner's view, from progressing
to the idea of spiritual science.
For the connection between
Steiner and Brentano, see
Florian Roder, 'Franz Brentano
in der Begegnung Rudolf
Steiners,' in *Die Drei* (1988)3,
197–219; also Bernardo Gut, 'Die
Klassifikation seelischer
Phänomene und der
Fortbestand der Individualität.
Versuch an einem Topos der
Philosophie Franz Brentanos,'
Die Drei (1988)2, 118–135.
Helpful on Brentano's historical
setting in relation to the emer-
gence of important ideas is B.
Smith (ed.), *Structure and Gestalt:
Philosophy and Literature in
Austro-Hungary and her Successor
States* (Amsterdam 1981). As
Brentano has come to be seen
increasingly as tentatively reach-
ing toward ideas which led to
Husserl's Phenomenology, and
thence to Existentialism, etc. the
closeness of his project to
Steiner's has the effect, as Owen
Barfield says, of sometimes
bringing the latter 'almost mod-
ishly up to date' (*Case for
Anthroposophy* p.16).

6. Steiner, *Anthroposophie.
Psychosophie. Pneumatosophie*
(Dornach 1931) p.79.

7. Steiner, *Eleven European Mystics*
(New York 1971) pp.210–211.

8. Steiner, *Wisdom of Man*, pp.143–53.

9. Steiner, *Theosophy* (London 1965) pp.18–20.

10. The first stage in the project for a human science, or anthroposophy, is indeed the extension and deepening of our understanding of bodily existence, and of the senses: see *Foundations of Human Experience* (New York 1996) pp.159ff.

11. Steiner, *Anthroposophy. An Introduction* (London 1983) p.95.

12. C. Unger, *Aus der Sprache der Bewusstseinsseele* (Basel 1954) pp.16–17.

13. Born, cited in Barrow and Tipler, *The Anthropic Cosmological Principle* (Oxford 1988) p.459.

14. Cited in Barrow and Tipler, loc. cit.

15. Steiner, *The Karma of Materialism* (London and New York 1985) pp.104–5.

16. Steiner, *The Gospel of St Matthew* (London 1965) p.136.

17. J. Piaget, 'The Myth of the Sensory Origin of Scientific Knowledge' in *Psychology and Epistemology: Towards a Theory of Knowledge* (Harmondsworth 1972) pp.45–62.It is well-known that Thomas Kuhn applied Piaget's type of questioning to the history of science: *The Structure of Scientific Revolutions* (Chicago 1970) p.vi and n2.

18. See Appendix 2.

19. The somewhat tortuous complexities of these modern, sophisticated versions of empiricism are rigorously looked into by J.L. Austin, *Sense and Sensibilia* (Oxford, London and New York 1962). Extensive discussion also in G. Warnock, *Berkeley* (Harmondsworth 1969). Attempts to break away from the old analysis of *sensa* for a more integrated view, as proposed by Steiner, have still been few: Jonathan Westphal draws my attention to the refreshing approach of J.J. Gibson, *The Senses as Perceptual Systems* (Boston 1966). Steiner's notion of thought and sensations each being essentially *incomplete* (a particularly interesting aspect of his view) might recall the ideas of his near contemporary, the Cambridge philosopher G.F. Stout, that 'the sensum is, "by nature" fragmentary and incomplete; we are bound to take it as belonging to a wider whole': and Stout was likewise taking off from Brentano's work, which led progressively him to modify the empiricist-Idealist tradition from which he never quite broke free, however: see John Passmore, *A Hundred Years of Philosophy* (Harmondsworth 1968) pp.194–7. Cf. Steiner, *Goethean Theory of Knowledge*: 'We meet with a concrete percept. It confronts us as a riddle. Within us the impulse manifests itself to investigate its "What?" — its real nature — which the percept itself does not express' (p.52).

20. Steiner, *Philosophy of Freedom* pp.41–2.

21. Steiner, *Foundations of Human Experience* pp.37–8. Cf. Wittgenstein, *Philosophical Investigations* (Oxford 1972) I,1 and the fuller exposition of the rationalist misunderstanding of the very nature of explanations at I,87: 'As though an explanation as it were hung in the air unless it were supported by another one. Whereas an explanation may indeed rest on another one that has been given, but none stands in need of

another — unless we require it to prevent a misunderstanding.' Some of the radical philosophical implications of this realization are worked out in Williams, *Groundless Belief. An essay on the possibility of epistemology* (Oxford 1977). The indispensable introduction to Wittgenstein, stressing the 'subtle anthropocentrism' which motivates his later philosophy in particular, is still: David Pears, *Wittgenstein* (London 1971).

22. One might be tempted to suppose that some aspects of things simply have to be acknowledged — basic shapes, colour-properties, etc. But a little historical consideration confirms Steiner's point-of-view. Take cloud-shapes: surely people must see that some clouds are rounded, some stratified, some wispy, and so on? Yet in fact no one saw clouds as falling 'obviously' into such types until the nineteenth century! What made the cloud-types obvious was not that the perceptual differences force themselves on us, but that Luke Howard came to them with the new scientific, analytical attitude. Similarly trees, like clouds, have been scrutinized by artists over centuries, and featured in countless landscape-paintings; aspects of their movement and texture, colour, mass, etc. have been repeatedly rendered by devoted observation and technique. Yet in classic art it is almost never possible to identify the species. Attention to differentiating features came only with a particular analytic approach. There was nothing about the different trees that *made* the artists show features that mark off one

species from another, despite their loving attention to the detail of their appearance! Colour-features too can be described in different ways, and there is nothing external which *makes* anyone classify them in our way. Steiner repeatedly drew attention to the fact that the ancient Greek (Homeric) colour-language classes together the colour of dark-red wine and the deep blue of the sea.

23. Steiner, *Philosophy of Freedom* p.76.

24. Steiner, id., pp.76–77.

25. Barfield, 'Rudolf Steiner's Concept of Mind,' in his *Romanticism Comes of Age* p.249.

26. Steiner, *Philosophy of Freedom* p.70.

27. Steiner, *Philosophy of Freedom* p.14.

28. Marjorie Greene mentions the example of scientists who believe that just getting the results into published form gives them the status of knowledge, and is intrinsically valuable.

29. See B. Gut, *Informationstheorie und Erkenntnislehre* (Stuttgart, n.d.) *passim.*

30. N. Davidson, *Astronomy and the Imagination* (London, Boston and Melbourne 1985) pp.3–4.

31. Steiner, 'Mathematics and the Occult,' in *Anthroposophical Movement,* V (1928) 28, 217–22.In the usual processes of measurement and calculation we remain within the picturable and perceptible, but with the development of the infinitesimal calculus by Newton and Leibniz 'we stand on an important boundary line. We are mathematically led out beyond what is perceptible to the senses, and yet we remain so far within the real that we calculate

the non-perceptible.' This does not yet bring us to any spiritual reality as such, but it crosses the boundary into the non-representable which modern science has needed to traverse, and so enabled 'life to flow into natural science' (pp.219–20). Science which has reached such a point is methodologically open, it would follow, to the complementary methodology of spiritual science, and ultimately must require it as the completion of its own development. Further attention to what happens 'in full consciousness' during the operation of the calculus (p.221) is, I take it, the point at which the anthroposophical methodology would come in.

32. *Anthroposophie. Ein Fragment* pp.42–3.

33. See further Steiner, *Anthroposophie, Psychosophie, Pneumatosophie* pp.11–31; a full account of Steiner's theory of the senses in: E.H. Lauer, *Die zwölf Sinne des Menschen* (Schaffhausen 1977). Wider perspectives on human sensory-bodily experience in Steiner, *Foundations of Human Experience* pp.134ff; and a lesser known but important phenomenological sketch in *Man in the Light of Occultism, Theosophy and Philosophy* (London 1964) pp.92–118. On the 'incarnational' meaning of anthroposophical science, see further below, pp.103–5.

34. M. Warnock, *Imagination* (London and Boston 1976) p.192 on the basis of a long exploration of Wittgenstein on 'seeing aspects' leading up to the famous duck-rabbit, and, still more widely, of phenomenolog-ical ideas going back to Brentano (p.142) which show that ultimately 'we cannot separate concepts from perceptions, nor one aspect of a thing from another. Perceiving it *is* perceiving it as an object and as falling under a concept' (p.147). Steiner had taken in these implications in a leap!

35. Steiner, *Riddles of Philosophy* pp.195–6.

36. Cf. the reflections in Iris Murdoch, *The Sovereignty of Good* (London 1970), p.24ff. Goethe's fascinating account of the 'sensuous-moral' significance of colours was of course highly influential in Steiner's scientific thought: see Steiner's phenomenological description in his lectures on *Colour* (London 1996). Other attempts have been made to explore 'significant' aspects of perception, e.g. in terms of the 'adverbial' awareness that extends beyond the percept: see discussion in D. Emmet, *The Nature of Metaphysical Thinking* (London and New York 1966) pp.42ff ; and, for the relationship to aesthetic feeling, R.G. Collingwood, *Principles of Art* (London and New York 1958) pp.204ff.

37. Steiner, *Anthroposophie, Psychosophie, Pneumatosophie* p.127. Steiner's aesthetic ideas were again largely shaped by Goethe, see his *Goethe als Vater einer neuen Ästhetik* (Dornach 1963). Otherwise it might be admitted that Steiner was a little too apt to fall back upon Schiller's *Aesthetic Letters* in many of his lectures; but then, as now, Schiller's impressive ideas were relatively little appreciated.

CHAPTER 3

1. Edo Pivčević, *Husserl and Phenomenology* (London 1970) pp.23–44.

2. Husserl, *Cartesian Meditations* (The Hague 1960).

3. This is the so-called 'intentional inexistence' of the object, strongly insisted upon by Brentano: 'Every mental phenomenon is characterized by ... the intentional inexistence of the object, ... what we would call relation to a content, or direction upon an object, which is not here to be taken for something real' (*Psychology from the Empirical Standpoint*). I can indicate (recognize, tell someone about, etc.) my friend John across the square, and the fact that I meant John remains the case even though it should turn out that I was mistaken and John was not in the square at all. Although Phenomenology was to retain the 'transcendental' approach (i.e. arguing from what we *must* think if we are to make sense of things), the whole metaphysical side of Kantianism, with its pseudo-explanatory 'things in themselves' is essentially swept away as soon as we realize that meaningful knowledge can be explicated in this way from within, and does not require justification from metaphysical entities.

4. Jean-Paul Sartre, 'Intentionality: A Fundamental Idea of Husserl's Phenomenology,' cited in Schmidt, *Maurice Merleau-Ponty* p.18.

5. 'It would then be found that the words, vowels, and phonemes are so many ways of "singing" the world, and that their function is to represent things not, as naive onomatopoeic theory had it, by reason of an objective resemblance, but because they extract, and literally express, their emotional essence': M. Merleau-Ponty, *Phenomenology of Perception* (London and Henley 1962) p.187.

6. Op. cit. p.141.

7. The subtitle of Steiner's *Philosophy of Freedom*. In the first instance, of course, the subtitle is an echo of E. von Hartmann — but then, he too was inspired by Brentano to give philosophy a basis in 'science' and especially psychology.

8. Above, pp.88–9.

9. *Case for Anthroposophy* pp.26–7.

10. Ibid. p.44.

11. Lacan, 'The Mirror-Stage as Formative of the Function of the I,' in his *Écrits: A Selection* (New York 1977), pp.1–7; discussion in Schmidt, *Maurice Merleau-Ponty* pp.74ff: 'Any philosophy directly issuing from the *cogito*,' i.e. from the thinking self, is undermined, argues Lacan, by the conclusion of psychology that the ego arises as a function of 'misrecognition,' tearing the subject out of unconscious self-centredness only through the illusory 'desire of the other' (p.6).

12. Steiner, *Philosophy of Freedom* p.224.

13. Steiner, *Philosophy of Freedom* p.225.

14. Loc. cit.

15. Steiner, *Philosophy of Freedom* pp.225–6. By this Steiner clearly means that he rejects the shift to a 'transcendental' self, cf. p.77: 'Moreover, it does not mean a modification of some "ego-in-itself" standing behind the perception of the subject ....'.

16. Husserl too was to turn phenomenology toward the developmental,

at least in the latter years of his life, showing perhaps that in the meantime the old issue with psychologism had not ultimately been resolved, and had not gone away. Schmidt's book on *Merleau-Ponty* is essentially concerned with the problems which continued to hang over the direction of Phenomenology, crucially experienced by Husserl's later followers. It can be argued that Steiner foresaw many of the solutions in terms of structural and developmental concepts which have in fact taken philosophy forward.

17. Cf. the example in *Philosophy of Freedom* pp.41–2.

18. Piaget, in *Psychology and Epistemology* (Harmondsworth 1972) pp.53ff.

19. Steiner, *The Karma of Materialism* p.105.

20. *Philosophy of Freedom* p.88.

21. See the passage quoted in *Philosophy of Freedom* pp.71–2.

22. Steiner, *Human Values in Education* (London 1971) pp.17–18.

23. One might note in particular that Marx established his social perspective in *The German Ideology* through a critique of Max Stirner's ethical individualism, which had proved so stimulating to Rudolf Steiner at this time. Steiner wanted to unite the insights of Nietzsche with Stirner's clarity of approach: see Steiner, *Friedrich Nietzsche* pp.123–6.

24. Welburn (ed.), *The Mysteries. Rudolf Steiner's Writings on Spiritual Initiation* (Edinburgh 1997) p.157.

25. Rightly stressed by P.L. Berger and T. Luckmann, *The Social Construction of Reality* (Harmondsworth 1971) pp.65ff. However, it is not clear to me why these authors back down on this insight when discussing the preliminary methodology of their approach. It is certainly true that 'to include epistemological questions concerning the validity of sociological knowledge in the sociology of knowledge is somewhat like trying to push the bus in which one is riding' (p.25). It is because here knowing is an active part of being in a society that a 'spiritual-scientific' method is indispensable: by giving them sociological knowledge we cannot avoid actively changing people and the society they know. The bus is pushed, and we cannot pretend we are not doing so! So some elements of the older 'programme,' with its supposedly theoretical emphases on 'Weltanschauungen' perhaps needs to be retained. The historical and cultural-evolutionary approach in Steiner's *Riddles of Philosophy* might ultimately be a model for the way forward in that sphere, to which one might add Owen Barfield's *Saving the Appearances* (New York n.d.).

26. Steiner, *Building Stones for an Understanding of the Mystery of Golgotha* (London 1972) pp.198, 200.

27. Steiner, *Philosophy of Freedom* p.169.

28. Schmidt, op. cit. pp.166–7.

29. See some of the exemplary studies of this process in Barfield, *Romanticism Comes of Age*, pp.84ff (consciousness soul); pp.126ff; general perspectives in relation to cultural evolution from Steiner in R. McDermott (ed.), *The Essential Steiner* (New York 1984) pp.212ff.

30. Sociology has more recently

arrived at some similar formulations. J. Huber notes that 'in the early '70s ... Claus Offe and Jürgen Habermas introduced the differentiation between the "socio-cultural system, political-administrative system and economic system" ... [and] these became fundamental analytic categories of German sociology'; more recently S.-Ch. Kolm developed his concept of an 'économie de réciprocité' linked 'with a broader membering of society according to the basic values of "liberté, égalité, fraternité"': 'Astral Marx,' in the journal *New Economy* 8 (Summer 1983), pp.3–6.

31. Berger and Luckmann, op. cit. p.30: 'These two statements are not contradictory. Society does indeed possess objective facticity. And society is indeed built up by activity that expresses subjective meaning.' Nevertheless I must confess to many difficulties with the supposed clarification of the foundations of everyday knowledge, pp.33ff.

32. P.L Berger, *A Rumour of Angels* (Harmondsworth 1971): a theology 'starting with man,' pp.66ff; 'relativizing the relativizers,' pp.43ff.

33. Steiner, *Foundations of Human Experience* p.74.

34. Steiner, *Theosophy* p.45.

35. Steiner, *Foundations* pp.74ff.

36. Steiner, *Foundations* p.75.

37. Steiner, *Goethean Theory of Knowledge* p.52.

38. A useful account in non-technical terms is E. Nagel and J.R. Newman, *Goedel's Proof* (New York 1960). Discussion also in J. Piaget, *Structuralism* (London 1971) pp.32ff.

39. Jean Piaget, 'The Myth of the Sensory Origin of Scientific Knowledge,' in his *Psychology and Epistemology. Towards a Theory of Knowledge* (Harmondsworth 1972) pp.45–62.

40. Steiner, *Human and Cosmic Thought* (London n.d.) p.12ff.

41. Although Steiner's analysis opens the way to a developmental-psychological approach, it by no means confuses the cognitive significance of the events with their subjective unfolding. Steiner is clear that 'psychologically, that comes first which in point of fact is derivative,' and that in the process of understanding something, 'we know that the concept which we have taken hold of is that real nature of the percept for which we have been seeking': *Goethean Theory of Knowledge* p.52.

42. Steiner, *Man in the Past, Present and the Future. The Evolution of Consciousness* (London 1966) p.15. Steiner had handled the *cogito* with beautiful circumspection in his main work, subtly refusing to allow the extrapolation of any kind of principle of 'being,' which could derive leverage, so to speak, from the certainty of the 'I think' part. 'Each object must first be studied in its relation to others before we can determine in what sense it can be said to exist': *Philosophy of Freedom* p.30. In this he follows the lead once more of Brentano, who vehemently opposed this kind of extrapolation of 'being': Pivčević, *Husserl and Phenomenology* pp.106–8. Steiner would presumably have objected to Heidegger's contrary development of Phenomenology as a study of supposed manifestations of 'Being' writ large.

43. Steiner, *Man in the Past, Present and Future* p.16.

44. Mary Warnock, *Imagination* pp.176ff, where the mental image is found a place in the post-Phenomenological account, under the 'proposition that images are our way of thinking of absent or non-existent things'. It is Sartre who has particularly interestingly developed the analysis of mental images as 'aspects of nothingness' (cited, p.177). Sartre is especially close to Steiner's view of thought as completing the perceptual range by placing it in a perspective or showing it in its relationship to ourselves, in the instance of the shapes on the carpet — which are partly concealed under the furniture. It is not that we fill in the shapes as an actual completing. We can picture to ourselves the full pattern if we wish, but that is not the main point. Knowing what is there before us in such a case is not such a completing, but consists precisely in that 'I have to think of them specifically as *not* part of the perceptual data I have. "I grasp them as nothing for me"': Sartre, *Psychology of Imagination* (cited in Warnock, op. cit. p.178).

45. Steiner, *Ancient Myths* (Toronto 1971) p.115.

46. *Philosophy of Freedom* p.40.

47. Penrose, *The Emperor's New Mind: Concerning Computers, Minds and the Laws of Physics* (Oxford 1999) p.534: mathematical thinking, he notes for example, strives for algorithms — but usual accounts of the matter ignore precisely that reaching out, striving aspect of the process. 'Once an appropriate algorithm is found, the problem is, so to speak, solved.' The computer- model which sees thinking as running on tracks, as it were, thus rests on a failure of observation — a failure to observe the 'hidden element' of thinking behind the resulting thought.

48. Steiner, *Outline of Esoteric Science.*

49. Steiner argues quite rightly that far from the brain producing thoughts, it is thinking which fashions the brain.

50. Steiner, *Goethean Theory of Knowledge* p.38.

51. Steiner, *Man, Hieroglyph of the Universe* (London 1972) pp.136–41.   Cf. Piaget, 'The individual does not understand himself except by adapting himself to the object. Thus man cannot understand the universe except through logic and mathematics, the product of his own mind; but he can only understand how he has constructed mathematics and logic by studying himself psychologically and biologically, or in other words, as a function of the whole universe': *Psychology and Epistemology* pp.82–3; this leads to the idea of the circle of the sciences as complementary viewpoints (p.83).

52. Steiner, *Man in the Past, Present and Future* p.38.

53. For a useful summary of Piaget's researches on these aspects of cognitive development, see his *Play, Dreams and Imitation in Childhood* (London 1962) pp.269ff.

54. Steiner, *Philosophy of Freedom.* See pp.36ff.

55. Some comments on the resistance of philosophers to developmental approaches in Wolfe Mays, 'Introduction' to Piaget, *The Principles of Genetic*

Epistemology (London 1972)
pp.5–6.

56. Rudolf Steiner frequently discussed details of child-development, naturally in his educational courses. Basic orientation in *Foundations of Human Experience*, pp.147ff.

57. He developed it in his essay *Philosophy and Anthroposophy* (London and New York 1929).

58. Steiner, *Die Suche nach der neuen Isis, der göttlichen Sophia* (Dornach 1980) p.31

59. *Three Streams in Human Evolution* (London 1965) pp.16–17.

60. Cf. the remarks of Merleau-Ponty, *Phenomenology of Perception* (London and Henley 1962) pp.22–32.

61. Steiner, *The Influences of Lucifer and Ahriman. Man's Responsibility for the Earth* (Vancouver 1976) p.28. Steiner emphasises that by 'becoming more subjective where the external world is concerned' he in no way means 'bringing in fantasy pictures' but 'bringing interest, alert attention and devotion to the things of immediate life' (loc. cit.)

62. By ignoring the fact that it was based on a (concealed) particular perspective, the system naturally invited a 'flip' to the opposing perspective, which Karl Marx duly provided: turning the idea-world into mere 'ideology,' the material activity of the subject now became the only reality. Obviously this does nothing to solve, but only displaces the inherent problem in the underlying question of orientation. Cf. 'The Eternal in Hegelian Logic and its Antitype in Marxism,' published as Lecture IX in Steiner, *Spiritual Science as a Foundation for Social Forms* (London and New York 1986).

63. We must expect also to discover unexpected new aspects to the objective world as we change our relationship to it. See for example, *Karma of Materialism* p.43!

64. *Foundations of Human Experience* pp.183–4.

65. *Foundations of Human Experience* p.185. Steiner is clearly right that it is the activity of thinking, based on the special relationship just outlined, which brings about the special elaboration of the nervous system, not vice versa: 'The materialists maintain that the brain thinks ... but this is as false as to assert that the speech-centre formed itself, whereas it has acquired its form through human beings having learned to speak. And so the speech-centre is the product of speaking. Similarly, all cerebral activity, even within recent times, is the result of thinking and not the other way around. The brain is plastically modelled through thinking.' Steiner, *Mysteries of the East* p.73.

66. Steiner, *Die Suche nach der neuen Isis* loc. cit.

67. Steiner, *Philosophy of Freedom* p.140.

68. Steiner, *Anthroposophical Leading-Thoughts* p.80 (no.110)

69. Or the hairline balance would require such finesse of judgment that it might work, perhaps, in some Henry Jamesian world where unhurried and infinitely delicate discriminations are the norm. Could this have been what Steiner had in mind? The urgency of everything he wrote and said suggests otherwise.

70. Steiner, *Egyptian Myths and Mysteries* (New York 1971): 'Only if humanity looks forward will life again become spiritual ...

consciousness must become apocalyptic' (p.25). The figure of Michaël who fights the ahrimanic dragon of materialism had been for Steiner from far-back the emblem of the modern conscious spiritual path. See the 'Michaël Letters' which accompany the *Leading-Thoughts*; also Steiner, *The Mission of the Archangel Michael* (New York 1961).

71. Steiner, *Leading-Thoughts* p.185 (nos. 162, 164).

72. Kuhn, *The Structure of Scientific Revolutions* (Chicago 1970)

73. Steiner, *Outline of Esoteric Science* pp.14ff.

74. Cf. O. Barfield, *Saving the Appearances*. Without reference to the evolution of consciousness, the kind of insights which stem from Kuhn's analysis lead to the miasma of Foucault's 'structureless structuralism': cf. the devastating attack in Piaget, *Structuralism* (London 1973) pp.128ff (relation to Kuhn, p.132). For all Foucault's obvious brilliance, only when he brought his insights into relation to history did he produce some valuable results.

75. Steiner, *Philosophy and Anthroposophy* pp.11–12.

76. Steiner, *Karma of Materialism* p.143: 'Man believes that he knows his own self. But in what sense does he know it? If you have, say, a red surface and cut a hole in it and look through into darkness, i.e. to where there is nothing, you will then be looking at the red surface, and see the hole as a black circle. But you are looking into nothingness. Likewise in your inner life, you see your own self in the way you see the black disk in the surrounding red. What man

believes to be a perception of his "I" is in fact a hole in his soul-life ....'

77. Steiner, *Theosophy* pp.35–7.

78. Steiner, *Origins of Natural Science* (London and New York 1985) p.81 (and generally pp.79–82).

79. R. Swinburne, *The Evolution of Soul* (rev. ed. Oxford 1997). In contrast, there is the notion of a self-brain interaction in a production such as Popper (see his 'Knowledge and the Mind-Body Problem' — in M.A. Notturno, *Defence of Interaction*, New York and London 1994 — which, apart from the up-to-date scientific references, still seems to have come straight out of the age of Leibniz. In his main contribution to the mind-body problem, the 'First Meditation' in *A Way of Self-Knowledge* (New York 1999), Steiner emphatically denies any such 'dualistic' model (see pp.103ff).

80. From a report by L.K. Cass and C.B. Thomas, cited in Jerome Kagan, *The Nature of the Child* (New York 1984) p.101 and generally, pp.99–111. Anthroposophical work with those in need of 'special care of the soul' has been based decisively on the possibility of reaching, behind even severe traumas, this human spirit or capacity of development and inner renewal. Cf. T. Weihs, *Children in Need of Special Care* (rev. ed. London 2000).

81. Kagan, op.cit. p.111.

82. See Steiner, *Theosophy* ch. II.

Chapter 4

1. Steiner, *The Spiritual Foundation of Morality* p.57.

2. *Spiritual Foundation* pp.49–50.

3. See Steiner, *Philosophy of Freedom* pp.162ff.

4. Steiner, *Zur Geschichte und aus den Inhalten der erkenntniskultischen Abteilung der Esoterischen Schule* (Dornach 1987) p.124.

5. Stephan Körner notes the trend and the backwardness of ethical thought in the twentieth century. 'The general movement of philosophical attention towards the analysis of concepts and conceptual systems had its effect on moral philosophy, although the conceptual tools of moral thinking had, in comparison with those of science and mathematics, undergone very little change ... [The] questions which received most attention were those questions of traditional ethics which were analytical': *Kant* (Harmondsworth 1967) pp.158–9.

6. Below, pp.

7. C.G. Jung, *Answer to Job* (London, Melbourne and Henley 1984) p.108 and *passim.*

8. *Cf. Steiner, Evil* (London 1997). Steiner gives the telling example of the 'wound' from strong sunlight which evolves into the light-sensitive eye. The senses are a healing of an invasion of the outer world which we accept in transformed guise as the beauty and pleasure of sensation. 'True as it is that the eyes convey to us the beauty of the world of colour, they could nevertheless only come into being through injury caused by the heat of the sun to places particularly sensitive to light. Nothing in the way of joy, happiness, blessedness has come about except through pain. To refuse pain and negation is to refuse beauty, greatness and goodness': Steiner, *Karma of Materialism* p.55

(see generally pp.54ff).

9. A Goethean expression.

10. See the fine demonstration of Steiner's method in his *Man — Hieroglyph of the Universe* pp.11–23.

11. *Spiritual Foundation of Morality* p.30.

12. *Spiritual Foundation of Morality* pp.14; 18–19.

13. [See further the comments in our Conclusion, pp. 218ff.]

14. Morality becomes metaphysical, when philosophers try to prove that it 'must' be valid, over and beyond any situation we actually encounter. See Appendix 2 for more on Steiner's response to Kant's version of the argument in particular.

15. Hare, *Freedom and Reason* (Oxford 1963); and cf. the more recent restatement of the same approach in his *Moral Thinking* (Oxford 1981); still more 'inspired by Kant' is the attempt to provide a transcendental rationale for moral judgments in the work, for instance, of C. Illies, *The Grounds of Ethical Judgment* (Oxford 2003). More pertinent to the type of approach adopted here, on the other hand, and eloquently expressive of the need to move on from the traditional relegation of all that is not fact to the 'subjective,' might be the observations of Hilary Putnam, *The Collapse of the Fact/Value Dichotomy* (Harvard and London 2002).

16. Above, pp.84ff, and see Appendix 1.

17. This is similar to the illuminating approach of Macmurray, *The Self as Agent*. It is important, however, that Steiner starts with the awareness, rather than the agent as such. We are more than we do — that is what Steiner means by

stressing the moral-perceptive power of the self. We are an agent in a situation, for his thought, rather than a product of it, because of our consciousness which extends beyond the situation as such. Further discussion in the papers published as *The Royal Institute of Philosophy Lectures. Vol.I. The Human Agent* (London and New York 1962).

18. It would only be possible to overthrow the difference 'in degree' much later, when biology had shown that male and female were versions of the same human form, rather than different 'creations': it would clearly be unfair to expect Milton to have been able to make use of this scientific breakthrough back in the seventeenth century.

19. See her play *The Rover,* and in particular her defensive 'Postscript,' included in Behn, *Oroonoko, The Rover and Other Works* ed. Janet Todd (Harmondsworth 1992) p.248.

20. *Philosophy of Freedom* pp.204–5.

21. Steiner, 'Truth, Beauty, Goodness' in *Art in the Light of Mystery Wisdom* (London 1970) p.106.

22. Steiner, 'Truth, Beauty, Goodness' p.108.

23. Steiner, *Spiritual Beings in the Heavenly Bodies* (Vancouver 1981) p.8. The spiritual world is consistently characterized by Steiner in terms of the coinciding of actuality and morality: see for example *Evolution of Consciousness* p.192.

24. M. Scheler, *The Formalistic Principle in Ethics and the Non-Formal Ethic of Values.* The 'formalism' referred to is Kantian generalizing morality; 'non-formal' translates *materielle,* which is used not in the sense of 'materialism' but of specific and concrete, morally objective values.

25. The term intuition rather misled other readers of Steiner, such as A.V. Miller, 'Rudolf Steiner and Hegel,' *Anthroposophical Quarterly* 17(1972)4, as though this meant that 'pure thinking is incapable of penetrating to absolute truth,' a view which Miller 'corrects' in good Hegelian terms (p.76) — with the slight drawback, however, that this requires believing in the metaphysical pretensions of Reason. Intuition of course has none of the common associations of 'less than fully conscious' which often attach to the word in English, but means an individual spiritual-moral perception of a specific content. It is interesting that some have actually seen Hegel as coming to the verge of a moral individualism like Steiner's in his account of the 'conscientious consciousness,' which in the *Phenomenology of Spirit* seems to be the highest stage of moral awareness; in the *Encyclopaedia,* however, it is replaced by the State and by the Absolute spirit and its values: see the interesting discussion in J.N. Findlay, *Hegel. A Re-Evaluation* (London and New York 1958) pp.128–9.

26. Cf. comments of the biblical scholar J.A. Soggin, *Introduction to the Old Testament* (London 1989) p.312: Old Testament morality is based, he says, on a trust in the divine governance of history: 'it is a matter of specific decisions of faith, of taking each case by itself .... The believer is not assailed with a norm ... but is called on for active commitment in a particular situation'

(giving examples, notably from Isaiah). It may actually be unfortunate that the Ten Commandments are so well known in the Old Testament context, while the inner setting to which they belong is so little understood. Ancient Judaism in fact experienced the Commandments as anything but the negative restrictions so often portrayed, resulting in a travesty of their historical meaning. It seemed more to the Jews a privilege that God had opened to them his intentions, allowing them to share in his purposes — rather as if, on a trivial level, the factory manager has called in the work-force to share in the plan for the future of the firm, rather than assigning them only their humble task on the production line! Far from feeling constrained, the singer in Psalm 119, 29–30 calls on God to 'give me the grace of thy Law: I have chosen the way of thy Truth'. While other nations seemed to be buffeted by the tide of history, God had shared with his people the inner meaning, the direction of its events, so that they could consciously commit themselves to furthering his will. This was a moral experience in Steiner's terms — quite different when 'law' is divorced from its historical reality.

27. In P. Foot (ed,), *Theories of Ethics* (Oxford 1974) pp.9; 83ff.

28. Steiner, *Philosophy of Freedom,* p.134.

29. Searle, 'How to Derive "Ought" from "Is,"' in Foot, *op. cit.* pp.101–114.

30. Foot, op.cit. p.9.

31. Cf. Mary Douglas, *Natural Symbols* (Harmondsworth 1973) pp.59–76.

32. See further Appendix 2, p. 231

33. Op. cit. p.60.

34. Op. cit. p.48.

35. Op. cit. p.76.

36. The view of *karma* as 'retribution' for past crimes, a sort of cross between popular misunderstandings of Buddhism and a Hollywood interpretation of the Old Testament, that is held by no serious student, is by now mainly limited to tabloid journalists and Ministers of Sport.

37. Steiner, *Theosophy* pp.81ff.

CHAPTER 5

1. To give just a single instance, from the religious domain: it was certainly from Rudolf Steiner, via the writings and translations of his influential pupil Edouard Schuré, that Teilhard de Chardin drew the concept of 'the cosmic Christ'. But how many of the latter's numerous religious and scientific admirers are aware of this fact?

2. The distaste for history is nowhere flaunted more ostentatiously than in R. Dawkins' introductory remarks to *The Selfish Gene* (New York and Oxford 1989): 'Living organisms had existed on earth, without ever knowing why, ' he writes, 'for three thousand million years before the truth dawned on one of them. His name was Charles Darwin.' (p.1) Notice the way that the origin of the idea becomes an event with no human dimension: it is just a matter of seeing how things are, or not. Dawkins cites with approval the still more extreme comment on the question of life from G.G. Simpson: 'All

attempts to answer that question before 1859 are worthless, and we will be better off if we ignore them completely.' Thus only a few previous thinkers had an 'inkling' amid their superstitious confusion! In reality, of course, evolution had been considered by many thinkers from Greek times onward, and it had been elaborated by religious Christian thinkers too. If it had not had wide appeal, that may have been to do with the fact that competitive natural selection did not become a widespread social experience until the nineteenth century post-Industrial Revolution era. Medieval humanity lived in a feudal hierarchical society where differences were elaborately labelled, and unsurprisingly they were particularly interested in aspects of nature that suggested hierarchy and the emblematic. Future changes in society and consciousness will doubtless bring out other relationships in the natural world, and people will wonder how it was that no one saw them before. Dawkins is also interesting for his spacemen (well, he does say his book should be read like science-fiction): the first question aliens would ask about humanity on arrival, he suggests, is, 'Do they know about evolution yet?' — another anti-historical feature, I would suggest, that is perhaps really a leftover from the notion of beliefs being vouched for by divine approval (heavenly voice, angel, and so on). The idea arrives like a revelation, and not like one that was developed by historical human beings.

3. Barfield, *Romanticism Comes of Age*, p.18.

4. Steiner had directly participated, one might say, in the very birth of Modernism, in the circles connected with Otto Erich Hartleben and others in Berlin from 1897: here he edited the *Magazine for Literature*, discussed 'modern art' and drama (such as Maeterlinck), took part in the founding of '*Die Kommenden*,' and so forth: see Ch. Lindenberg, *Rudolf Steiner* (Hamburg 1992) pp.57–60; and for more detail, the contributions of Lindenberg and H. Köhler in Oldenburg (ed.), *Zeitgenossen Rudolf Steiners* (Dornach 1988) pp.9–27, 29–43; W. Kugler, 'Zeichen des Aufbruchs. Rudolf Steiner im Kreis der "Kommenden,"' in the journal *Die Drei* (1985), 607–618. In these and related quarters the criterion of 'modernity' first attained priority. For a general introduction, see M. Bradbury and J. McFarlane (eds.), *Modernism* (Harmondsworth 1976). The publication of Rudolf Steiner's *Philosophy of Freedom* is included in their table of 'significant events' (p.576).

5. S. Prickett, *Romanticism and Religion* (Cambridge 1976).

6. Steiner, *Theosophy*, see in particular the discussion in Addenda pp.142–3. It would have been easy to join in the attempt to revamp 'vital force' in scientific theories (no doubt a reference to the fashionable *élan vital*), but with more critical acumen Steiner notes, 'in view of modern scientific developments, the more consistent logic of those who refuse ... to hear of any such "life-force." "Life-force" does not belong to what are today called "forces of nature" ... No one in this domain will be

able to get beyond shadowy abstractions,' by unjustifiably carrying over material ideas into the spiritual domain. No progress is possible unless a thorough-going reorganization of our ideas is undertaken — 'unless it is recognized that to reach what transcends the workings of inorganic forces in life is only possible through a mode of perception that rises to vision of the supersensible.' In the 'First Meditation' in *A Way of Self-Knowledge*, Steiner argues that after death the body is subject to chemical and physical laws: 'such physical and chemical laws do not relate to the physical body any differently than they relate to any other lifeless thing in the outer world. Therefore, one cannot but conclude that this indifference on the part of the outer world arises not just after death, but actually exists throughout human life ... To expect that progress in our understanding of nature will lead to our learning more about physical laws which govern bodily processes as mediating the life of the soul is an illusion': *A Way of Self-Knowledge* (New York 1999) pp.109, 112.

7. Cf. J. Hemleben, *Rudolf Steiner und Ernst Haeckel* (Stuttgart 1965). On Steiner and evolution cf. also the important assessment in N. Macbeth, *Darwin Retried* (New York 1976).

8. Cf. Steiner, *Christianity as Mystical Fact* (New York 1997) pp.173–5. Steiner's answer to this dilemma is that we need to understand science as the latest stage in the 'human' truth, descended from earlier forms of truth (p.175); otherwise we will look for that

human fulfilment somewhere else than in knowledge.

9. Published as Steiner, *Eleven European Mystics* (New York 1971); he covers similar ground again in his brilliant lecture-course on *The Origins of Natural Science* (London and New York 1985).

10. The fact that religion accepted the myth made it worse. When religion fell back on its own traditional myth along the lines just mentioned, that science was wrong because it denied religion (Genesis v. Geology) it was only completing the disaster. The 'Luciferic' myth that science is human self-glorification lacked the all-important other half of the picture, unconsciously permitting the one-sidedly 'Ahrimanic' justification of materialistic science in fact. Religion was left in a position to do little more than lament the loss of the spiritual from most people's experienced world. Few apart from Steiner, it seems, escaped the powerful bifurcation of ideas, and sought for its own sake ways to rescue science from the aridity of the Ahrimanic, which was rapidly turning a human and spiritually enriching activity of knowledge into a tortured attempt to deny our own place in knowledge, and so its spiritual significance, freezing ourselves out.

11. See now B.J. Dobbs, *The Janus Face of Genius. The Role of Alchemy in Newton's Thought* (Cambridge 1991); and still more spectacular evidence of the need to understand the consciousness of the time, L. Principe, *The Aspiring Adept. Robert Boyle and his Alchemical Quest* (Princeton 1998).

12. P. Gay, *The Enlightenment: The Rise of Modern Paganism* (New York and London 1977) p.313.

13. Op. cit. p.324.

14. Modern philosophical discussion of the issues here derives from H. Butterfield, *The Whig Interpretation of History* (London 1951). An apt example comes from the literary and cultural historian David Morse, even dealing with so recent a time as the Romantic revolution, when he observes the danger of Whiggishly 'tracing themes' in a past culture. The result, he notes, is all too easily that the 'investigator fails to understand the parameters both of his own discourse and that which he studies ... He offers an illustration of contemporary understanding through an assortment of curious material gathered from the past, a sort of beach-combing on the shores of time — so that what we learn is what we know already': *Perspectives on Romanticism* (London and Basingstoke 1981) p.xiii. Morse's study is perhaps especially interesting for the problems it raises about the methods employed — so often glossed over and disguised in other works.

15. Steiner, *Christianity as Mystical Fact* pp.174–5.

16. Steiner, *op. cit.* pp.144ff.

17. Steiner, *The Fifth Gospel* (London 1995) pp.9ff.

18. Owen Barfield, *Speaker's Meaning* (London 1967) pp.56ff.

19. Barfield, *Speaker's Meaning* p.56 points out that this is just as true of the 'physical' component in the meaning, which many modern theorists which to treat as if it could be separately experienced from the beginning, as a basis for 'metaphorical' developments in language.

20. Cf. J. McGann, *The Romantic Ideology* (Chicago and London 1983) p.2. Lisa Jardine shows a rare self-consciousness in this field. She is remarkable not least for her engaging directness on the subject of her own thinking and rethinking. In her historical and cultural investigation centred on Shakespeare, she takes her start from the 'new historicist' view that we can know only the 'material traces' of events, which for many signifies the death-knell of a world with coherent presences, and our condemnation to the 'radical indeterminacy' of the self-defeating constructs we place upon them. Yet on reflection she counters that 'it is by no means the case that this inevitably leaves us in a position of radical indeterminacy. In fact, I begin to believe that it only appears to lead us in such a direction if we are committed (wittingly or unwittingly) to the view that what textual remains yield, in the way of an account of the past, is evidence of individual subjectivity,' i.e. a particular idea of the fixed definable 'self': Jardine, *Reading Shakespeare Historically* (London 1996). Thus she becomes aware, as Steiner urges, of the hidden element of our own thinking. Instead of allowing herself to be simply drawn into the process of demonstrating ever more histrionically our inability to attain such fixities of our own presupposition, she opens herself to the ideas e.g. of Stephen Greenblatt's discussion of the rather different way that Renaissance people constructed their 'self'. This, with its anthro-

pological background, is actually an interesting step toward a Barfieldian perception of changing consciousness.

21. On this 'antecedent unity' and the concept of change (in a somewhat more biological framework), cf. further Barfield, *What Coleridge Thought* (Oxford 1971) pp.42–3.

22. The issue is interestingly raised in cultural-historical terms by David Morse once more. While rejecting the myth of modernity's special status, when he considers the implications of understanding the different structures of past mentalities: he wishes to conclude that 'there are no individual ways of looking at the world; collective ways are the only ways we have' (*Romanticism. A Structural Analysis* (London and Basingstoke 1982) p.10). The significance of events, and implicitly those who bring them about, is accordingly denigrated in favour of structures, meaning discourses in the sense of possible understandings of what occurs.

He acknowledges with some unease that in this case 'structures would appear to determine, not particular events but the particular type of events that would or could happen. Certainly I, at any rate, would be prepared to embrace this somewhat daunting conclusion, even if to do so might appear somewhat unprofitable, since it is hard to know what the implications of commitment are' (op. cit. pp.8–9). But in this personal aside we actually reach the heart of the matter. For so long as we stay outside full involvement in historical relationship, looking on at the structures of past viewpoints, individual uniqueness dissolves into mere manifold variations of collective discourse — as if a meaningful conversation consisted of any sequence of statements as long as they were all linguistically correct. If on the other hand, the historian were to undertake an assertion of what we need to grasp from Romanticism (in this case), for the future of our culture today, he would stand in a moral and fully historical relationship that would immediately clarify the implications of commitment that otherwise remain so uncertain. The uniqueness of the historical situation would then be a powerful experience, replacing the illusion of uniqueness as just a varied perspective: the latter would be the illusion polar opposite in fact, to that created by the myth of a time 'after the watershed'. But of course we do not normally require academic exponents to have this kind of 'committed' relationship at all to the time they study. Owen Barfield is a brilliant but rather lonely example.

23. A fascinating perspective on Ford and his ideas, with major reference also to Steiner, is the article by J. Westphal, 'Henry Ford — Objective Idealist,' *Golden Blade (1979)*, 115–36. For scientific resistance to history, see for example the comments of Barrow and Tipler, *The Anthropic Cosmological Principle* (Oxford and New York 1988) pp.9–11. (It would be a fascinating diversion to follow up their tantalizing question as to whether the history of the attempt to find pattern would really prove an exceptional case — see their p.11.)

24. See T.E. Hulme, *Speculations*.

Essays on Humanism and the Philosophy of Art (London and New York 1987): a book in its original edition (1924) vastly influential on early twentieth-century writers and cultural theorists, from T.S. Eliot down. See particularly the comments on classicism vs. Romanticism, pp.116–7.

25. Barfield, *Romanticism Comes of Age*: he adds that the issue has since been confused by Darwin's 'desperate attempt to fit into the essentially timeless framework of mechanical causality, the completely incompatible notion of *metamorphosis* — of the gradual change of one species into another'. The essence of Steiner's view, he rightly goes on to characterize as the spiritual conception of 'man's self-consciousness as a process in time, with all that this implies' (pp.188–9).

26. Steiner, *Goethean Theory of Knowledge* ch. XIX ('Human Freedom,' under the general heading of the 'spiritual or Cultural Sciences' (*Geisteswissenschaften*), pp.109ff. Barfield picks up on Steiner's indications here, and in his later work sees history reaching maturity, rather as natural science did in the nineteenth century. 'Just as science began life as a department of philosophy and then emerged into a separate existence in its own right, so history itself is today emerging from the position it has too long occupied as a sub-department of science into a separate existence as a parallel and autonomous method of cognition, as a valid approach to experience as a whole': Barfield, *Speaker's Meaning* p.19. The

spiritual-scientific clarifying consequences of this approach also for 'nature' and 'prehistory' he contrasts with the conventional modes of thought, which are well characterized as involving 'a sort of leapfrogging movement backwards and forwards at the same time' (p.90). These ideas are finely developed in his last chapter (pp.92ff).

27. Op. cit. pp.112–3.

28. Steiner, *Riddles of Philosophy* pp.xxi–ii; also 5ff. It is often assumed that Steiner took his sequence of stages (epochs) of civilization from theosophical sources. However, the notion of a developmental series applied to human civilizations, each working out in the fullness of life-experience the possibilities of a particular stage, more likely came to him *via* Hegel. One can see the similarities immediately in the religions which document the progress of the Spirit, although Steiner has substituted the concept of an evolution which is not in any sense 'deducible' apart from its historical reality. See Hegel's *Lectures on the Philosophy of Religion* (London and New York 1974): vol. II, pp.11ff (Indian religion); pp.70ff (Persian religion of Light and Darkness); pp.101ff (Egyptian); pp.170ff (Judaism); pp.229ff (Greek religion of art)— and compare e.g. Steiner, *Gospel of John* pp.28–36.

29. Steiner, *Anthroposophical Leading Thoughts* (London 1973), p.114.

30. A revolt by the French populace 'because they have no bread' could have amounted to no more than just another revolt, temporarily upsetting social

equilibrium — but if those taking part in it at the time had a new perspective on the potential for change, it could become the French Revolution. History comes into being with the interpretation, and 'causes' cannot explain the course of events: it is surely meaningless (despite Marxist wishful thinking) to have to suppose that such revolts were always proto-revolutions, whether people realized it or not, as when one historian would have us believe that the Romans and their slaves were engaged in a 'class struggle'. Thus the 'ideal' component, which is to say, the interpretation that is put on events, actually makes the historical reality, and it can be made only by free individuals who thereby introduce something new. The attempt to deprive this spiritual-ideal factor of its role, turning it into mere ideology (i.e. passive reflection of supposed historical-economic 'forces') because of the dogmatic assumptions of materialism, always fundamentally undermines serious historical understanding, e.g. in the way Marxism tries to rig the pattern of history by importing into past situations modern presuppositions such as the perception of 'class' rivalries.

31. It is necessary therefore to go beyond evolution (= the modification of existing structures) to grasp the spirit, the spirit which is the active agent powering evolutionary change itself but which emerges in its pure form in history. The reverse side of the coin is seen in Rudolf Steiner's spiritual cosmology, where the conservation of morphologies that have been produced naturally predominates since the subject-matter is the world of existing forms and structures. The unique direction of spiritual history is not denied, however, and a brilliant reconciliation between the evolutionary building-up of forms and the historical process is sketched out. One may compare the resulting 'cosmic history' with Whitehead's idea that the laws or patterns of nature would be found to change gradually: A.N. Whitehead, *Adventures of Ideas* (Cambridge 1947) p.143. Steiner's solution, whereby the spirit does not use its freedom to gain illusory (luciferic) independence but re-engages morally with nature, is expressed in the idea of the future relationships between the spirit and nature as higher-level recreations of past stages. In short, we can regain the same kind of belonging-with-nature we had in the primal stages of our emergence, but with the addition of our free self-consciousness. The future is a reflection or transformed version of the past, but on a higher level because of what we have attained (=history). This 'regaining on a higher level' is one of the few major ideas in Steiner's thought which are linked to German Idealism, cf. Hegel's pattern of transcendence/preservation expressed in his idiosyncratic use of the term *aufheben*: But Steiner's version is freed from the metaphysical idea of transcendence, whereby the spirit moves beyond nature, and turned into an 'incarnational,' anthroposophical idea: our self-consciousness, instead of being the goal and apogee of the world-process, is a turning-point

and a moral responsibility for the greater world we help to bring into being.

32. *Goethe's Theory of Knowledge*, p.108.

33. Steiner, *From Symptom to Reality in Modern History* (London 1976) (the original title refers to *geschichtliche Symptomatologie*).

34. He observed that the religious issues which precipitated the Thirty Years' War remained in all essentials unresolved when it came to an end in 1648, but rather that 'the outcome of the peace of Westphalia, the changed situation in relation to the past, had nothing whatsoever to do with the causes of the conflict in 1618' (op. cit. pp.37–8).

35. Op. cit. pp.68–9. I may perhaps mention a personal observation, in however small a way illuminating the somewhat analogous situation in present-day Ireland. I understood what 'history' means when a lady in Northern Ireland said of some people that they had no regard for 'our money,' i.e. Irish currency, but dealt only in sterling. In her eyes, she was living in Ireland; to the others, there was a border. What we have here is not a disagreement, which would imply a shared understanding of the terms involved. Two radically unconnected viewpoints have emerged. The elements here do not fit together into a 'present' or single pattern, and the basis for interaction and resolution is lacking. The emergence of the different viewpoints requires an essentially historical account, and the uniqueness of perspective on each side cannot be assimilated to a generalizing sociological model, since there is no common recognition of belonging to 'a society' but rather conflicting allegiances which do not have even a space to exist in the other's point of view. Something essential to historical understanding is thereby, tragically, highlighted: but perhaps also the realization of the way historical change can come about in the future through the emergence of new meanings can give new hope.

36. Op. cit. pp.74ff: Steiner gives examples of the way we bring death-forces into modern life through the Ahrimanic aspect of intellect (mechanical, manipulative knowledge). But this should not be seen negatively. That it is part of our becoming free, we have seen in a previous chapter. To object to it in historical terms would be like saying 'Because man is born to die, therefore it would be better if he were never born' (p.79).

37. That is not to say he rejected the 'convergent' programme of natural- and spiritual-scientific methods as earlier conceived, but compare his comments in the late (1925) Preface to *Outline of Esoteric Science* pp.1–2. As an indication of the focus for Steiner's later approach, especially expressed perhaps in the *Karmic Relationships* volumes, note that it was in the latter context that he returned to consider again the subject of human freedom: *Karmic Relationships* vol.I (London 1972) pp.45–59.

38. The emergence of historical treatments of many subjects previously in the domain of science is one of the most interesting 'symptoms,' in Steiner's sense, of the changing consciousness we can experience today.

39. Steiner's insistence on the changing meaning of 'sleep' and 'death' was in marked contrast to theosophical interpretations, which sought to find in their own accounts of these phenomena the explanation of many traditional mystical ideas. Changing historical reality of death: *Outline of Esoteric Science* pp.269–70.

40. Berger and Luckmann, *Social Construction of Reality* p.37.

41. Goethe to Eckermann, in the *Gespräche*, 11 March 1828. Goethe believed that his incessant inner activity showed the reality of his spiritual being (for which he used in his own way the Aristotelian term 'entelechy'). His belief that this must find expression in a future existence despite his physical body perishing he considered a 'common sense' view in contrast to the metaphysical-rational attempts at a proof of immortality. One might also see it as a fundamentally historical mode of thought, and its is in a similar vein that one must take Steiner's conception of *karma* and reincarnation.

42. For its importance to Steiner in his development as a thinker, cf. the passages from his autobiography quoted in O. Palmer, *Rudolf Steiner on his Book 'The Philosophy of Freedom'* (New York 1975) p.103.

43. Steiner, *The Gospel of John* p.27. The background of the Logos-doctrine in ancient thought is notoriously obscure, and was connected by Steiner with the secret teachings of the Mysteries. But that the teaching in the Gospel of John could have the connotations Steiner describes is clear from parallels notably in the Hermetic literature of Graeco-Roman Egypt which often overlaps with early Christianity and contemporary Judaism: there Logos distinguishes man from the lower beings or animals which, even when they can make sounds, cannot articulate meaning; art and science are described as 'the actualization of what belongs to Logos'; Logos is also the power by which God made the world; and sent man down into the world bearing Logos and 'mind,' enabling him become conscious of the world and to recognize his Maker. The main passages are collected in C.H. Dodd, *The Interpretation of the Fourth Gospel* (Cambridge 1968) pp.28–9; and see and for the central place it held in Christian origins, Steiner, *Christianity as Mystical Fact* pp.154ff.

44. C. Lindenberg describes how Steiner pulled these ideas together in particular relation to the two boundary-experiences (i.e. luciferic and ahrimanic) for the *Leading Thoughts*. 'In the experience of this paradox,' he writes, 'that the world reflects back our own thinking, and that our self has originated from the world, lies the starting-point for anthroposophical self-knowledge. And it shows something further: that there can be a deepening of thought, through which one not only does not lose touch with the world, but attains to a world of spiritual reality': *Rudolf Steiner* p.141.

45. Steiner, *Wahrheit und Wissenschaft* pp.69f.

46. Steiner, *The Case for Anthroposophy* p.61.

47. Loc. cit.

48. Barfield, *The Rediscovery of*

Meaning and other essays (Connecticut 1977) pp.11ff.

49. George Steiner, *Real Presences* (London and Boston 1989) p.163.

50. Op. cit. p.134.

51. Steiner, *Die Geheimnisse der Schwelle* (Dornach 1982) pp.24–5.

52. G. Kühlewind, *The Logos Structure of the World* (New York n.d.). See especially pp.61ff for his account of the 'third reality' that is possible through language after passing from the initial wholeness (first reality), through the analytical and mechanical, to consciously 'bridging the chasm' (p.83).

Appendix 1

1. See *The Occult Movement in the Nineteenth Century* (London 1973) pp.62–3.

2. The moralizing interpretation of the two Powers, which even Nietzsche did not question though he turned it upside down in his *Thus Spoke Zarathustra*, is secondary: see Steiner's remarks in *The Gospel of Luke* (London 1964) pp.115–6.

Appendix 2

1. The disastrous consequences for Kantianism as a metaphysical system of this analysis are well brought out in a book by P.F. Strawson, with the impishly Kantian title, *The Bounds of Sense* (London 1966). One might add here that Steiner's admittedly patchy treatment of the Kantian system is basically a result of his responding not so much to the master as to the uses to which his thought was being put by the scientific neo-Kantians. Wittgenstein has shown in a more thoroughgoing way the inherent difficulties in the Kantian view of the boundaries. Cf. D. Pears, *Wittgenstein* (London 1971) pp.25–38.

2. Steiner, *Philosophy of Freedom*.

3. Steiner, ibid.

4. The accusation was that Steiner has neglected this aspect 'to an almost grotesque extent': Ravagli, 'Ist Rudolf Steiner ein Vertreter des monistischen Pantheismus?,' in G. Altehage (ed.), *Im Vorfeld des Dialogs* (Stuttgart 1992) pp.175–198 (190). Yet Kant's argument that freedom is implied by moral obligation (it would not make sense that we should do something if we cannot do it), and that this is 'practically' meaningful even though it contradicts our knowledge of causation and necessity — is admitted by Kant himself to be hedged with 'many difficulties' and 'is hardly capable of being clearly represented': quoted by S. Körner, *Kant* (Harmondsworth 1967) p.157.

5. Steiner, *Building Stones for an Understanding of the Mystery of Golgotha* (London 1972) pp.74–5.

6. Ibid. p.75.

7. As evidence of the radical divide from German Idealism, one may list a) Steiner's complete avoidance of the 'transcendental' thinking (i.e. moving from something to the idea of the necessary conditions of its existence) which is the basis of Kant's reformed metaphysics; b) Steiner's post-Goethean viewing of form and content in a developmental, modern way as interdependent, form on one level becoming content on another, whereas in Hegel still we have the idea of something that is essentially content and, built up to ever greater heights upon it,

essential form, resulting in a metaphysics essentially as old as the Aristotelian *hyle*; c) Steiner's complete rejection of the teleological mode of argument, which is still essential to post-Kantian e.g. Hegelian philosophy.

8. Steiner, *Human and Cosmic Thought* (London n.d.) pp.41ff.
9. In: Unger, *Principles of Spiritual Science* (New York 1976) pp.50–80.
10. Unger, op. cit.
11. Ibid.
12. Steiner, *Philosophy of Freedom* p.128; the article to which he refers has recently been published in translation as: Kreyenbühl, J., *Ethical-Spiritual Activity in Kant* (New York 1986).
13. Fichte, *Science of Knowledge.*
14. Letter of Fichte cited in M.H. Abrams, *Natural Supernaturalism* (New York 1971) p.349.

Chronology

1861   Rudolf Steiner born in Kraljevic (then in Austria) 27
        February
1879   Student in Vienna, studying mathematics and science
        as well as literature and philosophy; attends lectures by
        Brentano
1882–   Editing Goethe's natural-scientific writings. Work at the
 1897   Goethe-Schiller Archive in Weimar; later at the Nietzsche
        Archive.
1886   *Outlines of a Goethean Theory of Knowledge.*
1888   *Goethe — The Founder of a New Aesthetics*
1892   *Truth and Knowledge* (published version of Steiner's
        Ph.D dissertation on epistemology with special
        reference to Fichte)
1894   *The Philosophy of Freedom* (important additions 1918)
1897   Extensive literary and philosophical work in Berlin, e.g.
        in the Giordano Bruno Society (from which he was
        expelled for expressing positive views on Thomas Aquinas)
1899–   Lecturer at the Workers Educational College in
 1904   Berlin
1904   Married Anna Eunicke (1899; died 1911)
1900   *Nineteenth-Century Ideas of the World and Life* (later
        formed part of *The Riddles of Philosophy* (1914)).
1904   Theosophy: An Introduction to the Supersensible
        Knowledge of the World and the destination of Man;
        also Knowledge of Higher Worlds and its Attainment
1909–   *Anthroposophie, Psychosophie, Pneumatosophie* (lectures,
 1911   Berlin)
1910   *Anthroposophie. Ein Fragment;* also *An Outline of Esoteric
        Science.*
1910–   Rudolf Steiner's Mystery Plays produced in Munich.
 1913   Work with Marie von Sivers in the artistic domain,
        including the development of the new art of movement:
        Eurythmy (1912)
1911   Address to the Philosophical Congress at Bologna. *The
        World of the Senses and the World of the Spirit* (lectures,
        Hanover).
1912   *The Spiritual Foundation of Morality* (lectures, Norrköping)

1913   Anthroposophical Society founded independently of
       the Theosophical Society. Extensive travelling and
       lecturing throughout Europe, including a visit to
       London (1914). Building of the First Goetheanum, a
       carved wooden structure including theatre, meeting
       halls, integral painting and sculpture, etc., on a donated
       site in Dornach, Switzerland.

1914   Married Marie von Sivers
       The Riddles of Philosophy; also *Human and Cosmic Thought*
       (lectures, Berlin)

1917   *The Case for Anthroposophy* (Von Seelenrätseln)

1919   *The Study of Man* (lectures, Stuttgart)
       Ideas on the 'threefold social order' presented in
       lectures and books such as *The Inner Aspect of the Social
       Question*. Founding of the first Waldorf (Steiner) School,
       in Stuttgart. Speaks widely on educational issues.

1920   *The Bounds of Natural Knowledge* (lectures, Dornach)

1921   *Man as a Being of Sense and Perception* (lectures, Dornach)

1922   *The Origins of Natural Science* (lectures, Dornach)

1922– The First Goetheanum burnt down (New Year's Eve).
  1923 Plans for the concrete Second Goetheanum begun
       (opened 1928)

1923   Major new beginnings in medicine, agriculture,
       pedagogy, religion and science. Participates in the
       founding of Societies in the several European countries,
       prior to the refounding of the Anthroposophical
       Society, Christmas 1923.

1924   *Anthroposophy. An Introduction* (lectures, Dornach)

1924– Outer activity curtailed by illness, but continues
  1925 writing and working on his autobiography.
       Anthroposophical Leading Thoughts; also
       Fundamentals of Therapy (with Dr Ita Wegman)

1925   Died 30 March in Dornach

Select Bibliography

A. Primary

Works by Rudolf Steiner:
Anthroposophical Leading Thoughts. London 1973.
Anthroposophie. Ein Fragment. Dornach 1980.
Anthroposophie. Psychosophie. Pneumatosophie. Dornach 1931.
Anthroposophy. An Introduction. London 1983.
The Boundaries of Natural Science: with an Introduction by Saul Bellow, New York 1983.
Christianity as Mystical Fact. New York 1997.
Colour. London 1996.
Eleven European Mystics. New York 1971.
Evil. London 1997.
The Evolution of Consciousness. London 1966.
Friedrich Nietzsche. Fighter for Freedom. London 1960.
Fruits of Anthroposophy London 1986.
The Influences of Lucifer and Ahriman. Man's Responsibility for the Earth (1976)
The Inner Nature of Man. London 1959.
Goethe als Vater einer neuen Ästhetik. Dornach 1963.
The Gospel of St. John. New York 1962.
Human Values in Education. London 1971.
The Karma of Materialism. New York and London 1985.
Man as a Being of Sense and Perception. Vancouver 1981.
Man — Hieroglyph of the Universe. London 1972.
Man in the Light of Occultism, Theosophy and Philosophy. London 1964.
Man in the Past, Present and Future. The Evolution of Consciousness. London 1966.
Methodische Grundlagen der Anthroposophie. Dornach 1961.
Nature's Open Secret. Introductions to Goethe's Scientific Writings. New York 2000.
Origins of Natural Science. With Introduction by O. Barfield. London and New York 1985.
Outline of Esoteric Science. New York 1997.
Philosophy and Anthroposophy. London and New York 1929.
The Philosophy of Freedom, trans. M. Wilson. London 1999.
The Philosophy of Spiritual Activity, trans. R. Stebbing. New York 1963.
The Redemption of Thinking. A Study in the Philosophy of Thomas Aquinas. London 1956.

The Riddles of Philosophy. New York 1973.

The Significance of Spiritual Research for Moral Action. New York 1981.

The Spiritual Foundation of Morality. (Vancouver n.d.)

A Theory of Knowledge based on Goethe's World-Conception. 1968. New York.

Theosophy. London 1965.

Towards social renewal. London 1999.

'Truth, Beauty, Goodness,' *in: Art in the Light of Mystery Wisdom.* London 1970.

A Way of Self-Knowledge. New York 1999.

Wahrheit und Wissenschaft. Vorspiel einer Philosophie der Freiheit. Dornach 1980.

The World of the Senses and the World of the Spirit. Vancouver 1979.

Works by Rudolf Steiner collected or edited by others:

Barfield, Owen *The Case for Anthroposophy.* London 1970.

MacDermott. R, *The Essential Steiner.* New York and San Francisco 1984

Palmer, O. *Rudolf Steiner on his Book 'The Philosophy of Freedom'.* New York 1975.

Welburn, A. *The Mysteries. Rudolf Steiner's Writings on Spiritual Initiation.* Edinburgh 1997.

B. Secondary

Altehage, G. (ed.) *Im Vorfeld des Dialogs.* Stuttgart 1992.

Amrine, F. et al. (eds.), *Goethe and the Sciences: A Reappraisal.* Dordrecht. 1987.

Austin, J.L. *Sense and Sensibilia.* Oxford London and New York 1962.

Barfield, Owen *The Rediscovery of Meaning and other essays.* Connecticut 1977.

— *Romanticism Comes of Age.* Connecticut 1967.

— 'Rudolf Steiner's Concept of Mind,' in his: *Romanticism Comes of Age* (Connecticut 1967, pp.241–54)

— *Saving the Appearances. A Study in Idolatry.* New York, n.d.

— *Speaker's Meaning.* London 1967.

— *What Coleridge Thought.* Oxford 1971.

Barrow, J.D., and Tipler, F.J. *The Anthropic Cosmological Principle.* Oxford and New York 1986, 1998.

Berger, P.L. *A Rumour of Angels. Modern Society and the Rediscovery of the Supernatural.* Harmondsworth 1971.

— and Luckmann, T. *The Social Construction of Reality. A Treatise in the Sociology of Knowledge.* Harmondsworth 1971.

Bortoft, H. *The Wholeness of Nature: Goethe's Way toward a Science of Conscious Participation in Nature.* New York 1996.

Butterfield, *The Whig Interpretation of History.* London 1951.

Collingwood, R.G. *The Principles of Art.* London and New York 1958.

Davidson, N. *Astronomy and the Imagination.* London, Boston and Melbourne 1985.

Davy, J.(ed.), *Work Arising from the Life of Rudolf Steiner.* London 1975.

Dobbs. B.J. *The Janus Face of Genius: the Role of Alchemy in Newton's Thought.* Cambridge 1991.

Douglas, M. *Natural Symbols*. Harmondsworth 1973.

Emmet, D. *The Nature of Metaphysical Thinking*. London and New York 1966.

Findlay, J.N. *Hegel. A Re-examination*. London and New York 1958.

Foot, P. *Theories of Ethics*. Oxford and New York 1967.

Gay, Peter *The Enlightenment. The Rise of Modern Paganism*. New York and London 1966.

Gut, B. *Informationstheorie und Erkenntnislehre*. Stuttgart n.d.

— 'Die Klassifikation seelischer Phänomene und der Fortbestand der Individualität. Versuch an einem Topos der Philosophie Franz Brentanos,' *Die Drei* (1988)2, 118–135

— *Die Verbindlichkeit frei gesetzter Intentionen*. Stuttgart 1990.

Hacking, I. (ed.) *Scientific Revolutions*. Oxford and New York 1981.

Hare, R.M. *Freedom and Reason*. Oxford 1963.

Harwood, A.C. (ed.), *The Faithful Thinker*. London 1961.

Hegel, G.W.F. *Lectures on the Philosophy of Religion*. 3 vols. London and New York 1974.

Hemleben, J. *Rudolf Steiner*. Sussex. 1975.

— *Rudolf Steiner und Ernst Haeckel* Stuttgart 1965.

Hoffmann, David Marc *Zur Geschichte des Nietzsche-Archivs*. In the series *Supplementa Nietzscheana*. Berlin and NewYork 1991.

Holbrook, D. *Evolution and the Humanities* Aldershot 1987.

Huber, J. 'Astral Marx,' in the journal *New Economy* 8. (Summer 1983), pp.3–6.

Hulme, T.E. *Speculations. Essays on Humanism and the Philosophy of Art*. London and New York 1987.

Husserl, E. *Cartesian Meditations*. The Hague 1960.

— *Logical Investigations*. London 1970.

Jacob, M.C. *The Radical Enlightenment*. London, Boston and Sydney 1981.

Kagan, J. *The Nature of the Child*. New York 1984.

Kallert, B *Die Erkenntnistheorie Rudolf Steiners*. Stuttgart 1971.

Klingler, W. *Rudolf Steiners Menschenbild*. Phil. Diss. Basel 1969.

Koenig, K. *The First Three Years of the Child*. New York 1986.

Koerner, S. *Kant*. Harmondsworth 1955.

Kreyenbühl, J. *Ethical-Spiritual Activity in Kant*. New York 1986.

Kugler, W. 'Zeichen des Aufbruchs. Rudolf Steiner im Kreis der 'Kommenden,' in the journal *Die Drei*. 1985. 607–618.

Kühlewind, G. *The Logos Structure of the World*. New York 1986.

— *Stages of Consciousness*. New York 1984.

Kuhn, T.S. *The Structure of Scientific Revolutions*. Chicago 1970.

Lacan, Jacques *Écrits: A Selection*. New York 1977.

Lauer, E.-H. *Die zwölf Sinne des Menschen*. Schaffhausen 1977.

Lehrs, E. *Man or Matter*. London 1961.

Lindenberg, C. *Rudolf Steiner*. Hamburg 1992.

Macbeth, N. *Darwin Retried*. New York 1976.

Macmurray, *The Self as Agent*.

Marsella, A.J. et al. (eds.), *Culture and Self*. New York and London 1985.

Merleau-Ponty, M. *Phenomenology of Perception*. London and Henley 1962.

Meyer, T.H. D.N. Dunlop. *A Man of our Time*. London 1992.

Miller, A.V. 'Rudolf Steiner and Hegel,' *Anthroposophical Quarterly* 17(1972)4

Murdoch, I. *The Sovereignty of Good.* London 1970.

Nagel, E. and Newman, J.R. *Goedel's Proof.* New York 1960.

Nicholl, C. *The Chemical Theatre.* London 1980.

Oldenburg, A. (ed.), *Zeitgenossen Rudolf Steiners im Berlin der Jahrhundertwende.* Dornach 1988.

Passmore, J. *A Hundred Years of Philosophy.* Harmondsworth 1968.

Pears, D. *Wittgenstein.* London 1971.

Penrose, R. *The Emperor's New Mind: Concerning Computers, Minds and the Laws of Physics.* Oxford 1999.

Piaget, J. *Play, Dreams and Imitation in Childhood.* London 1962.

— *The Principles of Genetic Epistemology.* London 1972.

— *Psychology and Epistemology. Towards a Theory of Knowledge.* Harmondsworth 1972.

— "The Myth of the Sensory Origin of Scientific Knowledge" in: *Psychology and Epistemology: Towards a Theory of Knowledge.* 1972. Harmondsworth.

—, *Structuralism.* London 1971.

Pivčević, E. *Husserl and Phenomenology.* London 1970.

— (ed.) *Phenomenology and Philosophical Understanding.* Cambridge, London and New York 1975.

Principe, L. *The Aspiring Adept. Robert Boyle and his Alchemical Quest.* Princeton 1998.

Hilary Putnam, *The Collapse of the Fact/Value Dichotomy.* Harvard and London 2002.

Roder, F. 'Franz Brentano in der Begegnung Rudolf Steiners,' in the journal *Die Drei* (1988)3, 197–219.

Ryle, G. *The Concept of Mind.* Harmondsworth 1973.

Scheler, Max *The Nature of Sympathy.* London and Henley 1954.

Schmidt, J. *Maurice Merleau-Ponty. Between Phenomenology and Structuralism* Basingstoke and London 1985.

Searle, R. 'How to Derive "Ought" from "Is,"' in Foot, P. (ed.), *Theories of Ethics.* Oxford 1967.

Smith, Barry (ed.), *Structure and Gestalt: Philosophy and Literature in Austro-Hungary and her Successor States.* Amsterdam 1981.

Stein, *Die moderne naturwissenschaftliche Vorstellungsart und die Weltanschauung Goethes, wie sie Rudolf Steiner vertritt.* Stuttgart 1921.

Steiner, G. *Real Presences.* London and Boston 1989.

Strawson, P.F. *The Bounds of Sense. An Essay on Kant's Critique of Pure Reason.* London 1966.

Suigerman, S. *Evolution of Consciousness: Studies in Polarity.* Connecticut 1976.

Swinburne, R. *The Evolution of Soul.* Oxford 1997.

Tautz, J. *W.J. Stein. A Biography.* London 1990.

Unger, C. *Principles of Spiritual Science.* New York 1976.

— *Aus der Sprache der Bewusstseinsseele.* Basel 1954.

Wannamaker, O.D. *Rudolf Steiner's 'Philosophy of Spiritual Activity': A Student's Introduction and Analysis.* New York 1963.

Warnock, G.J. *Berkeley.* Harmondsworth 1969.

Warnock, M. *Imagination.* London and Boston 1976.

Westphal, J. *Colour. Some Philosophical Problems from Wittgenstein.* Oxford 1987.

—, 'Henry Ford, Objective Idealist' in *Golden Blade.* (1979), 115–36.

Whitehead, *Adventures of Ideas.* Cambridge 1947.

Williams, *Groundless Belief. An essay on the possibility of epistemology.* Oxford 1977.

Wittgenstein, L. *Philosophical Investigations.* Oxford 1972.

Index